T0184298

Communications
in Computer and Information Science　　847

Commenced Publication in 2007
Founding and Former Series Editors:
Phoebe Chen, Alfredo Cuzzocrea, Xiaoyong Du, Orhun Kara, Ting Liu,
Dominik Ślęzak, and Xiaokang Yang

Editorial Board

More information about this series at http://www.springer.com/series/7899

Vanessa Agredo-Delgado · Pablo H. Ruiz (Eds.)

Human-Computer Interaction

4th Iberoamerican Workshop, HCI-Collab 2018
Popayán, Colombia, April 23–27, 2018
Revised Selected Papers

 Springer

Editors
Vanessa Agredo-Delgado (iD)
Corporación Universitaria Comfacauca
Unicomfacauca
Popayán, Colombia

and

Universidad del Cauca
Popayán, Colombia

Pablo H. Ruiz (iD)
Corporación Universitaria Comfacauca
Unicomfacauca
Popayán, Colombia

and

Universidad del Cauca
Popayán, Colombia

ISSN 1865-0929   ISSN 1865-0937   (electronic)
Communications in Computer and Information Science
ISBN 978-3-030-05269-0   ISBN 978-3-030-05270-6   (eBook)
https://doi.org/10.1007/978-3-030-05270-6

Library of Congress Control Number: 2018963069

This Springer imprint is published by the registered company Springer Nature Switzerland AG
The registered company address is: Gewerbestrasse 11, 6330 Cham, Switzerland

Preface

The area of human–computer interaction (HCI) has as one of its central problems the insertion of the technological element (computer, handheld devices, etc.) within the social context, with considerable progress having been made in the area, and whose foundations derive from a wide variety of fields: computer science, cognitive psychology, social psychology, perceptive psychology, linguistics, artificial intelligence, and anthropology, among others. Like any research area, HCI has evolved, marking paradigms that govern the construction process of the technological element. These paradigms have allowed for the development of different design approaches, which are known as technology-centered design, in the user and in the apprentice. This knowledge area tells us about the relevance of each of the three elements of the equation: the human being (user), the computer/mobile device (system), and the interaction (information transmission in two ways).

This book contains a compilation of research works on topics related to HCI at the Ibero-American level (Colombia, Argentina, Peru, Mexico, Cuba, Costa Rica, Spain) in specialized areas such as: emotional interfaces, HCI and video games, computational thinking, collaborative systems, software engineering, and ICT in education. We present papers that describe models, design patterns, implementations, evaluations of existing applications, and systemic reviews; all of them very important aspects in HCI. In this way, the book can become a theoretical reference for Ibero-American researchers, spreading knowledge and demonstrating the research quality that is being developed on the subject at the Ibero-American level. This work is the result of the HCI-Collab Network (Collaborative Network to support the teaching–learning processes in the HCI area at the Ibero-American level), whose main objective is to structure a curricular proposal in the HCI area that serves as a model for various Ibero-American institutions that deal with these themes. In this way, the papers presented in this book are the basis for the study of several Ibero-American academic programs on HCI subjects in content terms, objectives, methodologies, resources, and evaluation mechanisms.

All paper submissions were reviewed by three experts. Authors removed personal details, the acknowledgments section, and any references that may disclose the authors' identity. Papers not satisfying these conditions were rejected without reviews. All contributions were written following the Springer template and the first anonymous version was submitted in PDF format.

The call for papers attracted 83 submissions in Spanish, English, and Portuguese; 30 were accepted, with the 22 best papers being invited to send an extended version as a long article in English, of which 18 accepted the invitation and are presented in this book. Reviewing was performed by national and international reviewers. Moreover, the EasyChair system was used for the management and review of submissions.

We are grateful to all authors who sent their articles, to the organizers, and to Springer.

August 2018

Vanessa Agredo-Delgado
Pablo H. Ruiz

Organization

Program Committee

Alexandra Baldaque	Universidade Portucalense, Portugal
Alicia Mon	Universidad Nacional de la Matanza, Argentina
Ana Molina	Universidad de Castilla - La Mancha, Spain
Andrés Solano	Universidad Autónoma de Occidente, Colombia
Antonio Silva	Universidad Central de Venezuela, Venezuela
Beatriz Grass	Universidad San Buenaventura, Colombia
Beatriz Pacheco	Universidade Presbiteriana Mackenzie, Brazil
Carina González	Universidad de la Laguna, Spain
Carlos Lara	Centro de Investigación en Matemáticas (CIMAT), Mexico
Cesar A. Collazos	Universidad del Cauca, Colombia
Clifton Clunie	Universidad Tecnológica de Panamá, Panama
Cristian Rusu	Pontificia Universidad Católica de Valparaíso, Chile
David Geerts	Katholieke Universiteit Leuven, Belgium
Fernando Moreira	Universidade Portucalense, Portugal
Francisco Gutiérrez	Universidad de Granada, Spain
Freddy Muñoz	Fundación Universitaria de Popayán, Colombia
Freddy Paz	Pontificia Universidad Católica del Perú, Peru
German Lescano	Universidad Nacional de Santiago del Estero, Argentina
Germania Rodríguez	Universidad Técnica Particular de Loja, Ecuador
Gisela Clunie	Universidad Tecnológica de Panamá, Panama
Gustavo Eduardo Constain Moreno	Universidad Nacional Abierta y a Distancia - UNAD, Colombia
Habib Fardoun	King AbdulAziz University, Saudi Arabia
Hamurabi Gamboa	Universidad Autónoma de Zacatecas, Mexico
Huiziloztli Luna-García	Universidad Autónoma de Zacatecas, Mexico
Ismar Frango	Universidade Presbiteriana Mackenzie, Brazil
Jaime Muñoz	Universidad Autónoma de Aguascalientes, Mexico
Jeferson Arango López	Universidad de Caldas, Colombia
José Jurado	Universidad San Buenaventura, Colombia
José Pow	Pontificia Universidad Católica del Perú, Peru
Josefina Guerrero	Benemérita Universidad Autónoma de Puebla, Mexico
Juan Gonzalez	Benemérita Universidad Autónoma de Puebla, Mexico
Juan Murillo	Universidad de Extremadura, Spain
Julio Ariel Hurtado Alegría	Universidad del Cauca, Colombia
Laura Aballay	Universidad Nacional de San Juan, Argentina
Luis Merchan	Universidad San Buenaventura, Colombia

Editorial Committee

Vanessa Agredo-Delgado	Corporación Universitaria Comfacauca Unicomfacauca, Universidad del Cauca, Colombia
Pablo H. Ruiz	Corporación Universitaria Comfacauca Unicomfacauca, Universidad del Cauca, Colombia

Contents

A Systematic Literature Review on Organizational Training Using Game-Based Learning

Mateo Hernández$^{(\boxtimes)}$ ⓘ and Julián Moreno$^{(\boxtimes)}$ ⓘ

Universidad Nacional de Colombia-Sede Medellín, Medellín, Colombia
{mahernandezsa, jmorenol}@unal.edu.co

Abstract. Offering training programs to their employees is one of the necessary tasks that managers must comply with. Training is done mainly to provide up-to-date knowledge or to convey to staff the objectives, history, corporate name, functions of the organization's areas, processes, laws, norms or policies that must be fulfilled. Although there are a lot of methods, models or tools that are useful for this purpose, many companies face with some common problems like employee's motivation and high costs in terms of money and time. In an effort to solve this problem, new trends have emerged in the last few years, in particular strategies related to games, such as serious games and gamification, whose success has been demonstrated by numerous researchers. According to the above, we present a systematic literature review of the different approaches that have used games or their elements, using the procedure suggested by Cooper, on this matter, ending with about the positive and negative findings.

Keywords: Training · Serious games · Gamification · Game-Based learning
Organizations

1 Introduction

Training is done mainly to provide up-to-date knowledge of a specific topic of the employee's functions, also to convey to staff the objectives, history, corporate name, functions of the organization's areas, processes, laws, norms or policies that must be fulfilled. In addition, training influences the competitive level of the organization [1].

The competitiveness of companies is reflected in the competitiveness of the talents they own, and creative talents are the basis of companies [2]. Nowadays, there are many methods for training the organization employees, in a literature review realized in [3] are identified 13 training approaches such as case study, games-based training, internship, job rotation, job shadowing, lecture, mentoring and apprenticeship, programmed instruction, role-modeling, role play, simulation, stimulus-based training, and team-training. Some of the above methods have the possibility of carrying out to distance, namely, remotely through online learning. As Van Noord and Peterson argue in [4], "Online learning is no longer a novelty—it is now an accepted, even expected, component of professional development."

V. Agredo-Delgado and P. H. Ruiz (Eds.): HCI-COLLAB 2018, CCIS 847, pp. 1–18, 2019.
https://doi.org/10.1007/978-3-030-05270-6_1

Online learning, that in this case is online training, provides many benefits, both for the organization and for employees. It provides flexibility in time and cost efficiency, and it has the advantage that at any time and in any place (where connectivity exists), the employee can acquire knowledge and receive training. Bouhnik and Marcus consider that online learning, which is equivalent in many respects to online training, has four advantages: (1) freedom for the employee to decide when to enter training; (2) there is no limitations in time, (3) you have more confidence to express your thoughts or opinions and (4) accessibility to online course materials [5]. On the side of disadvantages, some researchers state that one of the most important is that most participants in these programs fail to complete the modules because there are no limits on them, there is no empathy with the technology or there is no motivation with the virtual learning environment [6].

As an alternative to solve that problem and looking for deleting the gaps that exist between the employees and virtual training environments, Game-based learning (GBL) has come to play a significant role. Game-based learning business must align with the learning goals and outcomes of training and development, and clearly it has demonstrated that learning can be evaluated and achieved. On the other hand, the other term that appears is serious game. Serious games also are involved in training organizations, these types of games experiences drive personal change and transformation by generating an attitude of acceptance of the challenge, motivation to achieve, and constant innovation through participant commitments. Simulations push the participant into experiencing an immersive environment. Finally, gamification, as a collection of techniques, may be applied to the educational and workplace activities or used as a wrapper for GBL, serious games, and simulations [7]. As is mentioned in [8], every day more companies adopt these terms in areas like sales, human resources, products design and even in accounting. Therefore, the gamification can be the necessary tool for the employers carry out their training activities in the employees. These areas that seem to be tedious, else, it turns in entertaining and commits the employees [9].

According to the description above, a systematic literature review will be developed for finding the different approaches, models, methods, components, etc. that have an element of games, serious games, gamification or simulation which are looking for resolving the two problems: high costs and motivation in organization training. After that, discussion, conclusions and future works will be presented.

2   Method

This literature review will be developed using the procedure suggested by Cooper for synthesizing the literature [10]. This systematic procedure helped to (a) formulate the problem, (b) collect data, (c) evaluate the appropriateness of the data, (d) analyze and interpret relevant data, and (e) organize and present the results. The literature review will focus on the models that use elements, tools or components of games for developing the training process.

2.1 Formulating the Problem

Talking about training costs in organizations includes time, money invested in training, hotel reservations or other places such as auditoriums, event rooms, travel expenses, and time spent by employees outside of their workplaces is a cost to their employers. For instance, when a large number of employees exist, the training methods based in face-to-face, cannot meet such a large demand with cost and time efficiency [2]. This cost is generally reduced considerably with the influence that technology has on training programs, which directly improves its effectiveness [1].

To help solve the problem, we want to know the different training approaches that are proposed in the literature. Therefore, the following questions guided this review:

(1) What approach was used (Method and model)?
(2) What elements of game-based learning, serious games, or gamification were used?
(3) Was there a validation? With what purpose and what was the population involved?

2.2 Data Collection

The purpose of data collection was to find training approaches with any element of games applied in organizations since 2000, implementations, validations, study cases, etc. for then present the results obtained for the authors.

The following keywords were used: *game-based learning, serious games, educational games, gamification, organization, knowledge management, training, company, enterprise and employee.*

As shown in Table 1, the search terms were constructed taking account which Boolean OR is used to incorporate alternative spellings, synonyms or related terms that could have similar meaning, and Boolean AND is employed to link the major terms.

Table 1. Terms of search.

Major terms	Alternative terms
Game organizational training	game-based training; game-based learning; gamification; serious games; educational games organization; knowledge management; training; organization; company; employee; human resources

The databases used included Web of Science and Google Scholar, which in turn index results from Springer, IEEE Xplore, ScienceDirect, among others. The search was carried out in English, Spanish and Portuguese, and was applied to the title, abstract and keywords.

2.3 Data evaluation and analysis

The inclusion and exclusion criteria are presented in the Table 2.

Table 2. Inclusion/exclusion criteria.

Inclusion/exclusion criteria	
Inclusion criteria	• Terms fulfill the search string • Contributions to industry/professional conferences, workshops, and online publications • Publication date: 2000–2017
Exclusion criteria for titles and abstract	• Papers which do not mention any term related with games
Exclusion criteria for full text	• Papers which the term "training" is consider within physical activities, sports or workout context • Papers without "training" or learning (company/university context) term • Papers which only have concepts and definitions • Literature Reviews, surveys, summaries or papers with the same objective

2.4   Statistics and Relevant Data

Initially, the search generated a total of 207 papers that were the result of applying the first inclusion criteria. After this analysis, the exclusion criteria were applied by title and abstract, leaving a total of 117 papers. Finally, after reading full-text several papers were excluded, obtaining a total of 60 papers. Once the papers were selected, a descriptive statistical analysis of some relevant data was carried out.

In Fig. 1, it can be seen the trend that starts from the 2000s, in which the amount of papers, conference papers, book chapters, etc. in the topic of organizational training with game-based learning approaches has grown up constantly. It also demonstrates the growing interest of companies to use these tools based on the results they observe in their application. Since 2010, two papers fulfilled all the inclusion and exclusion criteria, 11 papers in 2014 and 13 for 2016. There is an atypical data and it is in the papers reported in 2015, in which only were reported 3 papers and no serious reasons were found. Finally, in the year 2017, 6 papers were reported, although it must be specified that the search was made in mid-August-September 2017, so probably currently there are many more papers.

Furthermore, a classification by type of the 60 analyzed papers was made and it was found that 78% of the papers have as source conferences, congresses, workshops, proceedings, etc. being the most representative value. On the other hand, 20% of the total corresponds to published papers and only 2% corresponds to book chapter.

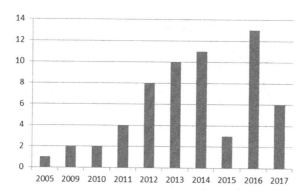

Fig. 1. Number of papers by year

3 Results

After performing a descriptive statistical of the papers that were analyzed, the guide questions will be answered according to what was found in the complete review in each of the papers. Additionally, some graphs will be presented that show in a better way the results found, as well as a brief analysis of them.

Approaches (Methods and models). To train the employees of an organization, multiple approaches and methods were found that contributed significant value to both the company and the employee. However, the use of a formal model/Framework of the literature, for example, Mechanics Dynamics Aesthetics (MDA), was not evident in any way to carry out the game design process to train the employees of the organization.

The models used by the authors in their papers were entirely their own approaches and implementations that they themselves created, adapted and adjusted to the needs they wanted to satisfy by applying the model, giving rise to models such as MAnaging System Change in Aviation (MASCA), ActionPlanT Industrial Learning, Collaborative Simulation and Training Object-Relation Model (C-STORM), Technology-Enhanced Training Effectiveness Model (TETEM), 3D Asymmetric Domain Analysis and Training (3D ADAT), etc.

Methods such as game-based training, lecture, programmed instruction, role-modeling, role play, simulation, etc. They were used in these approaches. The most used was game-based training which was expected due to the search terms.

In 90% of the analyzed approaches evidenced the use of technological platforms, virtual or online environments to offer training in the organization, while the remaining 10% corresponds to the use of educational games such as board games, Lego, card games, etc.

Elements of game-based learning. The elements of games used in the papers were classified in these 4 excluding terms: Gamification, Serious Game*, Virtual World/ Environment and Immersive/Simulation. Figure 2 represents the degree of play of each term from least to most.

Fig. 2. Grade of game elements.

Gamification. It consists of the application and use of game elements in contexts that are not game-based. In the reviewed papers, it was possible to demonstrate that gamification is an excellent bet that today companies have in their objectives. The typical elements used by the authors in their prototypes, models, platforms, etc. to train the employees of the organization were basically the following: Medals, Badges, Rankings, LeaderBoards, Levels, Avatars, Rewards, Acknowledgments, TeamWork, Discussions and Forums.

All of these elements were used in order to increase motivation, commitment and mainly the interest to train the employees of the organization.

The game elements of gamification were the second most used in the studies analyzed with 20%. Since the last decade, the tools of gamification have been a very important resource for the companies and not only in the field of training.

Serious Game*. Serious games are generally in which in addition to having fun and training, participants acquire learning on a specific topic. However, for this review, the * indicates that these serious games will only refer to didactic and educational games such as card games, board games, etc. It also means that does not overlap in any way with the other 3 categories, namely the serious game cannot represent a simulation, immersive game, an environment or virtual world, or contain any element of gamification, even though the concept can contain them. In other words, it was decided to make this exclusionary division in the classification.

Having said that, the review found serious games of all kinds such as card games, online game platforms, educational games, face-to-face games, games in a physical space called classroom, auditorium, etc. where participants through teamwork or individually had to make puzzle or go through stands that played the role of stages in a manufacturing process, also in some cases, a specific role were assigned by cards to along with their tasks where always the purpose was to add some entertainment and fun to the task of teaching a specific topic.

This type of serious games represents 15% of the total number of studies analyzed, being one of the least used by companies in personnel training processes.

Virtual World/Environment. The Virtual World/ Environment refer to the applications that try to simulate a real world or those virtual platforms that are not a simulation of the task that it wants to teach but that have as objective taught a specific subject is through a game.

Teaching how to care for the environment through a game like SimCity is a clear example of the elements of games that belong to this category.

In the papers reviewed, the use of Virtual World/Environment was demonstrated to train the employees of an organization where the employee has a profile, avatar or assigned character and in a world or interface virtual, solving problems, constructing elements within the game, both individually and collectively, answering questions, finding clues, learning key concepts, etc. that allowed him to complete the game while he acquired knowledge of the company or its future functions.

For example, Taskville, which visualizes productivity as an isometric city landscape, is an interactive visualization that aims to increase awareness of tasks that occur in the workplace. It utilizes gameplay elements and playful interaction to motivate continued use [A34].

Equal to Serious Games, 15% of the total studies reviewed were The Virtual World/Environments.

Immersive/Simulation: Immersive/Simulation refers to the reviewed studies that, within their contribution, developed an immersive or non-immersive simulation game, through which the employees of an organization were trained.

This type of game elements used represented 49% of the total papers reviewed, that is, in almost half of the papers games, environments or virtual interfaces were used, which through immersive or non-immersive simulation were trained the employees of the organization. The elements used were tools developed in game engines such as Unity3d and Blender, in order to recreate the reality in the environments and tasks in which it was required to train employees.

The graphic representation of the environments that simulated reality are usually cities, offices, laboratories, supermarkets, hospitals, manufacturing industries, etc. where employees enter an immersive or non-immersive world and simulate through some activity within the game the tasks on which they need training.

The premise of the authors when using these elements is that through the simulation a higher percentage of learning can be guaranteed by the employees since they are directly carrying out the activities that they will execute in the real world.

Validations. In 85% of the analyzed studies, there was a concrete validation of the prototype, model, framework or platform that through the use of game elements had as main objective the training of the employees.

- The main purposes of validating the approaches were generally the following:
- Test the serious game delivery mechanism.
- Test the gamification delivery mechanism.
- Evaluate the teamwork of the participants.
- Determine if the elements of games in training have better results than the traditional training methodologies.
- Measure simulation effectiveness.
- Increase motivation, interest, learning level and employee performance.
- Determine if is possible reduce the costs and time of organizational training with game-based learning.

The validations of the models, prototypes or approaches made by the authors were through real implementations in companies that needed to know some of the previous items. These companies from different sectors of the industry were discriminated in Table 3 according to the topic in which the employees were trained.

Analyzing the Table 3, it is clear that manufacturing is the topic in which the most companies train in their employees since it was found in 11 studies, almost 20% of the papers reviewed. The manufacturers of the market mainly are looking for through game-based learning to reduce production times using the minimum possible resources, which is called Lean Manufacturing. The Software and Management topics represented 10% respectively with 6 papers each. For the topics of game-based learning in software, the papers show evidence of modeling and global software development training, while in Management, many implementations of administrative training for project managers, CEOs, sales personnel, cashiers, customer service, etc. in specific functions of each profile or in transversal tools such as an ERP. Finally, 4 papers did not specify, or it was very complicated to classify it in one of the topics. Topics such as Cyber Security, Collaborative Learning with 3 papers and Employee Induction with 4, and the rest of topics like Tourism, Supermarket, Workplace and Engineering with 2 papers.

Table 3 contains references to the 60 studies of Appendix, classified by topics and type of element of games.

What was the population involved? The people involved are all of the groups of employees of each organization that were trained in the topic that the company required. Groups of 15, 25, 30 and even more than 10,000 employees, in the case of Deloitte, compose this population [A44]. In some cases, 2 subgroups were created, one group used game-based learning and the other group used traditional methodologies for training. The main objective of this division was making a result comparison.

In addition to these groups, administrative personnel such as managers, CEO's, the human resources department, etc. they also intervene in the validation process of the implemented prototypes. Some validations were made with undergraduate students, who were candidates to be hired in the companies so they were formed through training of the organization.

Table 3. References of studies by topics and game-based learning used.

Topics	Game elements			
	Immersive/Simulation	Virtual World/Environment	Gamification	Serious Game*
Manufacturing	[A1], [A4], [A5], [A7], [A12], [A40], [A42], [A51], [A55]	[A22]		[A38]
Management		[A49]	[A3], [A10], [A20], [A26], [A35]	

(continued)

Table 3. (*continued*)

Topics	Game elements			
	Immersive/Simulation	Virtual World/Environment	Gamification	Serious Game*
Software development	[A6], [A60]		[A18]	[A8], [A9], [A37]
Culture	[A59]			
Cyber security			[A6], [A19], [A21]	
Collaborative learning		[A48], [A50]	[A17]	
Employee induction	[A11]	[A54], [A29]	[A45]	
Tourism	[A23], [A56]			[A27]
Government	[A39]			
Supermarket	[A33], [A43]			
Workplace		[A34], [A53]		
Engineering	[A36], [A47]			
Banking	[A13]			
Business				[A14]
Biology	[A24]			
Transportation	[A25]			
Electricity	[A30]			
Military				[A31]
Aviation				[A32]
Employment health				[A41]
Environment	[A46]			
Formal education			[A52]	
Innovation				[A57]
Triage	[A58]			
Not specified	[A15], [A28], [A44]	[A2]		

4 Discussion

After answering the guided questions that were raised at the beginning of the review, some issues can be discussed according to the findings of the studies analyzed.

In general, all the studies reviewed showed more positive and satisfactory results than negative or without feedback. On average, each paper presented 80% of results in favor of GBL in organizational training and 20% against or neutral. Below we will mention the positive results of the validation of the use of game-based learning in organizational training in priority order:

- Reduction of costs and time in organizational training.
- Increase in the level of learning, motivation and interest of the employees of the organization.

- The use of game-based learning showed better results than traditional training methodologies in organizations.
- Using game-based learning enhanced attitude, knowledge, skills and competencies of the employees.
- The rate of dropouts of employees in the training courses was considerably reduced.
- The majority of employees had an adaptive and friendly reaction to the use of game-based learning in the training.
- Although not all implementations allowed playing in multiplayer mode, when it was present improved the collaborative learning in the team works.

The neutral and negative results that represent of the validations are described in the following items:

- In some cases, among potential learners with high experience and attitudes with games, game-based learning produces better outcomes than traditional methodologies (face-to-face, PowerPoint slides), but among potential learners with low experience and attitudes, game-based learning produces worse outcomes than traditional methodologies.
- In the implementation of some of the approaches, adult employees who were born in the 1970s or later, that is, are not digital natives, they are more prone to skepticism in the use of game-based learning in process training.
- In the implementation of some of the approaches, adult employees who were born in the 1970s or later, that is, are not digital natives, they are more prone to skepticism in the use of game-based learning in process training.
- In several approaches, the validation of the implementation was carried out through surveys of workers who were trained through the prototype or model proposed. When the workers' answers were analyzed, it was evident that the employees were not previously instructed to enter a gamified platform, a serious game*, a virtual world/environment or an immersive or non-immersive simulation game. Additionally, some mentioned that the games were not intuitive enough, practical, close to reality or simply their structure or game line was complex, thus, it did not motivate employees, its content was not appropriate or other reasons specific to the approach implemented.

Initially, it is clear that game-based learning in training for organizations is a trend that gets more strength year by year. Additionally, taking it to an online environment has also been a boom because of the technological advance is seen in most companies. This was demonstrated by the fact that 90% of the studies analyzed corresponded to online approaches.

After finding in the papers reviewed positive, encouraging and promising results in terms of the use of game-based learning in the training of employees in organizations, it can be said that the solution to the problems initially raised can follow the path of what was seen in the studies analyzed. The high costs, both in time and money, the lack of motivation and the low commitment of employees when offering training programs by organizations, are problems that companies had to face. Thus, companies proposed their approaches as a solution. However, some studies presented in their validations some troubles of the employees regarding the instructions prior to the game, their intuition, realism, structure, complexity and content. These negative aspects are considered the gap that must be tackled in the next approaches since it is necessary not to leave aside the aspects of the games that make their results a total success for the company and its employees.

According to the above, in the models or approaches of game-based learning in organizations, it is necessary to carry out a training session with the employees/players in which the objective, rules, competition, interaction, results and other necessary aspects of playing it properly are explained. In addition, the game itself must have a well-defined but straightforward structure, with identified roles, procedures, activities or tasks, content and resources with high quality, game history, etc. in such a way that the game diminishes its complexity (if it exists), be intuitive, motivating and really adds value to the organization, compared with other traditional training methodologies.

Another issue that was not adequately addressed by the implementations was the prior training of employees to enter the world of game-based learning. Some employees are reluctant to new practices; therefore, it can work on it before the game.

Finally, another of the missing characteristics was the multiplayer mode in the studies analyzed. This mode can contribute to increase entertainment, collaborative learning and interaction with other employees and only was present in some studies.

5 Conclusions

Offering training programs in organizations is essential for the performance of a company. Training the employee in order to he has up-to-date knowledge of his functions or the history, objectives, rules and structure of the organization, contributes to improving his productivity and motivation.

A systematic literature review was developed in which was evidenced that from 2005 to the present, research and studies on the topics of game-based learning in organizational training have been growing up. Companies have decided to implement it to reduce costs, time, increase the motivation and interest of employees and take advantage of other benefits that come with using games in organizations.

The companies have created their approaches, models, frameworks, prototypes, instead of the academic models of literature. Besides, companies used game-based learning through serious games*, gamification, virtual world/environment and simulation games immersive and non-immersive, the last one being the most used by companies, as the mechanisms of games in their training programs to solve the exposed problem.

In the majority of the studies analyzed performed a validation through the implementation of the approaches in different companies. The main training topics were Manufacturing, Software and Management. The majority of the population involved was small, medium and large groups of employees, consisting of workers, salespeople, managers, project managers, CEOs, etc.

The results obtained were generally positive, satisfactory and encouraging for all the implementations that were made in the analyzed studies. However, there was always something in common for improving and is what some employees said in the validation process such as lack of instructions previous to the game, the lack of a well-defined structure, games that are not intuitive for the employee, high complexity, etc.

Appendix

[A1]   Li, K., Hall, M., Bermell-Garcia, P., Alcock, J., Tiwari, A., & González-Franco, M.: Measuring the Learning Effectiveness of Serious Gaming for Training of Complex Manufacturing Tasks. Simulation & Gaming 48(6), 770–790 (2017). doi: 10.1177/1046878117739929.

[A2]   Allal-Chérif, O., & Bidan, M.: Collaborative open training with serious games: Relations, culture, knowledge, innovation, and desire. Journal of Innovation & Knowledge 2(1), 31–38 (2017). doi: 10.1016/j.jik.2016.06.003.

[A3]   Landers, R. N., & Armstrong, M. B.: Enhancing instructional outcomes with gamification: An empirical test of the Technology-Enhanced Training Effectiveness Model. Computers in Human Behavior 71, 499–507 (2017). doi: 10.1016/j.chb.2015.07.031.

[A4]   Perini, S., Luglietti, R., Margoudi, M., Oliveira, M., & Taisch, M.: Training Advanced Skills for Sustainable Manufacturing: A Digital Serious Game. Procedia Manufacturing 11, 1536–1543 (2017). doi: 10.1016/j.promfg.2017.07.286.

[A5]   Binninger, M., Dlouhy, J., Oprach, S., & Haghsheno, S.: Learning Simulation Game for Takt Planning and Takt Control. In: 25th Annual Conference of the International Group for Lean Construction, pp. 227–233 (2017). doi.org/10.24928/2017/0088.

[A6]   Holdsworth, J., & Apeh, E.: An Effective Immersive Cyber Security Awareness Learning Platform for Businesses in the Hospitality Sector. In: 2017 IEEE 25th International Requirements Engineering Conference Workshops (REW). Lisbon (2017). doi: 10.1109/rew.2017.47.

[A7]   Müller, B. C., Reise, C., Duc, B. M., & Seliger, G.: Simulation-games for Learning Conducive Workplaces: A Case Study for Manual Assembly. Procedia CIRP 40, 353–358 (2016). doi: 10.1016/j.procir.2016.01.063.

[A8]   Strecker, S., & Rosenthal, K.: Process Modelling as Serious Game: Design of a Role-Playing Game for a Corporate Training. In: 2016 IEEE 18th Conference on Business Informatics (CBI), pp. 228–237. Paris (2016). doi: 10.1109/cbi.2016.33.

[A9]   Valencia, D., Vizcaino, A., Garcia-Mundo, L., Piattini, M., & Soto, J. P.: GSDgame: A Serious Game for the Acquisition of the Competencies Needed in GSD. In: 2016 IEEE 11th International Conference on Global Software Engineering Workshops (ICGSEW), pp. 19–24. Irvine (2016). doi: 10.1109/icgsew.2016.11.

[A10] Alcivar, I., & Abad, A. G.: Design and evaluation of a gamified system for ERP training. Computers in Human Behavior 58, 109–118 (2016). doi: 10.1016/j.chb.2015.12.018.

[A11] Olexová, C., & Gajdoš, J.: Logistics Simulation Game Proposal – a Tool for Employees' Induction. Quality Innovation Prosperity 20(2), 53–68 (2016). doi: 10.12776/qip.v20i2.753.

[A12] Brauner, P., Philipsen, R., Fels, A., Fuhrmann, M., Ngo, Q. H., Stiller, S., Schmitt, M., & Ziefle, M.: A Game-Based Approach to Raise Quality Awareness in Ramp-Up Processes. Quality Management Journal 23(1), 55–69 (2016). doi: 10.1080/10686967.2016.11918462.

[A13] Allal-Chérif, O., Bidan, M., & Makhlouf, M.: Using serious games to manage knowledge and competencies: The seven-step development process. Information Systems Frontiers 18(6), 1153–1163 (2016). doi: 10.1007/s10796-016-9649-7.

[A14] Grund, C., & Schelkle, M.: Developing a serious game for business information visualization. In: Proceedings of the 22nd Americas conference on information systems (AMCIS), (2016).

[A15] Hamza, A., Pernelle, P., Ben Amar, C., & Carron, T.: Serious games for vocational training: A compared approach. In: 2016 IEEE/ACS 13th International Conference of Computer Systems and Applications (AICCSA), pp. 1–8. Agadir (2016). Doi: 10.1109/aiccsa.2016.7945712.

[A16] Nassal, A., & Tichy, M.: Modeling human behavior for software engineering simulation games. In: Proceedings of the 5th International Workshop on Games and Software Engineering - GAS '16, pp. 8–14. Austin (2016). doi: 10.1145/2896958.2896961.

[A17] Isdiyanto, & Rosmansyah, Y.: Gamification framework for designing online training and collaborative working system in Statistics Indonesia. In: 2016 International Conference on Information Technology Systems and Innovation (ICITSI), pp. 1–6. Bandung (2016). doi: 10.1109/icitsi.2016.7858238.

[A18] Butgereit, L.: Gamifying mobile micro-learning for continuing education in a corporate IT environment. In: 2016 IST-Africa Week Conference, pp. 1–7. Durban (2016). doi: 10.1109/istafrica.2016.

[A19] Baxter, R. J., Holderness, D. K., & Wood, D. A.: Applying Basic Gamification Techniques to IT Compliance Training: Evidence from the Lab and Field. Journal of Information Systems 30(3), 119–133 (2016). doi: 10.2308/isys-51341.

[A20] Di Bartolomeo, R., Stahl, F. H., & Elias, D. C.: GAMIFICATION AS A STRATEGY FOR TRAINING AND DEVELOPMENT. Revista Científica Hermes 14(14), 48–70 (2015).

[A21] Adams, M., & Makramalla, M.: Cybersecurity Skills Training: An Attacker-Centric Gamified Approach. Technology Innovation Management Review 5(1), 1–5 (2015). doi: 10.22215/timreview861.

[A22] Pons-Lelardeux, C., Galaup, M., Segonds, F., & Lagarrigue, P.: Didactic Study of a Learning Game to Teach Mechanical Engineering. Procedia Engineering 132, 242–250 (2015). doi: 10.1016/j.proeng.2015.12.476.

[A23] Petridis, P., Uren, V., Baines, T., Lameras, P., Pisithpunth, C., & Shi, V. G.: iServe: A serious game for servitization. In: 2014 International Conference on Interactive Mobile Communication Technologies and Learning (IMCL2014), pp. 237–241. Thessaloniki (2014). doi: 10.1109/imctl.2014.7011139.

[A24] Zafeiropoulos, V., Kalles, D., & Sgourou, A.: Adventure-Style Game-Based Learning for a Biology Lab. In: 2014 IEEE 14th International Conference on Advanced Learning Technologies, pp. 665–667. Athens (2014). doi: 10.1109/icalt.2014.195.

[A25] Hetherinton, D.: SysML requirements for training game design. In: 17th International IEEE Conference on Intelligent Transportation Systems (ITSC), pp. 162–167. Qingdao (2014). doi: 10.1109/itsc.2014.6957684.

[A26] Kampker, A., Deutskens, C., Deutschmann, K., Maue, A., & Haunreiter, A.: Increasing Ramp-up Performance By Implementing the Gamification Approach. Procedia CIRP 20, 74–80 (2014). doi: 10.1016/j. procir.2014.05.034.

[A27] Ahmed, A. M., Mehdi, Q. H., Moreton, R., & Elmaghraby, A.: Towards the use of serious games for effective e-government service. In: 2014 Computer Games: AI, Animation, Mobile, Multimedia, Educational and Serious Games (CGAMES), pp. 1–6. Louisville (2014). doi: 10.1109/cgames.2014.6934148.

[A28] Klemke, R., Ternier, S., Kalz, M., Schmitz, B., & Specht, M.: Immersive Multi-user Decision Training Games with ARLearn. In: European Conference on Technology Enhanced Learning, LNCS, vol. 8719, pp. 207–220. Springer, Cham (2014). doi: 10.1007/978-3-319-11200-8_16.

[A29] Allal-Chérif, O.: Using serious games to Recruit, integrate and train your employees: an exploratory study of practices. European Scientific Journal (ESJ) 10(10), 1–10 (2014).

[A30] Ribeiro, T. R., dos Reis, P. R. J., Júnior, G. B., de Paiva, A. C., Silva, A. C., Maia, I. M. O., & Araújo, A. S.: AGITO: Virtual Reality Environment for Power Systems Substations Operators Training. In: International Conference on Augmented and Virtual Reality (AVR'14), vol. 8853, pp. 113–123. Springer, Cham (2014). doi: 10.1007/978-3-319-13969-2_9.

[A31] Raybourn, E. M.: A new paradigm for serious games: Transmedia learning for more effective training and education. Journal of Computational Science 5(3), 471–481 (2014). doi: 10.1016/j.jocs.2013.08.005.

[A32] Zon, G. D. R., Corrigan, S., McDonald, N., & Maij, A.: A learning, training & mentoring framework (LTM) & the role of serious games to facilitate sustainable change in the aviation industry. In: 11th International Probabilistic Safety Assessment and Management Conference (PSAM'11). Helsinki, Finland (2012).

[A33] Oprins, E. A. P. B., & Korteling, J. E.: Transfer of Training of an Educational Serious Game: The Effectiveness of the CASHIER TRAINER. Simulations, Serious Games and Their Applications, 227–253 (2014). doi: 10.1007/978-981-4560-32-0_15.

[A34] Nikkila, S., Byrne, D., Sundaram, H., Kelliher, A., & Linn, S.: Taskville: visualizing tasks and raising awareness in the workplace. In: CHI '13 Extended Abstracts on Human Factors in Computing Systems, pp. 151–156. Paris (2013). doi: 10.1145/2468356.

[A35] Makanawala, P., Godara, J., Goldwasser, E., & Le, H.: Applying Gamification in Customer Service Application to Improve Agents' Efficiency and Satisfaction. In: International Conference of Design, User Experience, and Usability, LNCS, pp. 548–557. Springer, Berlin, Heidelberg (2013). doi: 10.1007/978-3-642-39241-2_60.

[A36] Korman, T. M., & Johnston, H.: Using game-based learning and simulations to enhance engineering and management education. In: 2013 IEEE Frontiers in Education Conference (FIE), pp. 701–703. Oklahoma City (2013). doi: 10.1109/fie.2013.6684916.

[A37] Li, C., Ranganathan, S., & Vijayachandran, S.: Games in the workplace: Revolutionary or run-of-the-mill? In: 2013 IEEE International Games Innovation Conference (IGIC), pp. 138–147. Vancouver (2013). doi: 10.1109/igic.2013.6659131.

[A38] Messaadia, M., Bufardi, A., Le Duigou, J., Szigeti, H., Eynard, B., & Kiritsis, D.: Applying Serious Games in Lean Manufacturing Training. In: IFIP International Conference on Advances in Production Management Systems. Competitive Manufacturing for Innovative Products and Services, vol. 397, pp. 558–565. Springer, Berlin, Heidelberg (2013). doi: 10.1007/978-3-642-40352-1_70m.

[A39] Buendía-García, F., García-Martínez, S., Navarrete-Ibañez, E. M., & Cervelló-Donderis, M. J.: Designing Serious Games for getting transferable skills in training settings. Interaction Design and Architecture(s) Journal 19, 47–62 (2013).

[A40] Carvalho, C. V. de, Lopes, M. P., & Ramos, A. G.: Digital serious games and simulation games - Comparison of two approaches to lean training. In: 2013 International Conference on Interactive Collaborative Learning (ICL) pp. 49–53. Kazan (2013). doi: 10.1109/icl.2013.6644534.

[A41] Roozeboom, M. B., Wiezer, N., & Joling, C.: Serious gaming used as management intervention to prevent work-related stress and raise work-engagement among workers. In: International Conference on Digital Human Modeling and Applications in Health, Safety, Ergonomics and Risk Management, vol. 8026, pp. 149–158. Springer, Berlin, Heidelberg (2013). doi:10.1037/e577572014-170.

[A42] Gomes, D. F., Lopes, M. P., & de Carvalho, C. V.: Serious Games for Lean Manufacturing: The 5S Game. In: IEEE Revista Iberoamericana de Tecnologias Del Aprendizaje vol. 8, no. 4, pp. 191–196 (2013). doi: 10.1109/rita.2013.2284955.

[A43] Mathieu, P., Panzoli, D., & Picault, S.: Virtual Customers in a Multiagent Training Application. In: Transactions on Edutainment IX, LNCS, vol. 7544, pp. 97–114. Springer, Heidelberg (2013). doi: 10.1007/978-3-642-37042-7_6.

[A44] Donovan, L.: The Use of Serious Games in the Corporate Sector. A State of the Art Report. Learnovate Centre 1–28. Dublin (2012).

[A45] Depura, K., & Garg, M.: Application of Online Gamification to New Hire Onboarding. In: 2012 Third International Conference on Services in Emerging Markets, pp. 153–156. Mysore (2012). https://doi.org/10.1109/icsem.2012.29.

[A46] Lui, S. M., Lemmon, C., Hamilton, J., & Joy, A.: Standardised training simulations: a case study of the water industry in Australia. In: Proceedings of the 6th European Conference on Games Based Learning (ECGBL), pp. 294–300. Cairns (2012).

[A47] Gedeon, T., Zhu, D., & Bersot, S.: Developing a Situated Virtual Reality Simulation for Telerobotic Control and Training. In: E-Learning and Games for Training, Education, Health and Sports, LNCS, pp. 13–22. Darmstadt (2012). doi: 10.1007/978-3-642-33466-5_2.

[A48] Wendel, V., Göbel, S., & Steinmetz, R.: Game Mastering in Collaborative Multiplayer Serious Games. In: E-Learning and Games for Training, Education, Health and Sports, LNCS, pp. 23–34. Darmstadt (2012). doi: 10.1007/978-3-642-33466-5_3.

[A49] Berger, F., & Müller, W.: Implementing High-Resolution Adaptivity in Game-Based Learning. In: E-Learning and Games for Training, Education, Health and Sports, LNCS, pp. 35–40. Darmstadt (2012). doi: 10.1007/978-3-642-33466-5_4.

[A50] Luna, A. S., Gouranton, V., & Arnaldi, B.: Collaborative Virtual Environments for Training: A Unified Interaction Model for Real Humans and Virtual Humans. In: E-Learning and Games for Training, Education, Health and Sports, LNCS, pp. 1–12. Darmstadt (2012). doi: 10.1007/978-3-642-33466-5_1.

[A51] Hauge, J. B., & Riedel, J. C. K. H.: Evaluation of Simulation Games for Teaching Engineering and Manufacturing. Procedia Computer Science, 15, 210–220 (2012). doi: 10.1016/j.procs.2012.10.073.

[A52] Landers, R. N., & Callan, R. C.: Casual Social Games as Serious Games: The Psychology of Gamification in Undergraduate Education and Employee Training. Serious Games and Edutainment Applications 399–423. Springer London (2011). doi: 10.1007/978-1-4471-2161-9_20.

[A53] Werneck, E., & Chang, M.: A Flash-Based Game for Employee Doing On-the-Job Training. In: Edutainment: 6th International Conference on E-learning and Games, LNCS, pp. 522–526. Taipei (2011). doi: 10.1007/978-3-642-23456-9_94.

[A54] Almeida, P., Pedro, L., Moita, M., Magalhães, R., Santos A., & Moreira, L.: Serious Games as an onboarding organizational tool for new employees. In: 6th Iberian Conference on Information Systems and Technologies (CISTI 2011), pp. 1–6. Chaves (2011).

[A55] Léger, P. M., Charland, P., D. Feldstein, H., Robert, J., Babin, G., & Lyle, D.: Business Simulation Training in Information Technology Education: Guidelines for New Approaches in IT Training. Journal of Information Technology Education: Research 10, 39–53 (2011). doi: 10.28945/1362.

[A56] Cantoni, L., & Kalbaska, N.: The Waiter Game: Structure and Development of a Hospitality Training Game. In: 2010s International Conference on Games and Virtual Worlds for Serious Applications, pp. 83–86. Braga (2010). doi: 10.1109/vs-games.2010.22.

[A57] Flores, M., Leon, N., & Aguayo, H.: The BREAK|THROUGH Game: A new way to learn innovation practices. In: 2010 IEEE International Technology Management Conference (ICE), pp. 1–8. Lugano (2010). https://doi.org/10.1109/ice.2010.7477032.

[A58] Jarvis, S., & Freitas, S. de.: Evaluation of an Immersive Learning Programme to Support Triage Training. In: 2009 Conference in Games and Virtual Worlds for Serious Applications, pp. 117–122. Coventry (2009). doi: 10.1109/vs-games.2009.31.

[A59] Zielke, M. A., Evans, M. J., Dufour, F., Christopher, T. V., Donahue, J. K., Johnson, P., Jennings, E. B., Friedman, B. S., Ounekeo, P. L., & Flores, R.: Serious Games for Immersive Cultural Training: Creating a Living World. In: IEEE Computer Graphics and Applications, vol. 29, no. 2, pp. 49–60 (2009). doi: 10.1109/mcg.2009.30.

[A60] Navarro, E. O., & Hoek, A. van der.: Design and Evaluation of an Educational Software Process Simulation Environment and Associated Model. In: 18th Conference on Software Engineering Education & Training (CSEET'05), pp. 25–32. Ottawa (2005). doi: 10.1109/cseet.2005.16.

References

1. Singh, H., Singh, B.P.: E-training: an assessment tool to measure business effectiveness in a business organization. In: 2015 2nd International Conference on Computing for Sustainable Global Development (INDIACom), New Delhi, pp. 1229–1231 (2015)

2. Li, S., Yang, C., Hou, Y.: Study on enterprise training design of MOODLE. In: 2010 International Conference on Computer and Communication Technologies in Agriculture Engineering, pp. 339–341. Chengdu (2010). https://doi.org/10.1109/cctae.2010.5543376

3. Martin, B.O., Kolomitro, K., Lam, T.C.: Training methods: a review and analysis. Hum. Resour. Dev. Rev. 13(1), 11–35 (2014). https://doi.org/10.1177/1534484313497947

4. Van Noord, R., Peterson, J.: Practical approaches for incorporating online training into staff development initiatives. In: World Library and Information Congress: 76th IFLA General Conference and Assembly, Gothenurg (2014)

5. Bouhnik, D., Marcus, T.: Interaction in distance-learning courses. J. Assoc. Inf.Sci. Technol. **57**(3), 299–305 (2006). https://doi.org/10.1002/asi.20277

6. Dutton, J., Dutton, M., Perry, J.: How do online students differ from lecture students? J. Asynchronous Learning Networks **90**(1), 131–136 (2002)

7. Ahmed, A., Sutton, M.J.D.: Gamification, serious games, simulations, and immersive learning environments in knowledge management initiatives. World J. Sci. Technol. Sustain. Dev. **14**(2/3), 78–83 (2017). https://doi.org/10.1108/wjstsd-02-2017-0005

8. Werbach, K., Hunter, D.: Gamification. Coursera (2014). https://class.coursera.org/gamification-003/lecture/preview. Accessed 20 May 2018

9. Gallén, S.: Gamification: a new approach for human resource management. Thesis in Business Management (2016)

10. Cooper, M.: Synthesizing Research: A Guide for Literature Reviews. vol. 2. Sage (1998)

Academic Emotions in Programming Learning: Women's Impact on the Software Sector

Beatriz Eugenia Grass[1(✉)], Mayela Coto[2(✉)], and César Collazos[3(✉)]

[1] San Buenaventura University, Cali, Colombia
beagrass@gmail.com
[2] Universidad Nacional de Costa Rica, San Jose, Costa Rica
mayela.coto.chotto@una.cr
[3] Cauca University, Popayán, Colombia
cacollazo@unicauca.edu.co

Abstract. This document presents an analysis based on a systematic review carried out on the most recognized topics related to academic emotions in the different mechanisms of research and emotional evaluation, trying to focus attention on the initial programming courses, based on the basic programming concepts, independently of the tool in which these concepts are applied, taking into account that the programming courses are considered relevant courses for the training of computer engineers; mechanisms for the evaluation of emotions are also identified. The main emotions in academic contexts are identified and the aim is to identify elements and analysis through the gender variable. Analyses are done focusing on academic emotions. Subsequently, the factors by which women are not linked to the area of software engineering are analyzed, from the perspective of the high drop-out rates due to the programming courses and the impact of the low participation of women in the software sector in the world order, taking into account the roles in which women perform satisfactorily in the software industry.

Keywords: Emotions · Affective states · Learning of programming
Teaching process of programming · Academic emotions

1 Introduction

The impact of emotions on academic processes transcends to the point of affirming that emotions are the stimuli to generate or not, the necessary motivation for the learning process to take place, whatever the subject matter that is being learned [1]. Academic emotions are a highly relevant element in making learning a reality [2].

Academic emotions can be a tool that can be used to reduce dropout [3]. For some years now, the Colombian government has been concerned about academic dropout rates, with critical figures appearing in engineering, computer science and careers related to software development [4]. These high drop-out rates generate professional abandonment, which directly impacts the software industry, stating that the gap between supply and demand is widening every day, since we do not provide enough engineers to the market who can develop software in the world [5].

© Springer Nature Switzerland AG 2019
V. Agredo-Delgado and P. H. Ruiz (Eds.): HCI-COLLAB 2018, CCIS 847, pp. 19–28, 2019.
https://doi.org/10.1007/978-3-030-05270-6_2

An exercise was carried out with female students from different Colombian universities in order to identify relevant milestones in their engineering training process. In focus group meetings with computer science students at Colombian universities, programming courses were identified as the main causes of school dropouts. These courses generate high levels of frustration and boredom in the students [6]. In most professions, academic dropout is directly related to a lack of motivation and frustrated learning processes. Another important factor relates to the economic possibilities of continuing to pay for university studies. In this paper, we will focus on the analysis of the first element, motivation to continue the vocational training process [3]. The lack of motivation causes students to seriously consider dropping out of their careers and increasing dropout rates in their profession [7].

In addition, an analysis of the behavior of women and men's participation in computer and software-related careers was conducted, identifying that the low participation of women is widespread throughout the world, with some exceptions in countries such as India [8]. In the focus groups, it was identified that the low participation of women in professions related to the software sector is due to the high dropout rate of women, and the lack of motivation in their initial courses, such as programming [9].

This article is organized as follows: In Sect. 2, the importance of programming in computer education is presented. Section 3 details the literature related to academic emotions. Section 4 presents the findings found in studies related to academic emotions in programming courses. In Sect. 5, the general conclusions derived from the analysis are presented.

2   Importance of Programming in the Software Sector

The development of software has been consolidated as an important activity in the economies of the countries in the world order. In Colombia, this is no exception, with revenues that will exceed 9.6 trillion pesos in 2015. In addition, sales have multiplied by 3.69 between 2010 and 2015. The figures show that the software industry in Colombia is growing at an accelerated pace and is also identified as an activity of great importance for the country's economy [10].

On the other hand, other countries with similar behavior are identified, countries in which the construction and sale of software products, takes on an important relevance, "the countries in which the software sector concentrated its exports in 2016 were: United States (26%), Ecuador (12%), Spain (12%), Mexico (9%), Chile (4%), Peru (4%) and other countries (20%)" [11].

Despite these optimistic figures, which show the production and sale of software as a promising sector in the short and long term, the opposite situation arises when analyzing that young people do not decide to train as engineers in the areas of software development, they consider this profession to be very difficult, as well as having a conception that they are professions that force professionals to spend a great number of hours in front of a computer. This figure is even more distressing when assessing the participation of women in the software industry. Through different publications, it has been considered that women play a leading role in the sector in areas such as software quality, testing, management, IT project management, analysts, requirements engineers, among others [12]. When the reasons for not studying these professions are identified, students argue the difficulties of mathematics and programming courses [2]. In the same way, they are investigated through focus groups [13]. The difficulties they face are mainly exposed in the initial programming courses. The students state that they are confronted with highly complex issues and that it is not an easy task for them to propose a solution when they were not taught subjects related to the development of computational thinking during their school years [14].

The programming courses generate a set of academic emotions at all levels. Students repeatedly experience emotions such as boredom and frustration when they do not achieve their goal, when programs do not work [15]. Historically, it has been possible to identify that these courses generate high levels of dropout and loss. In reviewing existing literature related to academic emotions, which has been the focus of much research, we have looked at topics such as: which topics are identified as the most difficult, which programming languages produce the most concern, strategies for teaching programming, and mechanisms for learning about programming [16]. In addition, motivation has been identified as the decisive factor for a student to learn. If a student is motivated, he or she will learn. This is why learning programming is a complex problem to solve when the emotions they experience are not properly managed, to be transformed into academic emotions that culminate in a learning process [17].

In academic contexts, there are elements that have been identified as important for motivating students. Motivation is fostered by some elements that are identified in the context of education, for example, collaboration. Collaboration is an alternative as a strategy for teaching programming [18]. Collaborative learning is an educational theory that involves two or more people working together to learn something, it is a theory that goes back years and comes back to life since the emergence of online educational models and with today's students who are digital natives. It is based on the general idea that people can learn more from each other through the exchange of experiences, knowledge and social interaction. Many authors who defend this theory argue that active exchange, debate and negotiation of ideas among peers increases interest in learning [19].

Collaborative elements have been evaluated as positive to be incorporated into teaching strategies, taking into account which collaborative practices and activities generate trust in group members and foster motivation. In an experiment carried out at the University of San Buenaventura, practices with collaborative elements were implemented, the results in relation to motivation and academic performance were superior, compared to the results obtained through traditional practices [13]. A similar situation causes the incorporation of game elements or gamification elements, in such a way that it has been tested, which contributes to motivation, when used and applied in educational environments [13].

Globally, a problem related to women's participation in the software industry is identified as a global concern. Some countries have lower numbers than others, but overall the numbers of women engineers in the software industry are alarming, so it is clear that this is being encouraged through the many efforts of governments and large software companies around the world to encourage women's participation in these organizations [20].

Studies carried out by organizations such as the United Nations (2015), entitled "The Software Industry and Computer Services: A Sector of Opportunity for the Economic Autonomy of Latin American Women [11]", and McKinsey Global Institute (2015), entitled "The power of parity: How advancing women's equality can add \$12 trillion to global growth [16]", highlight the need for more equal participation of both genders to ensure countries' economic growth, emphasizing women's own skills required to improve countries' economies.

The first study also identifies the roles of women with higher and better performance, who due to their low participation in the software industry, these tasks are assumed with less efficiency, generating reprocesses that increase the costs of software development. Figure 1 shows that the greatest presence of women is in roles such as functional analysis, detection of the needs of the software sector, identification of requirements, implementation and design of solutions (soft skills); while men focus more on coding roles, code development and support, among others (hard skills).

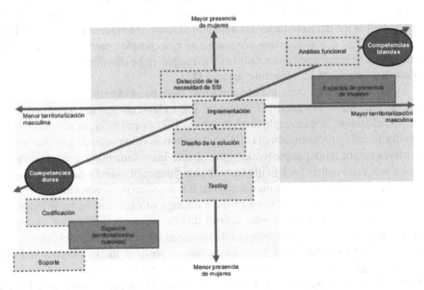

Fig. 1. Gender territorialization in the software industry in Latin America. Source: The software industry and computer services: A sector of opportunity for the economic autonomy of Latin American women (2013) [11].

As part of the analysis of the problems detected related to the low participation of women in the software industry, causes are identified such as the identification of these professions as professions that are labeled as male, which makes them discard the possibility of becoming engineers, due to cultural circumstances; in addition, when students are being trained as engineers, the courses that cause the highest drop-out rates are those of programming [21]. It is identified that the greatest cause of women's dropouts is found in programming courses, even in higher numbers than in mathematics courses, focusing on learning the first few years of programming [22].

In the focus groups held with women from five universities in Cali, information was identified in which they stated that when they manage to pass the first levels of programming, there is greater possibility that they will complete their training process as engineers [13].

3 Academic Emotions and Their Relationship to Gender

Theoretically, it can be said that students experience a rich diversity of emotions in academic settings. Learning and academic achievement are among the most important issues in the current life of our society, especially in terms of professions, social relations and the allocation of many types of resources, which are largely independent of individual achievement [7]. This implies that learning and achievement are unique and important sources of human emotion today, instigating a variety of self-referenced, task-related and social emotions (cf. also Schererer, Wallbott, and Summerfield, 1986). Furthermore, judging by the general functions of emotions for individuals, it can be assumed that emotions influence students' cognitive processes [23] and performance, as well as their psycho-logic, including research that academic emotions are significantly related to students' learning and performance variables [7].

To keep a student motivated, allusion to emotions should be made, focusing on research that studies academic emotions. An academic emotion is one that is directly related to achievement activities or outcomes of achievement [24].

In the 21st century, emotions once again become a subject of interest, which is approached from different disciplines, bearing in mind that these are times in which feelings and emotions are once again given importance [21]. The area of knowledge of computing also recognizes emotions as a subject of interest to contribute from this discipline to the evaluation of emotions, to measure them in real time, to build software that allows decision making in relation to the emotions that are identified in specific circumstances.

When applying collaborative academic practices, the students' commitment to achieving their learning is evaluated.

The academic emotions that are identified in a significant number (14) of papers related to emotions in educational settings are proposed in the following table (Table 1), this classification is made without distinction of gender, that is, any student, male or female, experiences the same academic emotions [25].

Female students experience the same academic emotions; it is a very interesting experiment to identify which of them more frequently, and whether there are some combinations of emotions that they experience more than others. The important thing is to identify what to do with the negative emotions, so that they can be minimized to provide motivation and later learning for the students, specifically in the programming courses. Women experience their learning processes differently [26].

Table 1. Mastery of academic emotions (Source of classification: [7])

	Positives	Negatives
Processes related to tasks	Enjoy yourself	Boredom
Social	Anticipated joy hope	Hopelessness
	Joy for success	Anxiety
	Satisfaction	Sadness
	Relief	Disappointment
	Flow	Shame and guilt
	Gratitude	Anger
	Empathy	Jealousy and envy
	Admiration	Contempt
	Sympathy and love	Antipathy and hatred

4 Findings of Academic Emotions in Teaching Programming

According to the analyzed texts, positive and negative emotions are identified in the educational field, which for research purposes, will be adopted as in many scientific articles, with the name of academic emotions. This concept is considered a general domain in education.

Anxiety is one of the academic emotions that appears repeatedly in the moments of learning programming, with intervals of representation between 15% and 25% of the analyses performed [7]. This emotion is seen as a negative academic emotion, as it can lead to emotions that affect learning, such as frustration or boredom. Academic emotions are generally studied after teacher instruction, as well as behavior in the face of academic tests, which involve assessment and subsequent grading [7].

The emotions that appear repeatedly in all the articles evaluated are most often: the enjoyment of learning, hope, pride and relief, as well as anger, boredom and shame [27].

The concept of emotion, that proposed by Schererer (1984), is taken up again, where emotions are seen as sets of interrelated psychological processes [7]. In addition to the categories of positive or negative emotions, an adjective is also identified that opens the classification into four groups as follows: positive activating emotions (enjoyment of learning, hope of success or pride); positive deactivating emotions (relief, relaxation after success, satisfaction); negative activating emotions (such as anger, anxiety and shame); and negative deactivating emotions (boredom, hopelessness) [28].

By investigating the presence of these emotions in women, the same emotions are identified, appearing at different times in their learning process. Women, by their very nature, are likely to express their emotions more openly. This could allow us to intuit that his experimentation with academic emotions is more fluid and elaborate.

When a search is made for information related to gender-differentiated academic emotions, the results are not detailed. General conclusions can be appreciated, taking into account that both men and women belong to the human race, and we should have similar experiences, but the nature of the woman, allows her to have a differentiated behavior before the situations that involve feelings and emotions. This would lead us to consider the possibility of studying their emotions in learning in a differentiated way, with the aim of identifying relevant elements in this sense [29].

In relation to emotions, an important number of research projects have also been identified, some focusing on programming issues, others on emotions in educational contexts [1, 5, 21, 26–28, 30–39]. Different types of emotions are identified, associated with learning states, but none of them deepen the differences in emotions between men and women.

5 Preliminary Findings

A significant number of publications related to academic emotions have been identified, and positive and negative academic emotions can be defined initially. Of all the publications analysed, five academic emotions can be taken into account: flow, commitment, anxiety, boredom, frustration. (the first two identified as positive in the learning process and the last three identified as negative emotions). These emotions are related to each other, depending on the context. All these emotions that are mentioned were directly identified in the contexts of the programming courses. With this we can conclude that of the fourteen articles reviewed in contexts of learning programming, this topic is of interest in many parts of the world, taking into account that they even propose the development of computational thinking from school stages, such as government bets, to make young people, more competitive and better educated, with respect to others.

The literature analyzed identifies elements and mechanisms that allow the measurement of emotions, which can be taken into account for this research, such as technological tools or hardware devices, or written tests that allow the identification of the perception of these emotions. They can provide real-time information to teachers so that they can make decisions to promote motivation in learning programming. But there is another set of tools to measure emotions, which is based on the application of instruments to identify the emotions that arise in the student's learning process.

No articles related to the particular emotions of the students were found, in all the investigations an analysis is made without distinction of gender, considering that men and women belong to the same race. Studies of identified emotions have been identified at the time of the programming exercises, but NOT with a gender distinction that allows us to conclude on the differences or similarities in this respect.

Academic emotions can be evaluated and identified through different mechanisms, written tests can be used to identify the emotions perceived at a given moment of the class, being considered as less invasive mechanisms, however, also considered less effective, because in a written test, you can write things far from what you have really experienced. Emotions can be assessed through hardware devices, which can reveal more accurately the emotion perceived by the student, but can be a more intrusive mechanism for carrying out the assessment. Likewise, academic emotions can be evaluated through a gestural comparison, physical elements, such as sweating, brain signals, through already proposed evaluation units.

In terms of emotions, important steps have been taken, bearing in mind that emotions are considered as triggers of learning processes, which is considered important for taking into account and carrying out effective teaching exercises. Knowing the emotions experienced by the students is an important element for the teacher to make decisions oriented to the achievement of the students' learning.

For the evaluation of emotions, mechanisms such as technology related to the emotion of speech, the emotion of facial expressions, the emotion of text, the emotion of body gestures and movement, the emotion of physiological states are identified [37].

Evaluating emotions from a gender perspective can increase women's chances of becoming part of the computer-related professions, when more efficient mechanisms can be proposed to achieve the learning of courses related to programming.

References

1. Astrolabio, E.: Emociones académicas: El Eslabón Perdido del Plan de Estudios, 94–107 (2015)
2. Fisher, A., Margolis, J., Miller, F.: Undergraduate women in computer science: experience motivation and culture. ACM SIGCSE Bull. **29**(1), 29 (1997)
3. Bosch, N., D'Mello, S., Mills, C.: What emotions do novices experience during their first computer programming learning session? In: Lane, H.C., Yacef, K., Mostow, J., Pavlik, P. (eds.) AIED 2013. LNCS (LNAI), vol. 7926, pp. 11–20. Springer, Heidelberg (2013). https://doi.org/10.1007/978-3-642-39112-5_2
4. Burton, L.J.: Higher education in a changing world (2005)
5. Won, J., Kang, M.: Computers & Education. The role of academic emotions in the relationship between perceived academic control and self-regulated learning in online learning. Comput. Educ. **77**, 125–133 (2014)
6. Lehman, K.J., Sax, L.J., Zimmerman, H.B.: Women planning to major in computer science: who are they and what makes them unique? Comput. Sci. Educ. **26**, 277–298 (2017)
7. Pekrun, R., Goetz, T., Titz, W., Perry, R.P.: Academic emotions in students' self-regulated learning and achievement: a program of qualitative and quantitative research. Educ. Psychol. **37**, 91–105 (2002)
8. Wilson, B.C.: Gender differences in types of assignments preferred: implications for computer science instruction. J. Educ. Comput. Res. **34**, 245–255 (2006)
9. Eccles, J.S., Wang, M.T.: What motivates females and males to pursue careers in mathematics and science? Int. J. Behav. Dev. **40**, 100–106 (2016)
10. Tiempo, P.: El Preocupante déficit de ingenieros en Colombia (2015). http://www.eltiempo.com/estilo-de-vida/educacion/p
11. Pérez-Bustos, T., Marquez Gutiérrez, S.: La industria del software y los servicios informáticos (SSI): un sector de oportunidad para el empoderamiento económico de las mujeres latinoamericanas. Capítulo Colombia – Informe de sistematización, **42** (2013)
12. Gabbert, P., et al.: ACM-W's New Programs for Recruiting and Retaining Women in Computing. ACM SIGCSE Bull. **39**(1), 247–248 (2007)
13. Ramírez, B.E.G., Collazos, C.A., González, C.S.: Gender differences in computing programs: Colombian case study. ACM Int. Conf. Proceeding Ser. pp. 4–6 (2016). https://doi.org/10.1145/2998626.2998670
14. Blum, L.: Transforming the Culture of Computing at Carnegie Mellon Why (and How) the Increase? 1–6 (2002)

15. Byrne, P., Lyons, G.: The effect of student attributes on success in programming. ACM SIGCSE Bull. **33**(33), 49–52 (2001)
16. Murphy, L., Westbrook, S., Richards, B., Morrison, B.B., Fossum, T.: Women Catch Up: gender differences in learning programming concepts. ACM SIGCSE Bull. **38**(1), 17–21 (2006)
17. Cohoon, J.M.: Recruiting and retaining women in undergraduate computing majors. ACM SIGCSE Bull. **34**(2), 48–52 (2002)
18. Collazos, C., Guerrero, L., Pino, J., Ochoa, S.: Evaluating collaborative learning processes. Groupw. Des. Implement. Use **2440**, 173–194 (2002)
19. González, C.S., Collazos, C.A., García, R.: Desafío en el diseño de MOOCs: incorporación de aspectos para la colaboración y la gamificación. RED. Rev. Educ. a Distancia (2016)
20. Mata, F.J. et al.: Gender Gap in Computer Science Programs from Costa Rican Public Universities Are Women Really Becoming Extinct? (2012)
21. Chetty, J., Westhuizen, D. Van der. " I hate programming" and Other Oscillating Emotions Experienced by Novice Students Learning Computer Programming. In: EdMedia World Conference on Educational Media and Technology, pp. 1889–1894 (2013)
22. Vitores, A., Gil-Juárez, A.: The trouble with 'women in computing': a critical examination of the deployment of research on the gender gap in computer science. J. Gend. Stud. 1–15 (2015). https://doi.org/10.1080/09589236.2015.1087309
23. Linnenbrink-Garcia, L., Pekrun, R.: Students' emotions and academic engagement: introduction to the special issue. Contemp. Educ. Psychol. **36**, 1–3 (2011)
24. Pekrun, R., Goetz, T., Frenzel, A.C., Barchfeld, P., Perry, R.P.: Measuring emotions in students' learning and performance: the Achievement Emotions Questionnaire (AEQ). Contemp. Educ. Psychol. **36**, 36–48 (2011)
25. Robins, A., Rountree, J., Rountree, N.: Learning and teaching programming: a review and discussion. Comput. Sci. Educ. **13**, 137–172 (2003)
26. Martin, C., Hughes, J., Richards, J.: Learning experiences in programming: The Motivating Effect of a Physical Interface. **1**, 162–172 (2017)
27. Linnenbrink, E.A.: Emotion research in education: theoretical and methodological perspectives on the integration of affect, motivation, and cognition. Educ. Psychol. Rev. **18**, 307–314 (2006)
28. Good, J., Rimmer, J., Harris, E., Balaam, M.: Self-reporting emotional experiences in computing lab sessions: an emotional regulation perspective. In: Proceedings of the 23rd Annual Psychology Programming Interest Group Conference (2011)
29. Davies, D., et al.: Creative learning environments in education-a systematic literature review. Think. Ski. Creat. **8**, 80–91 (2013)
30. Rosas, S.: The Achievement Emotions Questionnaire-Argentine (AEQ-AR): internal and external validity, reliability, gender differences and norm-referenced interpretation of test scores development and adaptation of instruments to measure test anxiety has been con. Revista Evaluar **15**(1), 41–74 (2015)
31. Martin, C., Hughes, J., Richards, J.: Learning experiences in programming: The Motivating Effect of a Physical Interface **2002** (2017)
32. Connolly, T.M., Boyle, E.A., MacArthur, E., Hainey, T., Boyle, J.M.: A systematic literature review of empirical evidence on computer games and serious games. Comput. Educ. **59**, 661–686 (2012)
33. Talug, D.Y.: Lifelong learning through out today's occasions namely social media and online games. Procedia - Soc. Behav. Sci. **46**, 4431–4435 (2012)
34. D'Mello, S., Graesser, A.: Dynamics of affective states during complex learning. Learn. Instr. **22**, 145–157 (2012)

35. Simões, J., Redondo, R.D., Vilas, A.F.: A social gamification framework for a K-6 learning platform. Comput. Human Behav. **29**, 345–353 (2013)

36. Pekrun, R.: The control-value theory of achievement emotions: assumptions, corollaries, and implications for educational research and practice. Educ. Psychol. Rev. **18**, 315–341 (2006)

37. Lachmann, H., Ponzer, S., Johansson, U.-B., Benson, L., Karlgren, K.: Capturing students' learning experiences and academic emotions at an interprofessional training ward. J. Interprof. Care **27**, 137–145 (2013)

38. Daniels, L.M., et al.: Individual differences in achievement goals: a longitudinal study of cognitive, emotional, and achievement outcomes. Contemp. Educ. Psychol. **33**, 584–608 (2008)

39. Pekrun, R., Goetz, T., Daniels, L.M., Stupnisky, R.H., Perry, R.P.: Boredom in achievement settings: exploring control-value antecedents and performance outcomes of a neglected emotion. J. Educ. Psychol. **102**, 531–549 (2010)

An Empiric Study of the Use of Mobile Technology by Users with Intellectual Disability

Alfredo Mendoza-González[1]([ORCID]), Huizilopoztli Luna-García[2][ORCID],
Ricardo Mendoza-González[3][ORCID], Cristian Rusu[4][ORCID],
Jorge I. Galván-Tejada[2][ORCID], Hamurabi Gamboa-Rosales[2][ORCID],
José G. Arceo-Olague[2][ORCID], José M. Celaya-Padilla[2][ORCID],
and Roberto Solis-Robles[2][ORCID]

[1] Instituto de Investigación, Desarrollo e Innovación en Tecnologías
Interactivas, A. C., Moscatel 103, Aguascalientes, Mexico
mendoza.uaa@gmail.com
[2] Universidad Autónoma de Zacatecas, Jardín Juárez 147, Zacatecas, Mexico
{hlugar,gatejo,hamurabig,arceojgh,jose.celaya,
rsolis}@uaz.edu.mx
[3] Instituto Tecnológico de Aguascalientes,
Lic. Adolfo López Mateos Ote 99, Aguascalientes, Mexico
mendozagric@mail.ita.mx
[4] Pontificia Universidad Católica de Valparaíso,
Av. Brasil 2950, Valparaíso, Chile
cristian.rus@pucv.cl

Abstract. People with intellectual disabilities can use tablet computers and smartphones to enhance their learning and increase their independent living. Nevertheless, there is a dark side in the use of mobile devices, directed linked with distraction, dependency, and isolation, especially in young people. This research focuses in the question, what kind of activities does people with intellectual disability do with mobile devices? With this objective an empiric study was developed over a population of 25 teenagers of two countries: Mexico and Chile. It included direct observation, surveys, interviews, and active research over two uncontrolled and controlled scenarios. All observations, evaluations and analysis were divided in 3 groups: Usage focus, Performance, and Subjective appreciation, Results showed that the main usage of mobile devices by these teenagers was entertainment, being Youtube® the most popular application. The performance of users varies widely depending of the experience in the use of such devices, but all of them have troubles with text and tiny touchable objects. Users are really happy while using freely their mobile devices, it decreases when the activities area guided and limited by parents or teachers. Parents and teachers see with good eyes the use of mobile devices in classroom and home with educational meanings, but both declare their lack of knowledge in finding the right content.

Keywords: Human factors · Human-computer interaction · Accessibility

© Springer Nature Switzerland AG 2019
V. Agredo-Delgado and P. H. Ruiz (Eds.): HCI-COLLAB 2018, CCIS 847, pp. 29–43, 2019.
https://doi.org/10.1007/978-3-030-05270-6_3

1 Introduction

The use of mobile devices has reach almost all activities in human living, including communication, entertainment, health, science and education. The current design of mobile software and hardware makes possible that all benefits reach almost all people in society. The tablet computer and the smartphones are most popular mobile devices used in Latin America… used by almost all members of the society including children, older adults, people with disabilities, professionals, students, and many others.

The accessibility of technology in the information society era implies not only the ease of use of devices, but also the simplification of the services consumption, no matter the skills, capabilities and physical and intellectual condition [1]. It is well known that, around the world, people with disabilities are regular users of technology including computers, game consoles, mobile devices, and wearable devices; nevertheless, it is less known the porpoise of use they have, are they used for educational porpoise, or for entertainment? Are they being fully used? Are they making a real change in their lives? And more important, how the people with disabilities and their relatives find this new technology?

This research is focus in analyzing how people with intellectual disabilities interact with tablet computer and smartphones and what is the impact that they make in their academic and personal living. Authors applied the Action Research methodology to understand better the problem from the participants' side, involving ethnographic activities, empiric evaluations and active participation in real scenarios. 25 teenagers with mild and moderate level of intellectual disability were the essential part of this study, 15 of them were from the city of Aguascalientes in Mexico, and 10 of them were from Viña del Mar, in Chile. The study involved also, all people around them: relatives, teachers and therapists.

The remainder of the paper is organized as follows: Sect. 2 presents a theoretical background of the study, including the learnability and gamification foundations, a summary of Down syndrome, and the most important researches related with this work. In Sect. 3 the research methodology is described. A detailed description of the proposed method is presented in Sect. 4. The experimental work is described in Sect. 5. Results are presented and discussed Sect. 5. Finally, our conclusions are presented in Sect. 6.

2 Theoretical Background

2.1 Intellectual Disability

Disability is the inability to accommodate to the world as it is currently designed [1].

Around the world, there are many terms to name people with disabilities; the United Nation Organization (UNO) on its Convention on the Rights of People with Disabilities mentions *person with disability* is the correct term to name a person that has limitations abilities or condition [2]. A person with disability, according with UNO and the World Health Organization (WHO), is an individual who manifests restrictions in the quality or quantity of activities that can develops, due to limitations on his/her intellectual or physical condition [3]. As referred by the UNO, the concept of disability has a dynamic focus "... *it is a concept that evolves and results from the interaction between people with disability and barriers imposed by the attitude of the others members of the society and the environment that limits their full participation and development in society, with no equality*" [2].

In May 22nd 2001, the executive committee of the WHO announced a classification for all disabilities entitled International Classification of Functioning, Disability and Health (ICF), it is based in the idea that: "*The term Disability includes deficiencies and limitations in activity, so as restrictions in participation, making emphasis in the negative aspects of the interaction between individuals with a certain condition and the contextual factors that affect him/her*" [3].

The Diagnostic and Statistical Manual of Mental Disorders (DSM) from the American Psychiatric Association, on its 5th edition defines *Intelectual disability*, also called Transtorn of the Intellectual Development, as the limitations in the intllectual function, and in the adaptative behavior in the conceptual, social and pragmatic domains [4]. The DSM-5 mentions that all people with intellectual disability has difficulties in memory where their development is usually low, affecting mainly the language learning generating troubles in auditive learning, razoning and problem solving. About the motricity development in people with disability begins late and retards the progress in other academical and personal habilities, such as hand writing, tools manipulation including digital devices [4].

The prevalesence of intellectual disability around the world, according with a 2011 meta-analysis of international studies is 10.37/1000 or 1.04% [5]. A follow-up meta-analysis of international studies, extending the work of [5], found the ID prevalence of children/adolescents and adults to range from .05 to 1.55% [6].

2.2 Disability Context in Mexico and Chile

In Mexico, the National Council of Statistic, Geography and Informatics (INEGI, by its name in Spanish *Instituto Nacional de Estadística, Geografía e Informática*) defined the term *person with disability* as "... *a person with some limitation on his/hers physical or mental that reduces his/her capabilities to develop activities in house, school, or work, such as walking, dressing, taking showers, reading and writing, among others*" [7]. This is the official term used on its National Population Census and Inter-census surveys.

Approximately 6% of Mexicans lives with some kind disability, and around 450 thousand has intellectual disability [7, 8].

In Chile the Law 20.22 dictates the adoption of the term defined in the UNO Convention, stablishing, according with the law, the rules of equality on opportunities and the social inclusion of people with disabilities [9]. The prevalence in Chile of people with disability reaches almost the 20% of the total population, being around 373 thousand people with intellectual disability [9].

Talking about learning development, people with intellectual disability take more time in learning new things and completing activities, in comparison with their neurotypical pairs (people without intellectual disability). They require a broken down learning program, based in small activities with concrete objectives, enhanced with visual clues, explicit teaching of certain abilities, and repetition as the medium to retain such new information [10]. Also, people with intellectual disability have deficiencies in some receptive language domains that exceed those of the cognitive domain [11]. It has been found that people with disability obtain lower age-based scores, in the Test for Auditory Comprehension of Language (TACL-R) than other children of the same age with normal intellectual development [12].

2.3 Technological Context in Mexico and Chile

In Mexico the National Survey of Availability and Usage of Technology in Homes showed that 14.7 million of homes (nearly 45% of all homes in Mexico) have at least one personal computer, being nearly 55.7 million of computer users. About internet services, almost 13 million of homes (nearly 40%) have private internet connection, being around 62.4 million of people using internet services [13]. Other results of the same survey, Mexican people use internet services mainly for information consultation (88,7%), for communication purposes (84.1%), multimedia entertainment (76.6%) and to socialize (71.5%). Nearly 80% of the population use mobile devices, and nearly 70% access to the internet with them.

In Chile, according with the Transport and Telecommunication Ministry around 85% of homes have at least one personal computer; 84.1% of the population have internet access, being a total of 15.3 million of internet users [14]. Results of the National Internet Usage and Accessibility Survey indicate that the main reasons of why Chileans use internet are: information consultation (92%), communicational purposes (89%), educational purposes (74%), entertainment purposes (60%) and social networking (55%) [4]. Using mobile technology nearly 74% of chileans have at least one mobile device; and more than 80% of all internet conections are made from mobile devices [15].

2.4 Related Work

As a Computer Science concern, humans are limited in their capacity to process information; this has important implications for design [16]. Evidently, knowing the user needs will help to reach the level of usability required by the user, in other words, when designer can translate user capacities, abilities and limitations to the design process, the system has a clear opportunity to be as expected by the user [16].

According with [17], nowadays the mobile devices are commonly used by people with disability and they are implemented, with more and more regularity, as complement in their academic programs. Mobile devices have been also proved as useful to support communicational capabilities, enhance job skills acquisition, and as entertainment providers to people with disability [18].

In [19] authors presented a study about the efficiency of interventions based on mobile technology for people with intellectual disability. They analized 78 individuals with intellectual disorders, all of them sharing limitations in cognitive functions (bellow the normal range), communication skills, and adaptative capabilities; including individuals with autthism, developmental disability, mental retardation and multiple intellectual disability. Authors found that the technology implemented did not required significant adecuations, in order to be used by the participants. As concluding remarks, authors mentioned that mobile devices are mainly used as an instructional tool, having interaction mainly with the teacher. This living away all beneffits of the use of such technoloy when students interact with it individually or in group, in-class activites or in extra-curricular activites, denying an enhancement in communication, social behavior, and even daily activities planning.

An exploratory study about the use of mobile devices as tools to help in communication for people with intellectual disability is presented in [18]. The first step of this research was to analize the different user-profiles. Then all changes in the communicational skills, derived from the use of these digital tablets were reported. The study was developed in Montreal, where 7 adults between 27 and 54 were tested while using iPad® computers. All participants have intellectual disability and were enrolled in a special education center; they also have 6 months using such devices at least at the moment of the test. Results showed that iPad® computers have the capability to be efficiently used as an augmentative and alternative communicational system for people with intellectual disability.

Focused on a pedagogic perspective, authors in [20] presented a study of the Information and Communications Technologies (ICT) by people with intellectual disability, particularly about the way they are used inside the learning process. Author refers that ICT are used mainly in two ways: one, as support of the learning activities, as a tool to guide and manage the academic content; and second, as augmentative and alternative communicational system. Author concludes that the usage of ICT inside the academic program of people with disabilities, not only enhances the acquisition of specific skills and abilities, but also develops the student's personal autonomy, enhancing self-esteem and life quality.

In [21], authors presented an exploratory study about the usage of internet services and mobile devices by adults with intellectual disability in Spain. The study involved 156 participants between 30 and 40 years old, all of them with intellectual disability. Authors found patterns in the consumption of such technologies, nearly equal to those of the neuro-typical (without intellectual disability) users. From results set, it is highlighted that 90% of participants owned a smartphone, and that only nearly 50% had internet access. The mobile apps, authors mentioned that just the 22% of participants used one for text messaging.

Examples of scientific work about how people with a specific intellectual disability can be benefitted with mobile technology, are:

- In [22], authors presented how people with Down Syndrome achieve several tasks in job activities using mobile devices.
- In [23] authors presents how a mobile app called OrientingTool helps people with anterograde amnesia.
- Authors in [24] show how people with Alzheimer can be benefit with BigKey, a mobile app designed to make the keys of virtual keyboard easier to acquire.
- In [25] authors analyzed, throughout surveys, the use of computers and internet services by people with Down syndrome.

3 Research Methodology

The methodology used in this work is the Action Research Methodology, which implied knowing the research problem from the perspective of those affected with it. Researchers diagnose, plan the actions, applied the actions, evaluates the results of the actions over the problem, and identify all findings, all in an iterating process, to know the most they can about the problem [26]. Into this process we added an ethnographic study; it was based in [27, 28] and followed the next steps:

1. Definition of the study population
2. Application of surveys and interviews
3. Direct observation and active participation
4. Identification of usage patterns
5. Data analysis

These five stages in the ethnographic study allowed researchers to deeply know the characteristics of the participants and their social environment, so as their background as users of technology.

4 Experimental Work

All activities took place in two scenarios: real (uncontrolled) scenarios, such as schools, therapy centers and participants' houses; and in controlled scenarios, such as usability laboratories, and observation rooms. The stages of the whole experiment are listed next:

1. Knowing the participants background
2. Applying surveys and interviews
3. Interacting in real scenarios
4. Interacting in controlled scenarios

4.1 Knowing Participants

The study involved 25 participants with Down syndrome, 14 men and 10 women between 12 and 20 years old ($\overline{X} = 16.1$, $S = 3.9$); all of them were enrolled in an institute of special education. This institute evaluated all students in six points: Communication skills, Physical development, Self-direction, Social behavior, Literacy and Mathematics.

With a battery of tests, based in WISC-IV [29] and Valpar [30] tests, a multidisciplinary team assigned one of three levels for each student at each point, according in what they expected, considering age, and type and grade of disability. The objective of the evaluation, according with them, is to offer academic services according with student's needs: The multidisciplinary team evaluated each student with the next scale:

1. Communication skills: Grade for expressing ideas and emotions to others.
   (a) High: The student has no problems to communicating.
   (b) Appropriated: The student need some help to put together and to express some ideas.
   (c) Low: The student needs a lot of help to communicate.

2. Physical Skills: Grade to develop gross movements such as walking, running, crawling, etc.
   (a) High: There is not difficulties in movement.
   (b) Appropriated: The student has some troubles in coordination and precision.
   (c) Low: The student has difficulties developing any movement.
3. Self-direction: Grade to be independent in daily living and self-care, to follow schedules and to solve common problems.
   (a) High: The student is independent in daily living tasks, and has no troubles learning new ones.
   (b) Appropriated: The student needs help in some tasks, especially in the new ones.
   (c) Low: The student cannot do any daily tasks by him/her-self.
4. Social behavior: Capability to get integrated in social groups and to respect its rules.
   (a) High: The individual can socialize easily, has no trouble with social behavior rules.
   (b) Appropriated: The individual has some problems socializing, and understanding the accepted social behavior.
   (c) Low: It is very difficult for the student to get integrated in a social group.
5. Literacy: Ability to read and write.
   (a) High: The student can read and write without troubles.
   (b) Appropriated: Student can read and write simple sentences.
   (c) Low: The student cannot read and write.
6. Math: Ability to solve problems involving numbers.
   (a) High: The student can solve additions, subtractions, and multiplications.
   (b) Appropriated: Student can read and write numbers, and identifying tens and hundreds, but has some troubles solving additions and subtractions.
   (c) Low: Student at much can read and write numbers.

Data for the 24 participants is shown in Table 1. No specific information about evaluation procedures and tests scenarios was provided by the institute.

4.2 Applying Surveys and Interviews

Surveys and interviews were focused in how people with Down syndrome have access and use mobile devices, including all kind of preferences: places, hardware, applications, purposes, etc. 95 people participate in this activity, between participants with Down syndrome, relatives, teachers and therapists, from Mexico and Chile.

We defined three different questionnaires, according with the next profiles:

- Users with Down syndrome, 15 questions.
- Parents and relatives of users with Down syndrome (25 questions)
- Teachers and therapists of users with Down syndrome (25 questions)

Table 1. Information about participants

Characteristic	Target users %
Communication skills	High: 37.5% Appropriated: 58.3% Low: 4.2%
Physical skills	High: 41.7% Appropriated: 54.2% Low: 4.2%
Self-direction	High: 37.5% Appropriated: 45.8% Low: 16.7%
Social behavior	High: 12.5% Appropriated: 87.5% Low: 0%
Literacy	High: 16.7% Appropriated: 70.8% Low: 12.5%
Math	High: 0% Appropriated: 58.3% Low: 41.7%

The differences between questionnaires types were for example the language used in the questions (going from simple to technical), the mode of how the questionnaires were presented to participants (with assistance and without it) and the mode of application (in group or individually). Despite the type of questionnaire, the core of all of them are the next ten questions (we use the term *individual* to refer to the users with Down syndrome):

1. Does the individual own a mobile device? Of what kind?
2. From whom, other devices used by the individual came from?
3. Which are the three main places where the individual uses mobile devices?
4. How much time, does the individual use mobile devices per day?
5. What activities does the individual mainly make over the mobile devices?
6. What are the most used applications by the individual?
7. Do you apply any rule or restriction in the use of mobile devices?
8. Have you ever received any usage recommendation? From what sources?
9. Does the individual use any mobile device as part of his/her learning process?
10. What advantages and disadvantages do you think the use of mobile devices by the individual brings?

Many other questions were derived from these five. Surveys applied to relatives and experts included multiple-choice questions, rating-scale questions, rank-order-scaling questions, and open questions; surveys applied to participants with Down syndrome were more flexible, to be sure that participants understand questions. Since the surveys were complemented with an interview (sometimes right after it, sometimes not), researchers could deeply inquire in relevant responses. Both, surveys and interviews were applied in participants' houses, classrooms, school offices, and therapy rooms, depending on the respondents' preference (or availability).

4.3   Interacting in Real Scenarios

To know how people with Down syndrome interact with each other, relatives, and teachers we made the next activities:

- Participation in academic activities
- Participation in extra-curricular activities
- Interviews with relatives, friends and teachers
- Visits to participants' houses

We did not limit the group of participants to only Down syndrome people. Since most of the activities took part in an Elementary School of special education, we hang out with all students. Nevertheless, interviews and visits were made only to those with Down syndrome.

Academic activities included all activities in classroom, such as painting, singing, reading, writing, dancing and so others. In these activities we took especially care about how teachers interacted with students, and the behavior that they evoked on them. Something to take in consideration is that, all researchers that were present in these activities, acted as members of the group since the beginning, just like new students incorporating in the group.

Extracurricular activities were in school, such as taking lunch, playing basketball and soccer, chatting, etc.; and outside school such as playing video-games, watching movies and going to parties. Here we analyzed how students interact each other. In all activities we talk with several teachers, relatives and friends about their Down syndrome boys and girls. They gave us all kinds of information: likes and dislikes, daily living, common behavior, peculiarities, etc. All this information was very useful for our work.

Computer classes were especially interesting. Due to the reduced number of available machines, teacher must place two students to each one. Since all activities were designed to work alone, students must take turns in participation. Nevertheless, we found out that working in pairs has a lot of benefits if activities were designed in a proper way, from which we can took advantage to enhance the learnability evaluation.

4.4   Interacting in Controlled Scenarios

We applied a set of activities inside usability labs and observation rooms in order to see how users with Down syndrome develop in such scenarios. Due to the availability of the scenarios and the available time of participants, only 15 of the 25 participated in this part of the research, some of them participate in more than one scenario. The activities were developed in four different places:

- Usability laboratory of the Institute of Research, Development and Innovation in Mexico, 5 participants.
- Usability laboratory of the Pontifical Catholic University of Valparaiso in Chile 5 participants.
- Observation room of APARID Association in Chile, 5 participants.
- Observation room of the Polytechnic University of Aguascalientes in Mexico, 5 participants.

Five activities were made in all the four controlled scenarios:

1. Using an already known application over an already known device (single).
2. Using an unknown application over an already known device.
3. Using an unknown application over an unknown device (single).
4. Using an already known application over an already known device (in pairs).
5. Using an unknown application over an unknown device (in pairs).

The activities were developed without researcher's intervention. At the beginning, one researcher provides general instructions to participants and only interrupts the session when the participant was stock or when the activity was completed. Behind the glass, commonly were two researchers, and one or two relatives of the participant. Sometimes there were a teacher, a therapist or another expert guest. Sessions, which included all 5 activities took around 25 min at maximum. From the 20 sessions applied, there were 10 fully completed, and the other 20 implied from 2 to 4 activities.

5 Results

Of the 25 participants, 6 of them have at least one mobile device, 4 have a smartphone and 2 have a smartphone and an electronic tablet. The ownership of the mobile devices was divided into owned by the user, with 26%, owned by the mother or father, with 60% and owned by other relative, 14%.

The places of use of mobile devices were the home of residence (70%), the home of a family member (40%), the workplace of one of the parents (30%) and public places (30%).

The daily time that users spend using mobile devices has an average of 3.5 h, taking a total of 26 h of use per week.

Regarding the activities that users perform on mobile devices, it was found that 80% of users primarily perform leisure activities, including entertainment, social networks, multimedia content and online or local games. 15% of users mainly use the device for academic purposes, including games and educational applications; and 5% for communication.

The applications most used by users were YouTube (70%), local games (20%), online games (5%) and other entertainment applications, including camera, social networks and messaging (5%). None of the participants declared the use of an internet browser.

Only 5 of the 25 participants have some kind of restriction in the use of the mobile devices, which is used for very specific purposes, for example, to complement school activities at home or for communication-only purposes. The rest of the participants use the devices without restriction in time and content.

12 of the parents have installed at least one recommended application, such recommendation was made by other parents (80%), by acquaintances or people close to the family (15%) and by teachers and therapists (5%). However, only 4 of them supervise and keep updated the set of installed applications, giving priority to those applications with academic content.

The use of mobile devices in the classroom was very limited. All the participants have used a mobile device at least once as part of the academic activities within the classroom, however, when inquiring about this fact, the teachers indicated that they use a mobile device on 1 of each 20 sessions, as an average, having 1 of each 10 the maximum. The minimum number of times that a teacher uses a mobile device in classroom, was one in the whole academic year.

The following Table 2 shows the advantages and disadvantages that participants and all interviewees found in the use of mobile devices.

Table 2. Advantages and disadvantages of mobile devices

Profile	Advantages	Disadvantages
Participants	• They are fun • You can do many things on them	• Battery last very little • They are tiny • They don't have good sound
Teachers and therapists	• Activities can be selected or adapted to each student • They allow interaction and communication throughout different channels	• It too difficult to close pleasant activities • There are no enough devices to all students • Require supervision
Parents	• Stimulate concentration • Control anxiety and stress levels • Motivate independence	• They are expensive • They are fragile
Other relatives	• They allow us to reach very diverse content	• They are hard to operate • They are too tiny • They are expensive

Based on the data collected, the following findings were determined. The frequency of use of mobile devices, according to the study region was on average: Mexico 15.13 h/wk (S = 6.03) and Chile 25.7 h/wk. (S = 8.28). Ownership of the devices, by people with intellectual disabilities, presented by country: Mexico 20% and Chile: 30%. The most common places of use in the Mexican and Chilean population are the home with 86.6% in the Mexican population and 80% in the Chilean population.

The purpose of activity that users perform on mobile devices is shown in Fig. 1. As can be seen, leisure activities dominated in both populations.

The most used applications according to the study region were shown in Fig. 2. In both populations YouTube dominated to a large extent, followed by games installed on the device, games available on the internet and other entertainment applications.

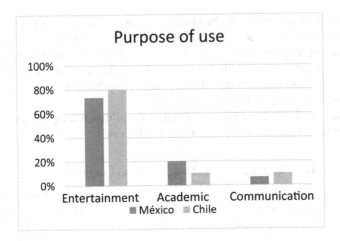

Fig. 1. Purpose of use of mobile devices

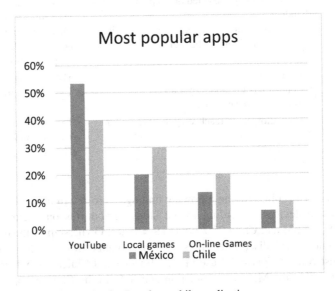

Fig. 2. Popular mobile applications

6 Conclusions

This paper reports the advantages and disadvantages of the use of mobile devices by people with disabilities. The findings were derived from an exploratory study conducted on a population of 25 young people with moderate intellectual disability, between 15 and 18 years old; involving participants from Mexico and Chile in order to expand diversity by taking advantage of their stay at the Pontifical Catholic University of Valparaíso by the first author.

Through the application of ethnographic research that included surveys, interviews and active participation with the young participants, their families and teachers, information was obtained about the objectives, places, frequent applications, among other relevant data regarding the use of mobile devices.

Among the most relevant results it was observed that one in four participants owns at least one mobile device, while 60% of the studied population uses a device provided by one of their parents.

The time of use of mobile devices was on average 20.5 h/week. About 80% of the participants mainly do leisure activities on mobile devices, with YouTube being the most used application, with nearly 50% of the population. Although parents, teachers and therapists know the advantages of using mobile devices in academic activities in the classroom, on average they are used in one of every 20 sessions.

This pilot study allowed to visualize generalities in the use of mobile devices by people with intellectual disabilities, denoting points of opportunity, where it is possible to carry out research. For example, in the realization of models of incorporation of mobile technology in special education, models of adoption and redirection of the purpose of use, models of approach and accessibility in digital contents for parents and academics, as well as analysis and evaluations of sites commonly used by said population, for example to extract design patterns, good practices and evaluation heuristics.

Aknowlegement. The authors thank those who participated in the tests developed in this research work, the young people who dedicated their time and effort in the surveys, interviews and other activities. Likewise, special thanks are given to the facilities and support of the Pontifical Catholic University of Valparaíso and the Fenix and Aparid foundations of the cities of Valparaíso and Viña del Mar in Chile, during the research stay carried out by the first author of this one job.

References

1. Vanderheiden, G.: Design for people with functional limitations. In: Handbook of Human Factors and Ergonomics (2012). https://doi.org/10.1002/9781118131350.ch51
2. UNO, Convention on the Rights of Persons with Disabilities, 13 December 2006. https://www.un.org/development/desa/disabilities/convention-on-the-rights-of-persons-with-disabilities.html. Accessed 1 Feb 2018
3. WHO, International classification of functioning, disability and health: ICF, Geneva, Switzerland: World Health Organization (2001). https://doi.org/10.1177/0883073814533595
4. APA, Diagnostic and Statistical Manual of mental disorders (DSM) 5, American Psychological Association (APA), Arlington, Virginia, USA (2014). https://doi.org/10.3928/02793695-20130207-01
5. Maulik, P., Mascarenhas, M., Mathers, C., Dua, T., Saxena, S.: Prevalence of intellectual disability: a meta-analysis of population-based studies. Res. Dev. Disabil. (2011). https://doi.org/10.1016/j.ridd.2010.12.018

6. McKenzie, K., Milton, M., Smith, G., Ouellette-Kuntz, H.: Systematic review of the prevalence and incidence of intellectual disabilities: current trends and issues. Intellect. Disabil. (2016). https://doi.org/10.1007/s40474-016-0085-7

7. INEGI, Encuesta Nacional de la Dinámica Demográfica, México: Instituto Nacional de Estadística y Geografía (2014)

8. INEGI, Censo de Población y Vivienda 2010, Instituto Nacional de Estadística, Geografía e Informática, Ciudad de México (2010)

9. SENADIS, II Estudio Nacional de Discapacidad, Santiago, Chile: Ministerio de Desarrollo Social (2015)

10. Parker, P.: Down Syndrome: A Bibliography and Dictionary for Physicians, Patients, and Genome Researchers. Icon Group International Inc. (2004). ISBN 0-497-11392-9

11. Troncoso, M., Del Cerro, M.: Síndrome de Down: Lectura y Escritura, Madrid, España.: Fundación Down 21 (2009)

12. Ruiz, E.: Programación Educativa para Escolares con Síndrome de Down, Madrid, España: Fundación Iberoamericana Down 21 (2012). ISBN 978-84-615-7500-8

13. INEGI, Encuesta nacional sobre disponibilidad y uso de tecnologías de la información en los hogares, Instituto Nacional de Estadística y Geografía, Ciudad de México (2012)

14. SUBTEL, Informe sobre acceso a internet, Subsecretaría de telecomunicaciones (SUBTEL), Ministerio de Transportes y Telecomunicaciones, Santiago, Chile (2016)

15. SENADIS, 7a Encuesta Nacional de Acceso y Usos de Internet, Servicio Nacional de la Discapacidad (SENADIS), Santiago, Chile (2015)

16. Dix, A., Finlay, J., Abowd, G., Beale, R.: Human-Computer Interaction, 3rd edn. (2003). ISBN-13 978-0-13-046109-4

17. Johnson, J., Blood, E., Freeman, A., Simmons, K.: Evaluating the effectiveness of teacher-implemented video prompting on an ipod touch to teach food-preparation skills to high school students with autism spectrum disorders. Focus Autism Dev. Disabil. 28(3), 147–158 (2013). https://doi.org/10.1177/1088357613476344

18. Lorah, E., Parnell, A., Whitby, P., Hantula, D.: A systematic review of tablet computers and portable media players as speech generating devices for individuals with autism spectrum disorder. J. Autism Dev. Disord. 45(12), 792–804 (2015). https://doi.org/10.1007/s10803-014-2314-4

19. Kim, J., Kim, C.: Functional technology for individuals with intellectual disabilities: meta-analysis of mobile device-based interventions. J. Spec. Educ. Apprenticeship 6(1), 3 (2017). ISSN 2167-3454

20. Luna, M.: Tecnología y discapacidad: Una mirada pedagógica. TIC y discapacidad 14(12) (2013). ISSN 1607-6079

21. Gutierrez, P., Martorell, A.: Las personas con discapacidad intelectual ante las TIC. Rev. Cient. Educomunicación 18(36), 173–180 (2011)

22. Kumin, L., Lazar, J., Feng, J., Bentz, W., Ekedebe, N.: A usability evaluation of workplace-related tasks on a multi-touch tablet computer by adults with Down syndrome. J. Usability Stud. 7(4), 118–142 (2012)

23. Wu, M., Baecker, R., Richards, B.: Designing cognitive help for and with people who have Anterograde Amnesia. In: Universal Usability. John Wiley and Sons, Hoboken (2007)

24. Al Faraj, K., Mojahid, M., Vigouroux, N.: BigKey: a virtual keyboard for mobile devices. In: Jacko, J.A. (ed.) HCI 2009, Part III. LNCS, vol. 5612, pp. 3–10. Springer, Heidelberg (2009). https://doi.org/10.1007/978-3-642-02580-8_1

25. Hu, R., Feng, J., Lazar, L., Kumin, L.: Investigating input technologies for children and young adults with Down syndrome. Univ. Access Inf. Soc. **12**(1), 89–104 (2013). https://doi.org/10.1007/s10209-011-0267-3
26. Reason, P., Bradbury, H.: Handbook of Action Research: Participative Inquiry and Practice, London (2001)
27. LeCompte, M., Schensul, J.: Designing and conducting ethnographic research: an introduction. AltaMira Press, Walnut Greek (2010)
28. O'Reily, K.: Ethnographic Methods. Taylor and Francis Group, New York (2005)
29. Weschler, D.: Weschler Intelligent Test for Children (WISC) IV. Pearson, London (2005)
30. V. International, Valpar Work Samples Test, Valpar International Corporation (2014)

An Information Visualization Application Case to Understand the World Happiness Report

Nychol Bazurto-Gomez[1]([⊠]) [iD], J. Carlos Torres[1]([⊠]) [iD],
Raul Gutierrez[1]([⊠]) [iD], Mario Chamorro[3]([⊠]) [iD], Claire Bulger[4]([⊠]) [iD],
Tiberio Hernandez[1]([⊠]) [iD], and John A. Guerra-Gomez[1,2]([⊠]) [iD]

[1] Imagine Group, Universidad de los Andes, Bogota, Colombia
{n.bazurto, cf.torres, ra.gutierrez, jhernand,
ja.guerrag}@uniandes.edu.co
[2] UC Berkeley, Berkeley, CA, USA
[3] Make it Happy, San Francisco, USA
marioachamorro@gmail.com
[4] World Happiness Report, San Francisco, USA
clairebulger@gmail.com

Abstract. Happiness is one of the most important components in life, however, qualifying happiness is not such a happy task. For this purpose, the World Happiness Report was created: An annual survey that measures happiness around the globe. It uses six different metrics: (i) healthy life expectancy, (ii) social support, (iii) freedom to make life choices, (iv) perceptions of corruption, (v) GDP per capita, and (vi) generosity. Those metrics combined in an index rank countries by their happiness. This index has been published by means of a static report that attempts to explain it, however, given the complexity of the index, the creators have felt that the index hasn't been explained properly to the community. In order to propose a more intuitive way to explore the metrics that compose the index, this paper presents an interactive approach. Thanks to our information visualization, we were able to discover insights such as the many changes in the happiness levels of South Africa in 2013, a year with statistics like highest crime rate and country with most public protests in the world. In the same fashion, the application illustrates recent Yemen's history, which in 2011 had a fall in the ranking, as in 2014 and onwards. Looking at the historical facts of this country, we see in 2011 a revolution began, explaining the fall in the happiness level, followed by a period of transition, that explains the peak in following years (2012–2013), finally, in 2014 the revolution continues, resulting in a civil war.

Keywords: World happiness · Coordinated and multiple views
Information visualization application

1 Introduction

The world happiness report is a survey which measures the happiness in almost all the countries of the world, this score happiness is sustained by several indexes, such as corruption, or life expectancy. This information, for sure, can be interesting for anyone,

V. Agredo-Delgado and P. H. Ruiz (Eds.): HCI-COLLAB 2018, CCIS 847, pp. 44–56, 2019.
https://doi.org/10.1007/978-3-030-05270-6_4

however, these reports are large, a little complex and their approaches to show its results had a lack of interactive visualization using a large bar chart to the ranking (which extends by several pages) and in a previous release, an image of a map with a color scale was used to highlight distribution of happiness.

For example, if one wants to determine how happy is a country, one can use a choropleth map and select a country to know the indexes and score associated with a text, but others might want to know how was that country in respect others, extremes for example, which countries are the nearest to his selection in the ranking, which countries are happier with respect your region, or what is the country with higher life expectancy. Also, it exists more than one version of the report, user maybe wants to compare how was his country over the last years, so we can't use a classic and simple visualization. So, how it is going to be exposed, a juxtapose and linked visualization can be used for these tasks, where the choropleth map is refreshed to express score, but also distribution of one index in all the world, allowing the user to explore not just about happiness, but indexes who are related, like corruption.

We evaluated this proposal using a usability test with people of different areas (engineering, math, and school environment), to corroborate advantages with respect last approach and possible future work.

Paper Organization. Section 2 briefly describes previous work on similar data such as OECD Better Life Index and the World Happiness Report itself. Section 3 illustrates the Visual Analytics basics applied to the particular problem: characterization of data and tasks. Then, we expose the design of this proposal, emphasizing the idioms used to encode. Finally, we summarize our results and experiments, conclusions and future work.

2   Related Work

It's important to take into account that the visualization has different perceptions and preferences depending on the user watching it [1]. For example, a bar chart is not always good for all the users: are not good enough for the scientific community users and the infographics [1] but for new media and government visualization is well received. So, we explored different idioms and tools that could satisfy a wide range of users and that handle similar data.

2.1   Previous Reports

In the last reports [2–5] we could see how there was an effort to represent the results in a way that there was as much data as possible but did not take into account that users could be interested in other information related.

In Fig. 1a, the graph that represents the level of happiness in all countries, where the survey is taken, shows the data that belongs to 2012. This bar chart is quite basic, no colors are used to represent additional information at the level of happiness. In the following year (Fig. 1b) it can be seen that they already include the use of colors to make comparisons with previous years and discriminate by ranking.

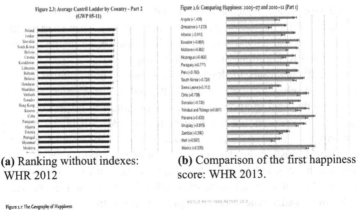

(a) Ranking without indexes: WHR 2012

(b) Comparison of the first happiness score: WHR 2013.

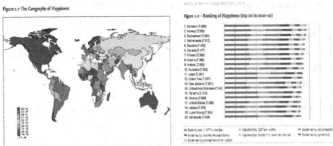

(c) Happiness through a choropleth map: WHR 2015.

(d) Ranking distinguishing per item WHR 2016 Update.

Fig. 1. Main visualizations already made for the World Happiness Report.

The following report is published in 2015, where a map showing the information of each country using colors was incorporated (and is the most common solution for this). But maps are often best when paired with another chart that details what the map displays, such as a bar chart sorted from greatest to least, a line chart showing the trends, or even just a crosstab to show the actual data. In this same report, the information for 2015 was not included, so in 2016 an up- date of the previous report was published, including comparisons with previous years.

It is highlighted that in none of the published reports is possible to interact with the data, they are simply demonstrative graphs that do not allow the community to investigate more about the data of the report or obtain insights from it.

2.2 OECD Better Life Index

This index is develop by Organization for Economic Co-operation and Development and tries to express how life is based in 11 topics which were identified as essential in quality of the same. Among topics are: Housing, Income, Jobs, Education, Health and Safety. Currently, OECD has a nice visualization for this data [6], letting user select index that is more interesting for him and see an- other data, like region (a very particular region, for instance Alberta, Canada) and summarize the topics values in this area. It uses right channels and marks for its data and there is sorting options which simplifies determine extremes per topic; however, its difficult compare entire world, appreciate distribution of one index and rankings are bounded.

2.3   Dashboard and Geographic Data

In the Whitepaper visual analysis guidebook [7] they suggest a configuration called dashboards. Basically, the dashboard is the main screen where all the detailed visualizations are placed. It gave us the first view of the problem. Dash- boards increase the analytical power of the visualization by showing multiple perspectives in the same location. They can also be used to combine multiple types of data in a single location (and this is our case).

On the other hand, to address the problem of displaying geographic data, the Linkoping University created an interesting solution [8] using coordinated views or dashboard, as we mentioned earlier, where they showed the geographic data of the world using a choropleth map together with idioms such as bar charts and scatter plots, and showed regional and countries data such as the ratio of the population or the average age, among many others.

2.4   Ranking

For countries ranking, based on one or a set of criteria we found: a bar chart is great for comparison and ranking because it encodes quantitative values as the length of the same baseline, making it extremely easy to compare values [7]. A sorted list of country names is a different kind of view and it fulfills the main task that consists of getting the max and min of the countries, the choice between ranking as a list or as a bar chart is given by the accuracy of the comparison. According to Robert K. most of the embellishments have an adverse effect on the accuracy of reading values when comparing bars [9].

In Fig. 2 is possible see a brief comparison between the current approaches for this data (and similar) and its limitations. As illustrates the World Happiness Report's visualizations have many difficulties. This, it is the result that there aren't interactions but several countries, extending the graphic along different pages. In addition, each idiom was focused on a task. On the other hand, the OECD is better in most of the aspects but the glyph idiom makes difficult some tasks. Its big advantage is the interactions, however, they just handle 38 countries.

3   Visual Analytics Tool Abstraction

We did the abstraction based on Tamara Munzner [10] framework which is com- posed for What, Why and How. This part just describes what (data abstraction) and Why (task abstraction).

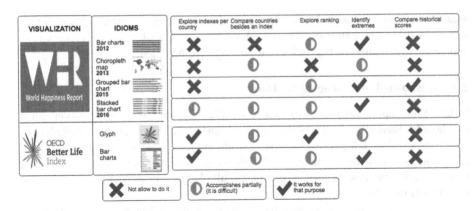

VISUALIZATION	IDIOMS	Explore indexes per country	Compare countries besides an index	Explore ranking	Identify extremes	Compare historical scores
World Happiness Report	Bar charts 2012	✗	✗	◖	✓	✗
	Choropleth map 2013	✗	◖	✗	◖	✗
	Grouped bar chart 2015	✗	◖	◖	✓	✓
	Stacked bar chart 2016	◖	◖	◖	✓	✗
OECD Better Life Index	Glyph	✓	◖	✓	◖	✗
	Bar charts	✓	◖	◖	✓	✗

✗ Not allow to do it   ◖ Accomplishes partially (it is difficult)   ✓ It works for that purpose

Fig. 2. Comparison between current approaches. Authors.

3.1 What

World Happiness Report data has 6 main indexes to define its happiness score ranking by country, these are:

- **Healthy life expectancy:** Calculated based on data from the World Health Organization (WHO), the World Development Indicators (WDI), and statistics published in journal articles.
- **Social support:** Its define by an average of answers to this dichotomous question, "If you were in trouble, do you have relatives or friends you can count on to help you whenever you need them, or not?".
- **Freedom to make life choices:** National average related to the answer to "Are you satisfied or dissatisfied with your freedom to choose what you do with your life?".
- **Perceptions of corruption:** Average of answers to this two question: "Is corruption widespread throughout the government or not" and "Is corruption widespread within businesses or not?"
- **GDP per capita:** It's the purchasing power parity (PPP) value of all final goods and services produced within a country in a given year, divided by the average (or mid-year) population for the same year. For the report was adjusted to constant 2011 international dollars.
- **Generosity:** It's the residual of regressing national average of response to the GWP question, "Have you donated money to a charity in the past month?" on GDP per capita.

All these, with the happiness score, are ordered quantitative sequential attributes.

As categorical attribute has "countries" which can be consider a geometric dataset too because have an implicit geometry and the quantitative attributes are associated with each one (table about each country).

3.2   Why

The main target of World Happiness Report is shows the ranking, that everyone can understand it. But we thought anyone must to be able to understand and interact with the indexes which are associated, in order to answer different user questions. With this and the data in mind five basic main task were identified to achieve:

1. *Present* the ranking, countries and their respective score (*feature*).
2. *Discover* happiness *distribution* in the world. The user can interact with each country to obtain details on demand.
3. *Identify* the happiness score and indexes by country (*features*).
4. *Locate* (knowing the country that I want to find (e.g. my country) a country and query how happy is it and how indexes are in this (*features*).
5. *Identify* which countries are happier and which ones less happy (*extremes*).
6. *Discover* happiness *distribution* in the different world regions. The user can interact with each country in those regions to obtain details on demand.

4   Design and Description of the Visualization

Continue with the Tamara's framework once what and why were established its possible think in the visual encoding of these task, its mean find the best options (channels and marks) for our tasks and data. So, considering the most important tasks and the state of art, we decided to use coordinate views (juxtaposed), which support the data and let the user discover interesting relationship between the different indexes.

4.1   Idioms: Encoding

This proposal is composed for 4 main idioms; Fig. 3 shows a view using the initial setup (score happiness as filter).

1. **A choropleth map:** This idiom supports the second and fourth tasks, preserves something familiar to the user and reuses their common knowledge of the world, in order to achieve everyone can understand easily the main idea. For this idiom its necessary choose the right channel, so, saturation it's perfect to express the happiness score or an index (something quantitative and sequential). User can **manipulate** the choropleth, in this case, map allows **select** and **navigate** by all the map. The idea of this design was let the user picks up on the map any country and apply a geometric zoom of that country. Moreover, it's presents a reduce action, when the proposed tooltip associated to this idiom provides to the user a **embedded** chart, with information about the ranking in the last years in a particular country (with mouse over action).

   On the other hand, to express the indexes data, we decided use two different idioms, which are affected by independent filters: parallel coordinates to show all indexes at the same time and bar chart per index.

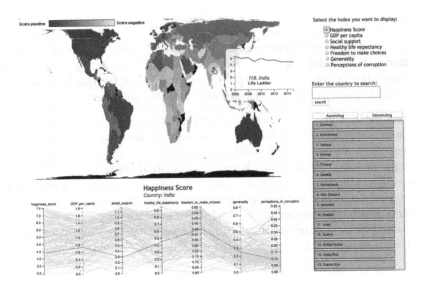

Fig. 3. World Happiness Report visualization. India is selected with happiness score as filter, and its historical scores are shown by a pop up over the country. This let us appreciate that India is descending across the years.

2. **Parallel coordinates:** Considering indexes have a different scale between them, it was necessary find a suitable idiom to show all together and avoid breaks expressiveness, selecting parallel coordinates. This idiom encodes expressing in different axis, and if there are interactions like selecting and highlight, linked with the map, makes possible establish relation between the general score in a country and its indexes. To avoid occlusion between different countries, saturation could be use. User can select and highlight one line which corresponds to a particular country and also filter items to get not only the information of a country but a set of countries with similar values in certain indexes. This idiom supports the third task in conjunction with the map.
3. **Bar chart:** This idiom let show and compare one index, visualizing the highest, lowest countries and the selected country by the user (there is a link between choropleth map and bars). Respect to selection on the map, highlights and selects a country.
4. **Ranking list:** We thought just the map isn't enough to express all the data, e.g., ranking needs to be express it with a better encoding, more directly: ordering, so a list with the values it's a simple alternative (spatially distributed text). This idiom let us support the first and fifth tasks. User can manipulate changing order, from lowest to highest position or vice versa and by a filter associated reduces shown items to the user.

5. **Bubble chart:** This idiom allows appreciating a different way to see the happiness, avoiding the possible bias produced for the choropleth map and the countries' size (user can understand that Russia is happier than Germany due to the area each country covers). This bias is handled using dots (bubbles) which its size is related with the happiness same as its color, and each one has a repulsion force to avoid overlapping. Additionally, the implemented filters for this idiom show a classification by happiness levels and by regions, supporting the sixth task (through arrange-separating the data).

4.2 Interactions

All the views are linked with shared data with purpose to give the user a richer experience with the data, letting him analyze and relation indexes between different countries and other characteristics. User can select in radio buttons which information he wants to see distributed on the map: about score happiness or a single index. If user selects score happiness as filter, he's going to see the parallel coordinates chart, which relations indexes of all countries. If user decides see information about an index, like generosity, a bar chart, instead parallel coordinates, is going to appear, as is possible see in Fig. 4, when sub Fig. 4a shows healthy life expectancy with Sierra Leone bar in center (it is the selected country by user) and let compares with his neighbors in values and extremes. Sub Fig. 4b shows how Venezuela has a freedom to make choices 4 units behind the highest, and Angola is one of the worst in this aspect (country with several problems with human rights).

The country selected could be updated when user picks up on the map other countries. Moreover, as soon as the user moves the mouse to through a country, embedded chart appears which is a chart line about the country positions in the ranking over the last years, even if user has an index selected, this chart appears to give the user a summarize about happiness.

On the other hand, there are several filters to help the users to find information quickly: there is a filter by country name which makes automatic selection and the country is zoomed in. Also, there is filters incorporated to parallel coordinates, in order to allow the users to combine indexes and ranges of his interest, in Fig. 6 appreciates an example, when countries with freedom to choices is between 0,10 and 0,15 and also have GDP per capita between 0,8 to 1,0 are highlighted.

Also, in order to make easier to find extremes, an ordering mechanism was integrated, listing in ascending and descending way, this works too when an index is selected affecting the bar chart.

Finally, the user can switch to a bubble chart visualization. This visualization has three presentations: a general view, a happiness level classification, and region classification. In Fig. 5 is possible to see the three data arranges and the detail offer when the user hovers a bubble. In Fig. 5a is possible see all the countries where the red color highlights the less happiest countries. Then, in Fig. 5b the bubbles are split by three levels: the highest, average and lowest happiness. In addition, Fig. 5c shows the bubbles classified by regions.

Previous proposal was implemented using a server in Amazon, this solution is web and the main technologies used were: D3, jQuery, Js, Topojson and HTML.

 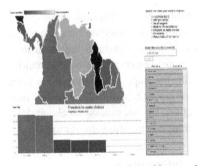

(a) Healthy life expectancy: Sierra Leone   **(b)** Freedom to make choices: Venezuela

Fig. 4. Bar chart for different index and countries. Authors.

5 Usability Test and Results

We ran a usability test with people from different areas and age: Music, math and Chemical students, systems engineers and math professionals, covering demographic diversity. In the first step, the subject had to explore current report, understanding about what it is. This step was repeated with our visualization. Usually, the first interaction that they had was with the map and then with radio buttons, trying to figure out relations between different components.

In general, all subjects agree with some aspects when interact with the report: It was a little hard to find a particular country, if they were lucky country searched was near to page opened. Also, know the values about indexes was complicated an they estimated.

On other hand, with our visualization they agreed on one thing: It easiest and didactic understand and learn about world happiness. Some suggestions were made about other interactions as select over the list and update all views, and a user told us about a different color for countries without data, because can be confusing, as darker color could be interpreted as "happiest color".

After exploring it free both scenarios, users had to solve the some tasks:

1. Can you identify what country is the least happy in the world?
2. Could you tell us how your country is and its indexes?
3. Can you tell us what country has highest life expectancy/generosity index?
4. How is your country respect of country with highest and lowest generosity index?

In the report, all of them had problems looking for its country and they highlighted it isn't friendly have to slide down by many pages to find the least happy country. The third and fourth tasks couldn't be determined with precision because is so complicate compares indexes between countries. By other hand, with visualization most of them

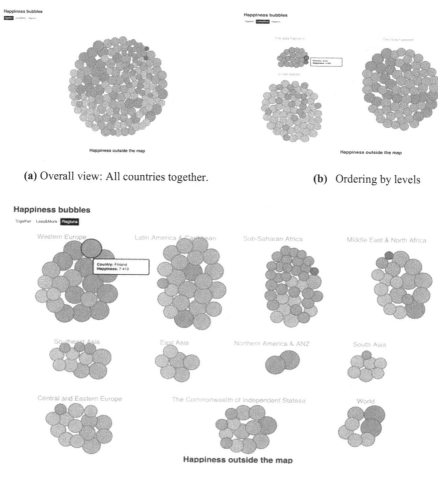

(a) Overall view: All countries together.   (b) Ordering by levels

(c) Arranging by regions: Western Europe is a happy place

Fig. 5. Bubble chart through the different data arranges. Authors

could do all the tasks and understand some interactions like bar chart was more complicated than other like a filter. In final feedback, they highlight the next things that they could do and the couldn't with report and was so interesting for them:

– It's possible find and interesting geographic correlation. You can see some clusters, countries who their culture and economics are related, for example places in occidental Europe presents a similar behavior and could be justified by his acquisitive power with GDP index, as Fig. 7 shows. This is lost with the report because barely you can compare indexes between countries.
– Historic positions in the ranking give you a panorama of growth of the country or let establish a relationship with possible conflicts in some areas, so this perspective brings an extra information about report who exposes separately these results.

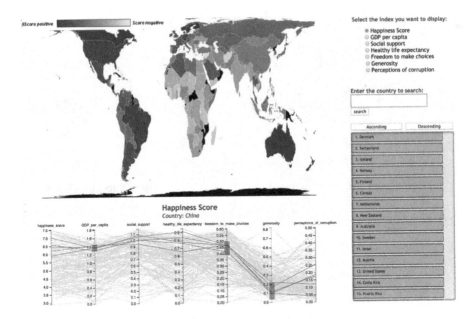

Happiness Score
Country: China

Fig. 6. Filter on parallel coordinates. Authors.

(a) Score happiness in Occidental Europe   (b) GDP index in Occidental Europe. Authors.
Authors.

Fig. 7. Interested case found by user: a geographic relationship can be appreciate. Authors

- It's possible see value for each index, so user doesn't need to estimate this.
- Allows evaluation from a single index over all countries, so it's interesting analyze how is perception of corruption is in the whole world.

  And we reaffirm the possibility to do this:

- Make easier to find a country and know its location.
- Find faster the extremes in indexes and compares with a particular selected country.
- The user doesn't need to see all ranking, he can use descending order if is looking for the worst 10 countries in kind aspect (score happiness and index).
- Get countries which have a similar behavior or are close in some indexes intervals.

General feedback was positive, visualization was seen as an easier way to handle the report results.

6 Conclusion and Future Work

The usability testing demonstrates visualization enables the regular users to take a more active role in the discovery process of exploring world, regional and country indicators.

Its main purpose was accomplished, improvement the way to the user solves main tasks and expressing the data in the correct way. Moreover, we have shown how a user can deduce and relate external information, looking for effects of politician regimens, conflicts, economic crisis and even events like realization of soccer world cup, this was a titanic labor with the report, because there isn't a perspective can give enough information without incurs in saturate users' mind.

Nevertheless, we identify two possible enhances. First, improve the visualization by regions through linking the bubble chart to others idioms, this as future work, when the work of Hans Rosling "Gapminder"[1] can serve as inspiration to incorporate a similar solution in the work already done, as it allows users see details on demand very intuitively.

Secondly, develop a version with texts more informative for the user, if the user doesn't know what is each index and its explanation, it could be a little confusing, maybe incorporate a menu with help or an animation about world happiness report.

World Happiness visualization was designed to work 100% from the browser, developed in D3 (JavaScript) with a backend that hosts the data. It's an open source project available at http://nycholbazurto.me/worldHappinessReport/viz/. Ultimately, we hope that it enables a new way for interested people in under- standing the report.

References

1. Borkin, M.A., et al.: What makes a visualization memorable? IEEE (2013). https://doi.org/10.1109/TVCG.2013.234
2. Helliwell, J., Layard, R., Sachs, J.: World happiness report, update. Technical report, World happiness report (2012)
3. Helliwell, J., Layard, R., Sachs, J.: World happiness report 2013. Technical report, World happiness report (2013)
4. Helliwell, J., Layard, R., Sachs, J.: World happiness report 2015. Technical report, World happiness report (2015)
5. Helliwell, J., Layard, R., Sachs, J.: World happiness report 2016, update. Technical report, World happiness report (2016)
6. Durand, M.: The OECD better life initiative: How's life? And the measurement of well-being. Rev. Income Wealth **61**(1), 4–17 (2015). https://doi.org/10.1111/roiw.12156
7. Tableau and Tableau Software: Visual Analysis Best Practices, Simple Techniques for Making Every Data Visualization Useful and Beautiful (2016)

---

[1] His work can be found at www.gapminder.org.

8. Jern, M., Brezzi, M., Thygesen, L.: A web-enabled geovisual analytics tool applied to OECD regional data. NCVA National Center for Visual Analytics, ITN, Linkoping University, Sweden, OECD, Paris, France (2015). https://doi.org/10.2312/ega.20091004

9. Skau, D., Harrison, L., Kosara, R.: An evaluation of the impact of visual embellishments in bar charts. In: Computer Graphics Forum (Proceedings EuroVis), vol. 34 (2015). https://doi.org/10.1111/cgf.12634

10. Munzner, T.: Visualization Analysis and Design. AK Peters Visualization Ser. CRC Press (2014). https://books.google.com.co/books?id=dznSBQAAQBAJ

ChildProgramming Evolution, A Method to Increase the Computational Thinking Skills in School

René Fabián Zúñiga Muñoz[1]([⊠]) [iD],
Julio Ariel Hurtado Alegría[1]([⊠]) [iD], Cesar Alberto Collazos[1]([⊠]) [iD],
and Habib Fardoun[2] [iD]

[1] University of Cauca, Popayán, Colombia
{fabianmunoz,ahurtado,ccollazo}@unicauca.edu.co
[2] King Abdulaziz University, Jeddah, Saudi Arabia
habib.fardoun@gmail.com

Abstract. ChildProgramming is presented as a model for the teaching of programming to groups of children between 10 and 12 years old, applying collaborative, ludic and agile development strategies. Since its appearance in 2013, different projects have been developed at the undergraduate and postgraduate levels at the Universidad del Cauca, where this methodology has been applied in case studies that have allowed its validation and adjustment, making contributions to the conceptual model on issues as: the identification of computational abstraction processes applied by children when proposing a solution, the performance of the groups taking into account the shared knowledge (transactional memory), also of the organization by gender in the work teams, to propose solutions to computational problems and the development of competencies related to computational thinking. In the present article a general revision of the evolution of the methodology is made, and for each one of the related works the objective of the work is exposed, the new component within the original model, a description of this additional component and the results of the Validation when applying the case studies. Likewise, the future of methodology is presented in terms of the work that is being developed and the proposals for future work.

Keywords: Computational thinking · Teaching · Education · Children
Transactive memory · Agile development · Gender · Gamification
Debugging

1 Introduction

Various proposals related to the possibility of initiating children in the development of computer applications consider the school environment as an appropriate environment for this experience. This type of learning has become a modern necessity in schools around the world. The development of computational thinking as a strategy to offer students the possibility of using computational concepts to propose solutions to problems in any field is considered a 21st-century skill [1]. There is the case of the

V. Agredo-Delgado and P. H. Ruiz (Eds.): HCI-COLLAB 2018, CCIS 847, pp. 57–69, 2019.
https://doi.org/10.1007/978-3-030-05270-6_5

International Society for Technology in Education (ISTE)[1], which in 2016 published some educational standards that include computer thinking as one of the primary competencies for technology literacy. The University of Cauca since 2012 undertakes the definition of a methodological proposal in which children are the protagonists of the development of computer solutions, developing mathematical and social logical skills, based on three aspects: playful, collaborative and agile development. Since its introduction, this methodology has evolved from the contributions that various groups of undergraduate and postgraduate students have proposed in topics such as: the identification of the processes of abstraction that children apply in the solution of problems, the gamification of the methodology, the application of the transactional memory in teamwork, the organization of the practices based on aspects related to gender and the implementation of debugging in the development process. All these contributions have been proposed with the best intention, and in that process, we have found that the authors of these extensions did not take into account a line of global evolution, nor an architectural base, beyond the original model. All this has led to the organization and presentation of various practices and resources that have made the model somewhat complicated for its understanding and application. Making its promulgation and organized evolution difficult, its development has been empirical so far. In this work, we present this evolution that we believe takes us to a process family, which is not required to be completed for its application. A partial selection of the family would result in a unique approach to the process; these novel approaches being necessary to facilitate their adoption. However, this derivation requires the flexible structuring of the methodology, which would also promote the future evolution of the family of models. In this paper, we review the development of ChildProgramming to identify extensions and extension points that allow proposing a conceptual architecture of the model with two purposes: 1. To facilitate the derivation of unique approaches and 2. To promote the organization of practices according to the needs real in the classroom.

2   ChildProgramming

This methodological proposal [2] was born under the conviction that all children are independent of their social and economic status that can address the issue of information technology, although they do not have sufficient technological resources. It arises as an idea to improve human capital in the medium term in matters related to software engineering. At this point, collaboration and the playful appear as instruments that allow teams of children to develop computer solutions through the application of some concepts of agile development processes. The conceptual model of the ChildProgramming methodology appears in Fig. 1.

The conceptual basis - ChP refers to the fact that in the process the child is taken into account aspects such as strategy, thinking, abstraction, creativity, intellectual development, individual and group behavior. The playful, collaborative and agile practices complement each other within the methodology, to the extent that

---

[1] http://www.iste.org.

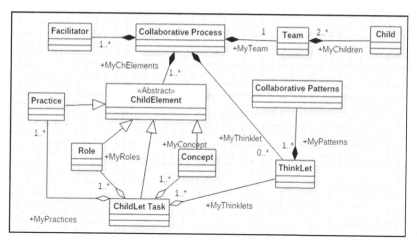

Fig. 1. Conceptual architecture of ChildProgramming.

pedagogical methods are designed and applied following aspects such as teamwork, learning by doing, innovation, trial, and error and the organization of work. Next, we present the life cycle of the ChildProgramming process.

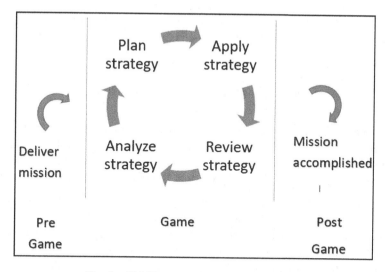

Fig. 2. ChildProgramming process life cycle

Figures 2 and 3 show the main phases and activities of the methodology, which must be carried out compulsorily and on which the contributions mentioned at the beginning of this article have been made. Each of these three phases has a specific objective; the pre-game has the purpose of establishing the mission (delivery of requirements), it must be detailed, each team member must know the objective and goals of each mission. They must obtain teaching the necessary materials for its fulfillment, and the teams identify tasks and carry out the first organization of duties among the members of the group, which allows to move on to the next phase. In the game phase, its objective is to develop the mission in such a way that a solution proposal is delivered at the end of the rounds. The rounds are iterations in which teams, as they move forward in solving the problem, must meet the following stages: Planning, applying, reviewing and analyzing the strategy.

In the post-game phase, the teams deliver the mission accomplished, this solution must meet the requirements proposed in the presentation of the activity, and the teacher makes an evaluation of the team's work, based on the objectives that he defined in the first phase.

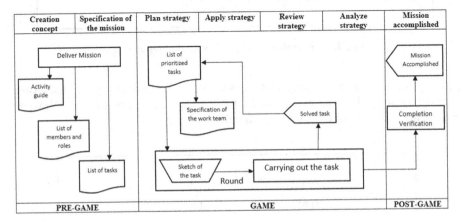

Fig. 3. ChildProgramming process flowchart

Additional to these are the Roles, Concepts, and Practices that constitute more specific elements and whose general definition is the following: Roles: Actors who intervene in the process in the activities of the class sessions as in extra work sessions. These are: Teacher, Team Leader, Work Team, Researchers or External Observers.

- Concepts: They allow the development of activities, they are those that integrate cognitive, collaborative and agile development aspects.
- Practices: It is an essential component, the work teams apply them, and these are divided into three parts, which have particular behaviors:
- Collaborative Component: includes accepting the conditions to develop the activity, developing team activity and committing to work as a team.
- Cognitive Component: refers to complying with the rules of the game, asking what is not understood and understanding the topic of the activity.
- Agile component: involves meeting with a partner and carrying out the task, using the entire workplace with the team to learn about the activity and doing the work efficiently, making it better and better.

3   The Evolution of ChildProgramming

Since the presentation of ChildProgramming in 2013, different initiatives have been developed with the purpose of complementing the methodology and contributing to the improvement of the practices defined in ChildProgramming; these contributions are presented below with the intention of showing how ChildProgramming is a methodology unique on which the complements provide particular ideas and processes. Next, we show the objectives of each of these works and their contribution to the aspects of the conceptual and architectural model within the methodology of children's programming. Its evaluation was carried out in a real educational environment applying several cases studies.

3.1   Identifying Abstraction Mechanisms

ChildProgramming-A [3] is a work focused on defining and applying an incremental method that facilitates the analysis and design in the development of software in teams in children of school age between 10 and 13 years. Based on the application of shared mental models as a basis for the organization, planning, and coordination of development tasks in the context of the ChildProgramming methodology.

Apply a refinement of the proposed practices in ChildProgramming, focusing on the development of computational thinking, from the application of the mechanisms of abstraction, incrementality in missions and shared thinking. In Fig. 4. It shows how the practices in ChildProgramming are refined to apply the three principles mentioned above.

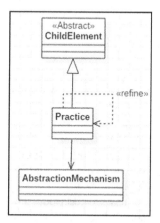

Fig. 4. Conceptual model of refined practices in ChildProgramming-A

At the conclusion of the research process, the following results are obtained:

The incrementality in the exercises favors the assimilation of the basic computational concepts, likewise, including an example within the guide generates a sense of relief in the work teams and the challenges are concluded satisfactorily. Children identify and use abstraction mechanisms such as generalization after applying the class practices that include the examples of guidance. This abstraction mechanism becomes an essential input so that they can later deduce concepts of abstraction such as decomposition, taking care in that the use of the guiding examples is more limited, because of the possibility that this will direct the children in a possible solution without giving rise to creativity. By organizing the work through shared mental models, the teams showed greater order and productivity, compared to the groups that did not apply this practice to share knowledge. ChildProgramming model count with enough structures for localizing the new concepts related with the abstraction mechanism, however the way as the practices are described requires some special description slots. To achieve this new slots, we refine the practice descriptor from the original. With this new descriptor, we defined the abstraction practices as follow: Are activities where the teamwork uses a template to register the evolution of the solution, these templates contains three columns (What I am going to do – What I am doing – What I finished), every team member must register and complete their task, this task is established by themselves. When all the work fills the third column, the mission is finish, and the team presents the solution to the teacher. In resume all the activities that the teacher defines must contain these elements:

- Incrementality
- Mental models
- By Example

Additionally, the study added the abstraction mechanism as new concepts:

- Decomposition
- Generalization
- Recursion

3.2   Gamification

ChildProgramming-G [4] aims to extend the ChildProgramming model by incorporating game mechanics and dynamics that allow increasing the performance of the work teams regarding quality, productivity, and behavior. In this paper, a characterization of the types of players is proposed, and the theme of incrementality in the mechanics and dynamics of the game is applied. Its evaluation was carried out in a real educational environment using two case studies. Figure 5 shows the contribution that has been proposed for the conceptual model of ChildProgramming, showing only the area included in the new entities that introduced.

In this proposal, there are two new GChildModel and GamiTool packages, as well as some packages that were modified to allow the application of gamification, by including teacher's activities in the planning, monitoring and closing stages of the tasks. At the conclusion of this research, the authors consider that gamification does allow better performance in the work teams, as it encourages learning and active participation of children in the process, as well as improving aspects related to socialization, teamwork and continuous improvement. The teacher has an essential role in the process because he is the one who must from the beginning plan and monitor the

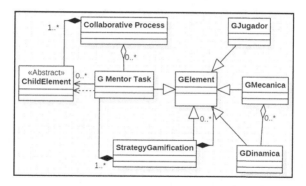

Fig. 5. Conceptual Model of ChildProgramming-G

performance of the teams within a gamified environment that he must design. Regarding the performance of the teams, it was possible to establish that productivity and behavior did show significant progress. However, quality is an indicator that was not possible to measure appropriately with the proposed study. Gamification completely add a package without change the original structure. A GElement extending ChildElement is defined and the new elements are defined by specialization from this concept, so each GElement is defined inside an independent package which can be managed as an extension package.

3.3   Transactive Memory

ChildProgramming-GTM [5] this paper presents several practices that are adjusted so that children's teams apply transactional memory as an exercise in planning and developing activities. We identified the components that should be taken into account to develop transactional memory systems in group work, measuring the effectiveness of this new approach for ChildProgramming was carried out taking into account three aspects (specialization, credibility, and coordination). Figure 6 shows the contribution that has been proposed for the conceptual model of ChildProgramming, shows only the area included in the new entities that are proposed, in this case, the ChildProgramming-G model is taken as reference.

The practices that pretend to apply the subject of the transactional memory are associated with the collaborative process also integrating elements of the development of the transactive memory. In the case of children, a new item appears, and it is related to the specialization (expert), which is the member that dominates a particular issue in the mission that developed. The transactional memory system includes practices for training thematic experts, who collaborate with the teams and share information while the mission developed. The transactional memory involves elements such as reward, interdependence of tasks, a search of resources, knowledge directory, knowledge exchange, and trust, differentiation of knowledge, equipment configuration and specialization. In this work it was evident the contribution in the behavior of the children, allowing to establish and recognize that there may be thematic experts that influence the planning and development of the tasks. The collaboration and the teamwork motive

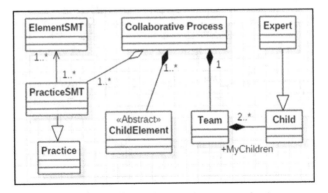

Fig. 6. Conceptual Model of ChildProgramming-GTM

adequately to the members to fight to achieve the reward, allowing higher efficiency in the solution. A redefinition of the Practices describes the new practices as PracticeSMT including new elements as ElementSMT to define the transactive memory. Practices include all the information regarding the practices that allow the development of the transactional memory system within the ChildProgramming-G process, facilitating the training of experts. ElementSMT consists of a name and a description that will enable describing the elements of transactive memory that associated with the PracticeSMT those elements are the base for the development of the practices proposed.

3.4   Gender

ChildProgramming-Gender [6] its proposal consists in presenting specific practices oriented to take into account aspects of gender diversity and inclusion when groups of children are involved in the design of activities related to computer programming. The evaluation of this research sought to increase the interest in computer issues away from the gender stereotypes that presented in society.

Figure 7 shows the conceptual model of ChildProgramming-Gender which extends from the ChildProgramming model.

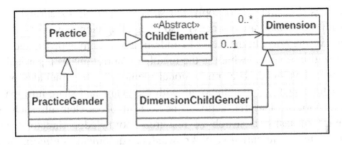

Fig. 7. Conceptual Model of ChildProgramming Gender

The practices and the gender dimensions contain specific information related to the theme of inclusion and diversity, these become input for the teacher to apply during the three phases of ChildProgramming. Teachers are those who seek to understand and analyze aspects related to genders, such as sexist practices, analysis of student interests and the promotion of equality. The practices have been complemented with activities, questionnaires, and references to didactic material that seek to eliminate gender stereotypes inside the classroom.

The performance of the team's increases in aspects such as productivity, quality, and behavior when the elements of gender are incorporated, the concepts of programming was adapted to the school environment with boys and girls maintaining attention and motivating participation in the development of the activities.

Practice Gender Class inherited from Practice; a Practice Gender inherits Practice fields such as Inputs_Practice_Gender and Outputs_Practice_Gender is identified with Id_PracticeGender and describes its attributes such as Name_PracticeGender, Orientation, Phases, Related_Activities, Related_Practices, Description_Practice, Strategies_monitoring_changes, and Indicators of problems, Expected behaviors and Notes. This class abstracts all the information related to the Gender practices that during the process the Professor will consider as input in the Pre-Game, Game, Post-Game phases.

3.5   Case Studies Review

All the research that complement ChildProgramming applied embedded studies cases and considered children teams as an analysis unit. Next, we present a review related to the study cases defined. Describing goals, research questions, research subjects, indicators, and meters.

Abstraction Mechanisms

Objective

Exploring the use of a set of abstraction mechanisms in children teams with ages between 10 and 13, using Increasing activities to allow present a problem-solving solution.

Research Question of Cases Studies

¿Which abstraction mechanisms are used by little children teams with ages between 10 and 13, of 9th grade to develop a good software solution using Scratch?

Research Subject

Focus: Exploring, pretend to study the performance of children teams.
Analysis unit: Teamwork by 5 or 6 students.
Information resource: Direct observation in 3 work sessions. They count with the same work conditions and theoretical and practice orientations.

Indicators and Metrics
Indicators

Team performance during the software development process.
Abstraction mechanisms used frequently.

Metrics

Team's behavior observed during each session work.

Teams productivity during each session work.

Group of abstraction mechanisms regularly presents in the teams works with most productivity.

Transactive Memory

Objective

Apply the ChildProgramming-G model with work teams of children between 9 and 11 years old. To observe the performance of the group under the methodology, also, analyze from direct observation the presence or absence of characteristics related to a transactional memory system.

Research Question of Cases Studies

Which characteristics of the transactive memory systems are presented implicitly under the ChildProgramming-G model with children of 5th grade?

Which are the practices that will make up the ChildProgramming-GTM model?

Which is the effectiveness of the ChildProgramming-GTM process model concerning Specialization, Credibility, and Coordination?

Research Subjects

Focus: Exploring, pretend to study the performance of children teams and how to incorporate a transactive memory system in the ChildProgramming-G model.

Analysis unit: Teamwork by 5 or 6 students.

Information resource: Direct observation in 8 work sessions. They count with the same work conditions and theoretical and practice orientations applying the ChildProgramming-G model.

Indicators and Metrics

Characteristics of the SMT perceived in the ChildProgramming-G model.

Set of practices that make up the ChildProgramming-GTM model.

Metrics

Perception of the researcher about the presence of the attributes of a TMS in ChildProgramming-G.

Validation of the development of transactive memory based on the degree of value interactions in the team.

Gender

Objective

Analyze the result of the study group concerning behavior, productivity, and quality of deliverables, which include aspects of gender diversity and distribution of groups by gender in teams of boys and girls aged between 8 and 12 years old in a public school.

Research Question of Cases Studies

How groups of children between 8 and 12 years old are organized and behaved, taking into account aspects related to inclusion and gender in solving problems in a public school?

Does ChildGender balance computer learning concerning behavior, productivity and quality in teams of boys and girls between 8 and 12 years old, considering inclusion and culturally established gender aspects?

Research Subjects

Focus: Exploring, pretends to demonstrate the organization, behavior, and performance of the work teams in the solution of different types of stereotyped activities. Analysis unit: 7 Teamwork by 5 or 6 students.

Information resource: Direct observation in 3 work sessions. They count with the same work conditions and theoretical and practice orientations applying the ChildProgramming-G model.

Indicators and Metrics

Indicators

Impact relation of the distribution of the organization of the team based on gender covering the behavior of the groups, their productivity and the quality of their results.

Metrics

Level of behavior observed in work teams.

Level of quality found in the work teams.

Level of productivity observed in work teams.

Degree in which children have stereotypes immersed.

The stereotype of the Activity.

Organization of the team regarding gender.

4 Discussion

Validation of different concerns, no assessment focused on computational thinking except the abstraction mechanisms extension. It requires of a new component related to the assessment and particularly, think about as computational thinking as be valuated and measured.

Different ways for extending the models and continuous evolution. It requires an extensible specification of the ChildProgramming meta-model.

5 Conclusions and Future Work

The methodology ChildProgramming as such constitutes a relevant input in the subject of the incorporation of the teaching of computer programming in school spaces for boys and girls. The works that have been developed around this proposal show that there is still a space that can be traversed to adjust a product that allows considering this methodology as something finished.

ChildProgramming as a general method is functional and allows adjustment and complement processes that can be applied as pieces that fit the methodological core and provide functionality and adaptability that teachers can take advantage of when deciding which approach they want to use. Figure 8 represents the connection between ChildProgramming and its extensions.

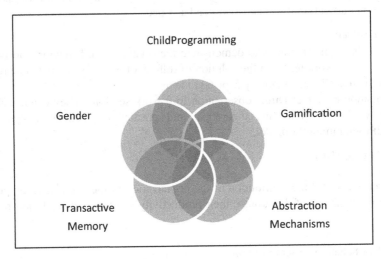

Fig. 8. Evolution of ChildProgramming

ChildProgramming-D is a new work proposal that is currently being carried out in the framework of undergraduate work. It proposes incorporating code debugging topics aimed at improving the quality of the products that are developed in each mission. Of the techniques and methods used in the subject of software purification applied to groups of children, which entails the construction of a conceptual model that complements the ChildProgramming model.

References

1. Moreno-Leon, J., Robles, G., Roman-Gonzalez, M.: Comparing computational thinking development assessment scores with software complexity metrics. Presented at the (2016). https://doi.org/10.1109/EDUCON.2016.7474681
2. Cruz, S.T., Rojas, O.E., Hurtado, J.A., Collazos, C.A.: ChildProgramming process: a software development model for kids (2013). https://doi.org/10.1109/colombiancc.2013.6637535
3. Zuñiga, R.F.Z., Alegría, J.A.H., Rodríguez, P.P.: Discovering the mechanisms of abstraction in the performance of work teams in children to solve computational problems. Sist. Telemática. **14**, 69–87 (2016). https://doi.org/10.18046/syt.v14i36.2216

4. García Potosí, A.A.., Hanner Fabián, O.M.: ChildProgramming-G: Extendiendo ChildProgramming con Técnicas de Gamificación (2014)
5. Zambrano Lasso, A.C., Gómez Calvache, V.Y.: Un Sistema de Memoria Transactiva para ChildProgramming-G (2017)
6. Manzano Quiñones, C.A., Moreno Vásquez, J.C.: ChildGender – Extendiendo ChildProgramming con Aspectos de Diversidad de Género (2017)

Collaborative Strategy with Augmented Reality for the Development of Algorithmic Thinking

Javier Alejandro Jiménez Toledo[1](✉) , César A. Collazos[2] ,
Manuel Ortega Cantero[3] , and Miguel Ángel Redondo[3]

[1] Institución Universitaria CESMAG, Pasto, Colombia
jajimenez@iucesmag.edu.co
[2] Universidad del Cauca, Popayán, Colombia
ccollazo@unicauca.edu.co
[3] Universidad de Castilla La Mancha, Castilla-La Mancha, Spain
{manuel.ortega,Miguel.redondo}@uclm.es

Abstract. The development of algorithmic thinking is one of the most important concerns in the teaching-learning processes that must be taken into account for the development of a first Computer Programming course under the imperative paradigm. This article presents the results of the research obtained by combining collaborative processes with augmented reality tools as a didactic strategy for the development of algorithmic thinking in fundament programming teaching. The research was developed with students of first course of computer programming under a quasi-experimental design with the application of post-tests, whose data obtained were analyzed with the Student's T-distribution. One of the activities of greater effort in the didactic area is to try to obtain maximum levels of attention in the student in each of the academic meetings in order to ensure better learning outcomes with the proposed strategies, for that reason, the study showed that the interactive didactic strategy enhanced the development of algorithmic thinking effectively.

Keywords: Collaborative strategy · Augmented reality · Algorithmic thinking
Computer programming

1 Introduction

Collaborative work as a didactic teaching/learning strategy, is an important research topic in the educational and computational field, due to its possible application to increase learning benefits especially in students of technical knowledge areas such as computer science, and specifically in courses related to computer programming [1].

Also, the use of certain emerging technologies allows a multimodal interaction, thus facilitating active learning. Among the different devices that offer this type of interaction, it is worth highlighting those that integrate Virtual Reality capabilities, which provide a natural learning environment where the student's actions in the physical world have an impact on the virtual world, which means being able to expand the capabilities of traditional learning systems of programming [2].

© Springer Nature Switzerland AG 2019
V. Agredo-Delgado and P. H. Ruiz (Eds.): HCI-COLLAB 2018, CCIS 847, pp. 70–82, 2019.
https://doi.org/10.1007/978-3-030-05270-6_6

This article presents the results obtained from implementing a didactic strategy that combines collaborative and immersive learning using augmented reality techniques for the development of algorithmic thinking with students of the first course of programming applied to the chapter on "capture and exit processes of data" in the professional program of System Engineering of the University Institution CESMAG (Colombia).

This article is structured in five parts: the introduction describes the importance of this study and the structure of the document; the theoretical fundament includes important conceptual elements, problem and background of the investigative process; the methodology describes the stages and roles used in the development of this study; the results show the research methodology proposed with the results obtained in the control and experimental group and finally the conclusions and future work show the obtained findings and the next derived studies.

2 Theoretical Fundament

In recent decades, there have been advances in the learning mechanisms, which can be grouped into three main advances: revolution in Information Technology and Communications, Progress of Pedagogy and Promotion of STEM teaching (Science, Technology, Engineering, Mathematics) in pre-university levels [3].

It is evident the existing preoccupation among the teachers of the first courses of programming with the results obtained in the learning process and, at the same time, there are many disadvantages that a student of first course of this discipline must face [4], Hence, to start learning programming has always been a complex process because it is a completely different discipline than previously studied by the novice at programming, since it requires a radical change in the way of thinking and analyzing things, even, in spite of having acquired the basic theoretical knowledge, a great difficulty has been detected when applying this knowledge to solving practical problems [5]. Programming teaching cannot be transmitted directly from instructors to students, it must be actively acquired by students [6].

In turn, the teaching of the fundamentals of programming is a field of study that has generated great importance due to the rise of software in all processes of human action, to the point of being present in devices with wearable technology [7]. Despite the current technological state, there are still problems related to the preparation of future software developers whose origin starts from the first programming course received, which is key to the training process that a developer of software solutions will have in its stage of learning and later in his professional life [8]; These drawbacks are presented by multiple situations: the lack of skills to program computers, the ignorance of the topics and even the lack of discipline in programming [9]. In addition, a recurrent problem in computer programming learning is that, although teachers explain grammar, students cannot create software by themselves and even some students give up learning [10]. The student's inspiration for learning and its appropriateness may be influenced by several environmental factors which include the learning approach and the social pressure of their classmates [1, 11].

In the study conducted by Affleck and Smith [12] it has been found that the main problem for beginning programmers is the access to prior knowledge and the adoption of a study approach, which goes beyond the explicit memorization of the knowledge necessary to apply and transfer concepts to new situations. For this reason, the formal logical representation methods such as diagrams, Pseudo-code, Nassi Shneiderman, Flow Diagrams, in other cases the paradigms such as the Object Oriented, Logical or Functional that are oriented towards the first programming courses, do not explicitly experience the results of operation and execution in a clear way in its initial phases [4].

Other methodologies for teaching the fundamentals of programming are based on the fact that students from the first course learn a programming language. For this, Xinogalos [13] determines that this methodology presents important problems of computational logic in the student, due to his concern over not having syntactic errors in the code that solves them without taking into account a true logical conception.

Many authors have proposed different strategies for learning the basics of programming. Some teachers begin this teaching in contexts related to the field of mathematics and geometry [14], others lead the student to propose solutions to problems through a cyclical process of "trial and error" [15], some teach programming in a particular programming language using its syntax and semantics, and others use algorithmic language that is general enough to allow its subsequent translation into any programming language [16]. Likewise, other teachers use a teaching/learning methodology based on problem solving, which sometimes involves the application of techniques such as peer-to-peer programming [1, 17].

On the other hand, algorithmic thinking consists in solving problems, designing systems, and understanding human behavior using the fundamental concepts of computer science [18]. There are different initiatives and educational tools to teach algorithmic thinking [19] as: ChildProgramming [20], Scratch [21], Alice [22], EDCIA [23], VPL [8], Entorno de integración de PBL and CSCL for the teaching of algorithms and programming in Engineering [24], Cupi2 [25], a tool and technique for teaching programming [26], Greenfoot [27], JeCo [28], ProLearn [5], PL-Detective [29], Collece [30], OOP Anim [31], DPE [32], ELP [33], BlueJ [27], Alice [34], Habipro [35], Algoarena [36], Sigacle [37], etc.

On the other hand, collaborative learning is the instructional use of small groups in such a way that students work together to maximize their own learning and that of others [38] where each member of the work group is responsible not only for their learning, but also for helping their classmates to learn, creating an atmosphere of achievement [39].

In collaborative learning, students work collaboratively. This type of learning is not opposed to individual work because it can be observed as a complementary learning strategy that strengthens the overall development of the student. Moreover, it is established that collaborative learning methods bring a renewal in the roles associated with teachers and students. In the case of teachers, three types are established: Teachers as Cognitive Mediator, Instructor and Instructional Designer [40].

On the other hand, Brown and Atkins [41] establish that the objectives of collaborative learning are focused on the development of comprehension and explanation strategies, with questions and answers. Discussion and debate serve, first of all, to develop communication skills with others and a precise use of language. Secondly, it generates the development of intellectual and professional competences, such as analyzing, reasoning, thinking critically, synthesizing, designing, etc. and, finally, collaborative learning also promotes the students' personal growth, which includes the development of communication and thinking strategies, the development of self-esteem, learn to work in a team [42].

For Jonhson, Jonhson and Holubec, collaborative learning is the instructional use of small groups in such a way that students work together to maximize their own learning and that of others students [43]. At the same time, Brufee considers collaborative learning as the composition of elements of consensus through collaboration in learning, voluntary participation in the process, non-foundational learning, change in the teacher-student relationship, the importance of work and dialogue between pairs where the authority of the professor and the validity of the contents are discussed thanks to the method [44].

Contrarily, although the concept of Augmented Reality (AR) dates from the 1960s, the first formal RA system was not developed until the 1990s by the Boeing company [45]. The most popular definition of AR is given by Milgram and Kishino who indicate that "the mixed reality is between a real environment and a pure virtual one and it is subdivided into 2: augmented reality (closer to reality) and virtuality augmented (closer to pure virtuality)" [46]. Also, augmented reality is a technology to merge the real environment with a virtual environment. It is based on the over-printing of virtual objects in reality in real time [47], allowing the user to interact with the physical and real world that surrounds it [48].

Thus, the RA is an interactive system that has as input the information of the real world and superpose to the reality new digital information in real time, this virtual information can be images, 3D objects, texts, videos, etc. [49]. During this process, the perception and knowledge that the user has about the real world is enriched [50].

Due to the above, and given the need of a changing world that demands the reinforcement of creative and innovative processes, the training of software developers becomes one of the strategic axes for a nation that wants to insert itself in the knowledge society and enhance its development [51].

3   Methodology

The methodological process carried out (Fig. 1) was based on the unit of studies called "analysis and design of data capture and output processes" for the course of "Introduction to programming" of the first semester of Systems Engineering of the Institution University CESMAG.

The methodological process of Fig. 1 contemplates the following elements:

3.1   Initial Setup

In which the teacher prepares prior to the class session materials and knowledge necessary to address the learning unit "Data capture and output". In this stage, the following activities were carried out:

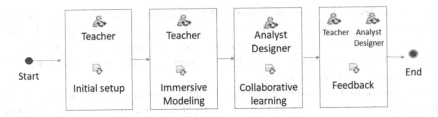

Fig. 1. Methodological process

- Identification of the course: area, component, credits, semester, teacher.
- Description of the course.
- Main skill.
- Definition of learning units with their corresponding subtopics.
- Design examples.
- Time estimation for explanatory topic development.
- Planning of resources and necessary materials for the proposed activities.
- Planning the physical distribution of students in the classroom.
- Design of tasks and evaluations.

3.2 Immersive Modeling

The teacher performs an initial motivation that consists of inculcating the student from his first programming course, with the existence of a series of important phases in the construction of software (independent of the existing software construction methodologies) which must be identified from early stages. Thus, among the initial phases proposed for a first course of Introduction to programming, it is recommended:

Requirement Collection Phase. The teacher must inform the student about the importance of collecting information as a significant stage in the construction of software projects. It is necessary for the teacher to commit the student to carrying out a good process of gathering information, so that the project has a higher probability of success.

For the present study, the artifact presented in Table 1 was taken as a mechanism for gathering requirements.

Table 1. Requirement collection form

System name	Requirements
A name is assigned to the problem provided by the teacher	Requirements are stated with keywords

Analysis Phase. It is necessary for the teacher to inform the student that after knowing and carrying out the requirement collection phase (which for purposes of the present methodological proposal will be taken through the approach of the problem), a process of information analysis is necessary.

In this phase, two artifacts are proposed: an input/output diagram and a sketch of a graphical user interface. This proposal considers the most elementary analysis object at the moment of conceiving a software project that is the "exit input diagram", with which it is possible to identify key elements such as conditional structures, repetitive structures, classes, general variables, variables of class, methods and other necessary elements in the fundamentals of programming.

Furthermore, in this phase, we created a series of examples that were implemented using an augmented reality software that takes the input/output diagram and presents it as an initial sketch of a graphic user interface equipped with technical elements suitable for a graphic environment, as shown in Fig. 2. In turn, such software also increases the reality by taking as a basis the graphical interface and presenting the commands and syntax of writing the source code in the C++ programming language.

Fig. 2. From input/output to the user interface with augmented reality.

Design Phase. In this phase the teacher will inform the student (who must know both the requirement collection phase and the analysis phase) that it is important to build a model that meets the requirements and elements made in the analysis phase. The artifact considered in this phase is the flow chart for algorithmic modeling.

Likewise, the software of augmented reality allows transforming the elements of the flow chart or graphic interface sketch into commands under a notation in the C++ programming language as shown in Fig. 3.

Coding Phase. The teacher will inform the student that after an appropriate software design process, the coding phase will have a high percentage of success. Also, the importance of design realization in any engineering process must be highlighted. The artifact for this phase is the pseudocode.

In this immersive modeling, the teacher must prepare the situations with which they will present the students before the class session so that, through a collaborative environment mediated by Jigsaw, there is a significant appropriation of the unit of competence addressed. At this stage, the following activities should be carried out: description of the course, definition of individual and group objectives, design of examples and tasks, estimation of the time for carrying out exercises and tasks,

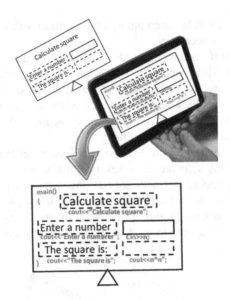

Fig. 3. From input/output to code with augmented reality.

planning of resources and necessary materials for the activities proposed, conformation of work teams and planning of the physical distribution of students in the classroom.

3.3 Collaborative Learning

In Fig. 1, we show both the roles, teacher and student who has the analyst and designer sub-roles, and the activities proposed in the methodological process of the present study, where the teaching role assumes characteristics of: cognitive mediator, instructor and instructional designer for the realization of an initial configuration of each concept oriented. On the other hand, the student has two sub-roles: Analyst and Designer, guided by collaborative principles that allow him to interact with the other colleagues in the case studies raised.

Supported by the model presented by Collazos and Mendoza [52, 53], the teacher as an instructional designer is the one who carries out the planning of the learning units as well as the learning and evaluation activities that will be carried out during the course [53].

In turn, the teacher as a cognitive mediator, is responsible for validating the knowledge acquired by the student through the use of various monitoring strategies that must go from direct observation with which you can show the interest and conceptual goals achieved, the use of verification questions, the realization of learning and evaluation activities which allow checking the learning of the topics directly.

Finally, the teacher as instructor must use the master class as a didactic strategy in which he is responsible for both the teaching of the concepts, in this case of the subject Introduction to programming, as to develop social skills and group work in students, besides, fundamentally collaborative activities, modeling positive interpersonal skills and leading them to practice [53].

Also, the student role according to the recommendations of Collazos and Mendoza [53], must have the following characteristics:

- Be responsible with learning and assume their own knowledge and self-regulation.
- Define learning objectives and problems that are meaningful to understand what specific activities relate to their objectives and at the same time use standards of excellence to assess how well they have achieved those goals.
- Be motivated to learn and have enthusiasm to solve problems and thus be able to understand abstract ideas and concepts.
- Be collaborative to understand that learning is social and to be "open-minded" about others' ideas and about articulating them effectively.
- Be strategic to continuously develop and refine learning and problem solving strategies.

Once the student understood the fundamentals of immersive modeling of the present proposal, exercises are carried out through a collaborative learning process with the Jigsaw method. To this end, the teacher followed the planning of the initial configuration, organizing the classroom in such a way that the students meet in groups of two and distributed throughout in the classroom, in addition, the teacher will be the person who will present the problem for each exercise proposed.

Each example must be analyzed by the two students each in the role of analyst and designer. I order to do this, each student will propose a solution from their role and share it with their base group partner, then each will meet another "pair" of another group to analyze each proposal and conclude a single and then these two will meet with others "Pairs" until half the group is reunited under one role and the other half with the other role which will obtain a solution to the exercise. Finally, each student will return to their base group to share the solution with their partner and both will propose the final solution.

3.4   Feedback

It is carried out by the teacher at the end of each exercise. It consists of concluding with the students, the final solution, the important and pertinent considerations to both the exercise and the subject treated. After making the feedback, the teacher will present the following exercise and it is necessary for both members of each group to exchange the roles.

4   Results

The research methodology proposed was developed under the positivist paradigm since it was based on scientific knowledge, with a quantitative approach that allowed the numerical examination of the data, using the analytical empirical method be-cause the data were treated with statistical techniques and under a descriptive re-search with an experimental design with two groups (control and experimental).

$$G_1 \quad X \quad O_1$$
$$G_2 \quad - \quad O_2$$

The research was conducted with two groups of different students of the first course of Introduction to programming. Thus, the first experimental group G1 was formed by 27 first-semester students of Systems Engineering corresponding to the academic period II-2017, to whom the experimental treatment X was applied and finally a subsequent O1 test was applied. The control group G2 consisted of 23 students of the I-2017 academic period of the same semester and course as the experimental group to whom no experimental treatment was applied and the scores obtained from the study topic were considered as O2. The characterization of the groups is shown in Fig. 4.

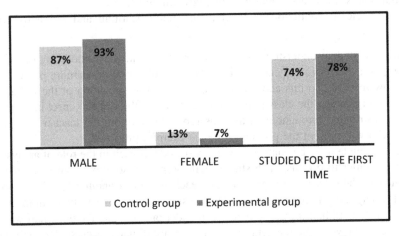

Fig. 4. Characterization of the control group and the experimental group

Once the investigative treatment for the experimental group and the traditional method in the control group were applied, four evaluation activities were carried out consisting in the application of two group workshops (with Jigsaw in the experimental team and group activities in the control team) with the participation of two students (40%) and two individual follow-ups (60%) with the purpose of establishing quantitatively the process of appropriation of such theme and whose results are shown in Fig. 5.

With the results obtained, we used the data technique called Parametric Analysis through the Student's T-distribution Probability Distribution, with which it is possible to test a hypothesis by examining the differences between two small, independent samples that in research processes come from the data obtained by the control group compared to the experimental group and that for the present study was parameterized with a 5% level of significance. Table 2 shows the results for the introduction to programming course.

Table 2 shows the success of the results of the application of the experimental treatment consisting of immersive modeling in a collaborative setting, where the

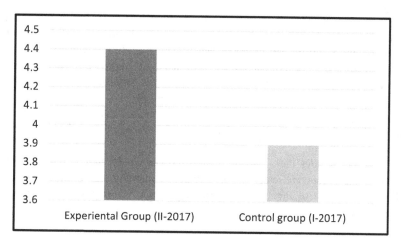

Fig. 5. Average score

Table 2. Student's T-test

Items	Experimental group	Control group
Observations	27	23
Statistic t	2,3396	
P(T <=t) one line	0,0118	
Critical value of T (one line)	1,6772	
P(T <=t) two lines	0,0235	
Critical value of T (two lines)	2,0106	

statistical results obtained for the experimental group G1 acquire a statistical value t (2.3396) greater at both the critical value of t of a tail (1.6772) as the critical value for two tails (2.0106) and the value of P (for one and two tails) which is less than 5% (0.0118 and 0.0235 respectively), which concludes that the difference of scores between experimental group and control group is statistically significant in 95%.

5   Conclusions and Future Work

As the main conclusion, we can state that by constructing a didactic strategy that takes the rigor of a topic and conjugates it with experiential technological processes in the students (augmented reality) together with a method of active participation (Jigsaw), more encouraging results are obtained in this difficult task that teachers of the first courses of programming have when the guide their students to the discovery and strengthening of algorithmic thinking that will be of vital importance in their role as future software builder.

The previous statistical analysis shows the incidence of the experimental treatment compared to the control group, establishing that by incorporating adequate didactic strategies, academic results are obtained that directly benefit the students.

The collaborative component carried out allowed higher levels of interaction between the students themselves and, at the same time between them and the knowledge, improving the interpersonal relations in the group.

In the study it was possible to verify that the combination of immersive interactive processes with elements of collaborative learning generate longer times of attention captured by the student.

Future work includes the inclusion of the study of conditional, cyclical structures, homogeneous and recursive data using collaborative learning and immersive modeling that allow the student of the first programming courses to acquire the learning in a meaningful way to their own experiences.

References

1. Revelo Sánchez, O., Collazos Ordóñez, C., Jiménez Toledo, J.: El trabajo colaborativo como estrategia didáctica para la enseñanza/aprendizaje de la programación: una revisión sistemática de literatura. TecnoLógicas **21**, 115–134 (2018). https://doi.org/10.22430/issn.2256-5337
2. Sánchez, S., et al.: Applying mixed reality techniques for the visualization of programs and algorithms in a programming learning environment. In: eLmL 2018: The Tenth International Conference on Mobile, Hybrid, and On-line Learning Applying, pp. 84–89 (2018)
3. Ortega, M., et al.: IProg: development of immersive systems for the learning of programming. In: Proceedings of the XVIII International Conference on Human Computer Interaction, Part F1311, p. 6 (2017). https://doi.org/10.1145/3123818.3123874
4. Jiménez, J., Collazos, C., Hurtado, J., Pantoja, W.: Estrategia colaborativa en entornos tridimensionales como estrategia didáctica de aprendizaje de estructuras iterativas en programación computacional. Investigium IRE Cienc. Soc. Humanas. **6**, 80–92 (2015). http://dx.doi.org/10.15658/CESMAG15.05060207
5. González De Rivera Fuente, M., Paredes Velasco, M.: Aprendizaje con programación Colaborativa. Aprendiz. con Program Colab. **5**(2), 1–33 (2008)
6. Ben-Ari, M.: Constructivism in computer science education. J. Comput. Math. Sci. Teach. **20**, 24–73 (2001)
7. Martos, C.: Zerintia. Innovando con madrid tour. Revista de turismo y patrimonio cultura. **12**(1), 239–241 (2014)
8. Hernández, G. Jiménez, R., Martínez, Á.: Creencias docentes sobre la importancia de la didáctica en la orientación de la enseñanza del primer curso de programación de computadoras. Rev. Univ. Docencia Investig. Innovación. **2**, 87–103 (2012)
9. Oviedo, M.: La enseñanza de la programación. http://bibliotecadigital.conevyt.org.mx/colecciones/documentos/somece2002/Grupo4/Oviedo.pdf
10. Hayashi, Y., Fukamachi, K., Komatsugawa, H.: Collaborative learning in computer programming courses that adopted the flipped classroom. In: International Conference on Learning and Teaching in Computing and Engineering, pp. 209–212 (2015). https://doi.org/10.1109/latice.2015.43

11. Sakhumuzi, M., Emmanuel, O.: Student perception of the contribution of Hackathon and collaborative learning approach on computer programming pass rate. In: 2017 Conference on Information Communication Technology and Society (ICTAS), pp. 1–5 (2017). https://doi.org/10.1109/ictas.2017.7920524
12. Affleck, G., Smith, T.: Identifying a need for web-based course support (1999)
13. Xinogalos, S., Sartatzemi, M., Dagdilelis, V., Evangelidis, G.: Teaching OOP with BlueJ: a case study. In: Proceedings of the 6th IEEE International Conference on Advanced Learning Technologies (ICALT 2006). IEEE (2006)
14. Bett, G., et al.: Desarrollo de Juegos como Estrategia Didáctica en la Enseñanza de la Programación. http://conaiisi.frc.utn.edu.ar/PDFsParaPublicar/1/schedConfs/4/120-429-1-DR.pdf
15. Murillo Rivera, M.: Exploring the teaching-learning process. Actual Investig. Educ. Explor. **6**, 28 (2006). https://doi.org/10.15517/aie.v6i1.9206
16. Szpiniak, A.F., Rojo, G.A.: Enseñanza de la programación (2007)
17. Jurado, F., Molina, A.I., Redondo, M.A., Ortega, M.: Cole-Programming: Shaping Collaborative Learning Support in Eclipse. IEEE Rev. Iberoam. Tecnol. del Aprendiz. **8**, 153–162 (2013). https://doi.org/10.1109/RITA.2013.2284953
18. Wing, J.M.: Computational thinking. it represents a universally applicable attitude and skill set everyone, not just computer scientists, would be eager to learn and use. Commun. ACM **49**(3) (2006). https://doi.org/10.1109/vlhcc.2011.6070404
19. Espino, E., González, C.: Estudio sobre diferencias de género en las competencias y las estrategias educativas para el desarrollo del pensamiento computacional. Rev. Educ. Distancia. **46**, 1–20 (2015). https://doi.org/10.6018/red/46/12
20. Hurtado, J.A., Collazos, C.A., Cruz, S.T., Rojas, O.E.: Child programming: una estrategia de aprendizaje y construcción de Software basada en la lúdica, la colaboración y la agilidad. Rev. Univ. RUDIC. 1 (2012)
21. MIT: Scratch (2008)
22. Mellon, U.C.: Alice (2003)
23. Fracchia, C., Baeza, N., Martins, A.: ECDIA: Entorno Colaborativo para el Diseño e Implementación de Algoritmos (2011)
24. Jiménez, J.A., Pavony Meneses, M.A., Álvarez, A.F.: Serna: enseñanza de algoritmos y programación en ingeniería Integration environment of PBL and CSCL for teaching algorithms and programming in engineering. Rev. Av. Sist. Inform. **5**, 189–194 (2008)
25. Villalobos Salcedo, J.A.: Proyecto Cupi2 – una solución integral al problema de enseñar y aprender a programar 10°, 1–37 (2009)
26. Pérez Calderón, R.: Una Herramienta y Técnica p ara la E nseñanza de la P rogramación (2008)
27. Kölling, M., Quig, B., Patterson, A., Rosenberg, J.: The BlueJ system and its pedagogy. Comput. Sci. Educ. **1**(13), 249–268 (2003). https://doi.org/10.1076/csed.13.4.249.17496
28. Myller, N.: Collaborative software visualization for learning: theory and applications (2009). http://doi.acm.org/10.1145/1513593.1513600
29. Diwan, A., Waite, W.M., Jackson, M.H., Dickerson, J.: PL-detective: a system for teaching programming language concepts. J. Educ. Resour. Comput. (JERIC) **4**(4), 1 (2005)
30. Redondo, M.Á.: Aprendizaje en grupo de la programación mediante técnicas de colaboración distribuida en tiempo real, pp. 351–357 (2004)
31. Esteves, M., Mendes, A.J.: A simulation tool to help learning of object oriented programming basics. In: 34th Annual Frontiers in Education, FIE 2004, pp. 811–816 (2004)
32. Jo, C., Arnold, A.J.: A portable and collaborative distributed programming environment the architecture of DPE (2003)

33. Truong, N., Bancroft, P., Roe, P.: A web based environment for learning to program, vol. 16 (2003)
34. University Carnegie Mellon, U.: Alice.org. http://www.alice.org/index.php?page=what_is_alice/what_is_alice
35. Vizcaíno, A., Contreras, J., Favela, J., Prieto, M.: An adaptive, collaborative environment to develop good habits in programming, pp. 262–271 (2002)
36. Suzuki, H., Kato, H.: Identity formation/transformation as the process of collaborative learning through AlgoArena. In: Proceedings of CSCL 1997, pp. 280–289 (1997)
37. Humphrey, W.S.: Introduction to the personal software process (1997)
38. Jonhson, D.W., Jonhson, R., Holubec, E.: Cooperation in the Classroom, 6th edn. Interaction Book Company, Edina (1993)
39. Monterrey, I.T.: Aprendizaje Colaborativo, técnicas didácticas, endizaje_colaborativo.pdf (2008)
40. Collazos, C., Guerrero, L., Vergara, A.: Aprendizaje Colaborativo: un cambio en el rol del profesor (2012)
41. Escribano González, A.: Aprendizaje cooperativo y autónomo en la enseñanza universitaria. Enseñanza Teach. Rev. Interuniv. Didáctica. 13, 89–104 (1995)
42. Lavigne, G., Vasconcelos Ovando, M.P., Sandoval, J.O., Salas, L.M.: Exploración preliminar del aprendizaje colaborativo dentro un entorno virtual. 12, 1–20 (2012). https://doi.org/10.15517/aie.v12i3.10295
43. Johnson, D.W., Johnson, F.P.: Joining Together: Group Theory and Group Skills. Allyn & Bacon, Needham Heights (1997)
44. Bruffee, K.A.: Collaborative Learning Higher Education, Interdependence and the Authority of Knowledge, 2nd edn. The Johns Hopkins University Press, Baltimore (1999)
45. Feiner, S., Macintyre, B., Seligmann, D.: Knowledge-based augmented reality. Commun. ACM 36, 53–62 (1993)
46. Hsiao, K., Rashvand, H.: Body language and augmented reality learning environment. In: Fifth FTRA International Conference on Multimedia Ubiquitous Engineering, pp. 246–250 (2011). https://doi.org/10.1109/mue.2011.51
47. Kato, H., Billinghurst, M.: Marker tracking and HMD calibration for a video-based augmented reality conferencing system. In: Proceedings of the 2nd IEEE and ACM International Workshop on Augmented Reality (IWAR 1999), pp. 35–51 (1999)
48. De La Torre Cantero, J., Martin Dorta, N., Saorín Pérez, J.L., Carbonell Carrera, C.: Realidad Aumentada, Un Enfoque Practico con ARToolKit y Blender, Madrid, España (2012)
49. Arribas, C., Gutiérrez, M., Gil, C., Santos, C.: Recursos digitales autónomos mediante realidad aumentada. Rev. Iberoam. Educ. Distancia RIED 17, 241–274 (2014). https://doi.org/10.5944/ried.17.2.12686
50. MIT: Faster Maintenance with Augmented Reality. Technol. Rev. 12 (2009)
51. Rodriguez Serrano, K.P., Maya Restrepo, M.A., Jaén Posada, J.S.: Educación en Ingenierías: de las clases magistrales a la pedagogía del aprendizaje activo. Ing. Desarro. 30, 125–142 (2012)
52. Aronso, E., Blaney, N., Stephan, C., Sikes, J., Snapp, M.: The Jigsaw Classroom. Sage, Beverly Hills (1978)
53. Collazos, C., Mendoza, J.: Cómo aprovechar el "aprendizaje colaborativo" en el aula. Educ. Educ. 9, 61–76 (2006)

Data Acquisition System for the Monitoring of Attention in People and Development of Interfaces for Commercial Devices

Alfredo Garcia[1]([⊠]) , Juan Manuel Gonzalez[1] ,
and Amparo Palomino[2]

[1] Facultad de Ciencias de la Computación, BUAP, Puebla, Mexico
alfredo_amigo18@hotmail.com, jumagoca78@gmail.com
[2] Facultad de Ciencias de la Electrónica, BUAP, Puebla, Mexico
Ampalomino@gmail.com

Abstract. The level of attention in people is associated with the efficiency in their intellectual activities, in their level of understanding and in the development of their creative ability. It is essential to know the behavior of the physiological variables involved in this process, with these variables the states of attention of a person can be determined with greater precision. Using this information, a person can have feedback on their cognitive activity and thus raise attention on the activity performed and consequently improve their cognitive performance. A common problem is the complexity of recovering the data by means of sensors since they are usually invasive and difficult to calibrate, they are usually single-user. So the signals can contain noise and generate an error in the diagnosis. In this work we propose the implementation of a non-invasive multi-user system, for the identification of the level of attention in people, based on at least two physiological variables of the user to determine it, as well as obtaining a better performance in reading the physiological variables, in the delivery of the final diagnosis and in the control of the level of attention of the people to improve their cognitive performance. Currently there are several commercial headbands used as sensors of brain waves. The manufacturers of these devices provide a graphical interface limited to specific applications. In this work, is shown a description of the development of data acquisition of three commercial brainwave diadems: Mindwave, MUSE and Emotiv Epoc. The data obtained are processed independently of the manufacturer's software to obtain the level of attention of the users, implementing a monitoring system for each commercial device.

Keywords: Attention level · Brain signals · Multi-user system
Graphic environment · Commercial brain computer interfaces and wireless

1 Introduction

There are several disorders that affect the level of attention of people both in their childhood and adulthood.

V. Agredo-Delgado and P. H. Ruiz (Eds.): HCI-COLLAB 2018, CCIS 847, pp. 83–97, 2019.
https://doi.org/10.1007/978-3-030-05270-6_7

One of the most recognized disorders is attention deficit/hyperactivity disorder (ADHD) and is usually diagnosed for the first time in childhood, and symptoms persist in adolescence and adulthood [1].

ADHD is characterized by lack of attention, impulsivity and hyperactivity. It has recently been estimated that affects 3.5% of school-age children around the world and is said to be one of the most common psychiatric disorders among young people. The biggest challenge for adults with attention deficit hyperactivity disorder (ADHD) is the management of information and tasks [2].

To know the degree of affectation that ADHD produces in people, it is necessary to have tools that can provide a feedback of the percentage of attention that the user has when executing a specific task.

Currently there is a variety of commercial devices that provide a quantitative level of concentration, meditation, relaxation and user care, but in some cases are achieved in an invasive way, affecting the user's response and consequently the final diagnosis.

Biofeedback training systems foster a specific mental or physical state in a user through a closed cycle of bio-feedback. These systems gather the physiological state of a person through the detection of hardware, integrate this state into a computer-based interactive system and present the comments so that the user can work to adjust their status [3–5].

In this research work it is proposed to implement a system to measure the level of attention in people, generating feedback in the form of a closed loop to carry out some action that helps to restore the user's level of attention.

This system will be a tool used as a basis in different areas for the analysis of user information required based on 2 biometric variables initially: brain waves and body posture.

A multi-user type system will be implemented, decreasing the delay in the response of the system, using a wireless communication and with the characteristic of being non-invasive and easy to use, in order to obtain a final diagnosis that reliably describes the level of attention of the user.

2   The Human Computer Interface

The human computer interaction (HCI by its abbreviations in English), is the study of the relation that exists between the human users and the computer systems that use to realize diverse tasks. The purpose of human computer interaction is to understand the processes, capacities and predilections that can be associated with the activities performed by users, involving understanding and knowledge of things such as memory, vision, cognition, hearing, touch and motor skills [6, 7].

2.1   Virtual Environments

Virtual environments are artificially generated spaces that simulate an environment with the appearance of reality -realistic or not- in which the user can interact. One of the most defining characteristics of these environments is that they give the user the sensation of being present in the virtual space.

2.2 Non-invasive Sensors

Portable sensors have garnered considerable recent interest due to their tremendous promise for a large number of applications. However, the absence of reliable non-invasive chemical sensors has greatly hampered progress in the area of detection in the body. Electrochemical sensors offer great promise as portable chemical sensors that are suitable for various applications due to their high performance, inherent miniaturization and low cost.

3 The Relationship Between States of Attention and Level of Attention

Emotions condition the interpretation of the messages we receive and the process of teaching-learning and development, both in face-to-face communication and through data networks (virtual learning environments or social networks) [8].

The feelings are the result of emotions and mean an affective mood that occurs in a person, emotions are psycho-physiological expressions, biological and mental states, can also be defined as adaptations of the individual to stimuli caused by the environment, it has been shown that emotions affect most human activities, among which are creativity, decision making and communication [9].

The role of automatic emotion recognition is growing continuously. This is because the importance of the reaction to the affective states of the user in the person-computer interaction has been accepted.

As computers become more and more sophisticated, whether professionally or socially, it becomes more important that they are able to interact naturally, that is, in a way similar to how they interact with other human agents. The most important feature of human interaction that guarantees that the process is done naturally, is the process by which we can infer the emotional state of others. This allows to adjust the patterns of behavior and responses, optimizing the interactive human-computer process [10].

4 The Cerebral Waves as a Physiological Variable of the Level of Attention

Electroencephalography was discovered by Hans Berger in 1924 (Haas 2003), and consists in obtaining an electrical signal of the functioning of the brain. It is divided into two groups:

- The invasive, where electrodes are implanted inside the skull of the patient, which despite the related natural complications, has in favor of the fact that the signal can be focused, distinguishing a specific area of the brain.
- The non-invasive, which record electrical potentials from the scalp, through pairs of silver conductive electrodes, which are used to read electrical signals. Small voltage differences between electrodes usually register values between 30 and 100 μV, so they should normally be amplified. Electrical activity occurs when neurons communicate [11].

4.1 Classification of the Signals of an EGG

The signals obtained through an EEG can be decomposed into 5 waves with different characteristics [11]:

Delta: These waves range from 0.5 to 4 Hz. They are the slowest waves and are present while a person sleeps. The production of these waves in the waking state, is related to the physical defects in the brain. Physical movement can cause artificial delta waves, but with an instantaneous analysis, only by observation of primary EEG records can this be verified or discarded.

Theta: It fluctuates between 4 and 7.5 Hz, are linked to inefficiency and daydreaming. In addition they are often related to access to unconscious material of the brain and states of deep meditation. The lower frequency waves of theta represent the thin line between being awake or in a dream state. Theta arises from emotional tension, especially frustration or disappointment. High levels of theta are considered abnormal in adults, and are also related to attention deficit hyperactivity disorder.

Alpha: Oscillate from 8 to 13 Hz, are slower and associated with relaxation and disconnection. Thinking about something peaceful with closed eyes gives an increase in alpha activity. In some way, alpha waves indicate a relaxed state of consciousness, without attention or concentration.

Beta: They are in the frequency range between 14 and 26 Hz, but are often divided into low beta and high beta to get a more specific analysis. The waves are small and fast, associated with focused concentration. When the movement is resisted or suppressed, or when solving a mathematical task there is an increase in the activity of the beta waves. A state of panic can also cause an increase in the level of beta waves.

Gamma: These waves are in the range of frequencies greater than 30 Hz. Their amplitude is very small, and their occurrence is rare, so they are related to certain diseases of the brain. It is believed to reflect the mechanism of consciousness. The beta and gamma waves together have been associated with attention, perception and cognition.

4.2 Commercial Devices to Measure Level of Attention

There are several commercial devices currently whose specific function is to determine the level of attention of people, through a graphical interface in most cases obtaining the measurement of a biometric variable. The most used biometric variable to measure the level of attention in people are brain waves, these are obtained through diadems with sensors. Some examples are the following:

MindWave. Developed by the manufacturer Neurosky (www.neurosky.com), it allows obtaining EEG signals through a headband-type interface that is placed on the head and powered by a 1.5 V AAA-type battery. It uses a wireless interface to communicate with the computer and acquires the signals through passive biosensors connected to an electrode that makes contact with the forehead. In addition, it has a reference terminal is connected to the earlobe. This feature is used to determine the origin of a signal. In the brain-computer interfaces, the location of the electrodes allows obtaining different representations of the EEG. The MindWave device has only one terminal placed on the forehead of the subject, in what is formally known as a prefrontal zone. Figure 1 shows the way in which the device is used [11].

Fig. 1. Correct positioning of the Neurosky MindWave headband.

Emotiv Epoc. Bases its operation on a set of sensors strategically located in different areas of the head; this in order to interpret the frequencies produced to detect the thoughts, feelings and expressions of the user.

The headset is responsible for receiving, encrypting and sending the signals through the communication port for post-processing, using a logical abstraction protocol called Emo-Engine. The SDK tools provided by Emotiv-Systems are used to access the signal registers in the equipment.

Emotiv Epoc has 3 Suites for the detection of input signals: Expressiv, which deciphers facial expressions; Affectiv, whose description is the emotional state of the user, and Cognitiv, whose interpretation is based on the conscious use of thoughts. Figure 2 shows the way in which the device is used [12–14].

Fig. 2. Correct positioning of the Emotiv-Epoc headset from Emotiv-Systems.

There are different types of BCI, which have particular characteristics in their design in the Table 1 are described some important technical characteristics of 8 different BCI devices, characteristics such as number and type of sensors, price or the option of a software development kit (SDK):

Table 1. Comparison of the brain computer interfaces.

Device	Price (Dollars)	Electrodes	Mental states	SDK	Released	Producer	Interface
iFocusBand	$500	1	8	YES	2014	iFocus Band	Bluetooth
MindWave	$99.9	1	2	YES	2011	NeuroSky	Bluetooth
Mindflex	$50	1	1	NO	2009	Mattel	
Emotiv EPOC	$399	14	3	YES	2009	Emotiv Systems	Bluetooth
Star Wars Force Trainer	$45	1	1	NO	2009	Uncle Milton	
MindSet	$199	1	2	YES	2007	Neurosky	Bluetooth
Muse	$299	4	5	YES	2014	InteraXon	
OpenBCI Ganglion B	$99	4	3	YES	2015	Open BCI	Bluetooth

4.3   Validation Instruments

To evaluate the validity of the intervention, validated questionnaires and scales should be used. These measurement techniques should be available in the language of the participants and should measure the key aspects of cognitive rehabilitation. For example, to evaluate the improvements of attention in longitudinal studies, the following scales and questionnaires could be used: Integrated Visual and Auditory Continuous Performance Test (VAT), Test of Variable Attention (TOVA), among others [4, 15].

4.4   Electronic Systems for Feedback

Classroom-related studies showed that environmental factors, such as cognitive assistive technology (CAT) and external location systems, can help people with cognitive disabilities [15].

An example is the battery of the attention training system. This electronically generated response cost system is placed on a student's desk and handled with a remote control that is given to the teacher. It is designed to send comments in order to increase the levels of attention related to tasks. This system was found to be more effective compared to a pre-existing classroom management program that used chip reinforcement [15].

Another example is the Watchminder, a vibrating wristwatch. This self-monitoring device aims to increase the task behavior of elementary school children. The results of this study proved effective for two out of three participants.

Socially expressive robots use gestures and other forms of nonverbal communication to express internal states and can be used to provide an affective expression of digital information [16]. People tend to perceive robots as social actors and attribute similar traits to humans, including mental states. This can contribute to the fact that instructions from physical robots are more reliable than those from on-screen agents and that robots can be more persuasive than on-screen agents when it comes to decisions in the physical world [15].

Learning objects (LOs) are important information resources that support traditional learning methods. To assess the impact, effectiveness and usefulness of learning objects, a theoretical, reliable and valid evaluation tool is necessary. An evaluation tool proposed in the literature consists of a cross-entropy metric to compare the LO design that uses the information provided by the visual fixations measured from a small focus group [17].

5 State of the Art of the Systems of Measurement of the Level of Attention in People

The research carried out on the implementation of a non-invasive and multi-user system, to identify the level of care in people is composed of the study of several stages:

- Types of non-invasive sensors currently used.
- Types of biometric variables used to measure attention states.
- Commercial devices implemented to measure attention statuses.
- Data acquisition speed of the biometric variables (sampling time).
- Software used for data processing.
- Applied technique to obtain data acquisition.
- Feedback techniques.

Figure 3 illustrates the diagram of the elements of the attention level recognition system using the closed-loop control technique.

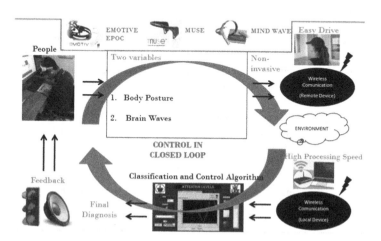

Fig. 3. System of identification of attention level in people.

Table 2 compares the physiological variables, applied techniques and impact with the levels of care obtained from various sources and scientific articles.

Table 2. Comparative table of physiological variables, applied techniques and impact on attention levels.

Ref	Variable physiological used	Technical applied	Relation and impact with the levels of attention
1	Facial gesturing	Digital image processing	Correlation of emotions with the level of attention of a person
2	Binaural waves (auditory waves)	Modification of the frequency range of the incident waves	Binaural waves cause a positive impact on mental states such as active concentration and creative visualization
3	Brain waves (Alpha, Beta, Delta, Theta and Gamma)	Wavelet transform	Using the Mindwave headband to read brain signals, which are classified into levels of attention
4	Brain waves produced by facial gestures	EmotivEpoc Suites: * Affective * Expressiv * Cognitiv	Use of the EmotivEpoc headband for the reading of brain signals, which are classified in levels of attention
5	Brain waves (Alpha, Beta, Delta, Theta and Gamma)	Classification of brain waves in emotions through their variations of frequencies	Correlation of emotions with the level of attention of a person
6	Brain waves (Alpha, Beta, Delta, Theta and Gamma)	Bayesian classification and search algorithm Hill Climbing	Correlation of emotions with the level of attention of a person
7	Facial gesturing	Digital image processing	Automatic feedback can improve a person's attention levels
8	Facial gesturing Body movements	Digital image processing Mouse movement	Application of tasks that require cognitive processes such as attention, memory and reasoning
9	Brain waves	Waves of the heart Classification of brain and heart waves in emotions through their variations in frequencies	Correlation of emotions with the level of attention of a person
10	Text	E-learning (Identification of emotions through the way of writing a text)	Correlation of emotions with the level of attention of a person

6 Implementation of Data Acquisition Systems for Commercial Devices

6.1 Implementation of MUSE Attention Monitor

InteraXon, manufacturer of the Muse headband, provides an SDK where the OSC (Open Sound Control) protocol must be decoded for the acquisition of data from the device. The Muse Interaxon SDK consists of a signal display called MuseLAB shown in the Fig. 4. In order to obtain the data from the virtual port, a graphical interface was implemented in Labview, which is shown in the Fig. 5, where an algorithm was developed to reflect the level of attention of the person. This monitor is mono-user type and its main characteristic is its sampling speed [18].

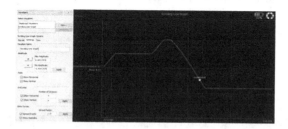

Fig. 4. SDK MuseLAB (Signals visualizer).

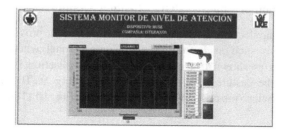

Fig. 5. Muse attention monitor implemented in Labview.

6.2 Implementation of MindWave Attention Monitor

NeuroSky, manufacturer of the MindWave headband, provides a free access SDK, this feature allows to perform a better interaction with the device and develop a multi-user interface, which is shown in the Fig. 6. Another application is Blink Detection whose function is the blink recognition shown in the Fig. 7 [18].

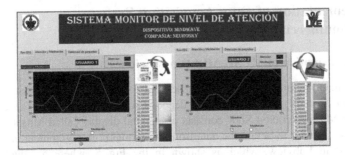

Fig. 6. MindWave attention monitor implemented in Labview.

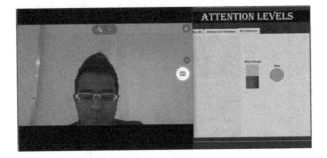

Fig. 7. SDK Blink detection (Blink recognizer).

6.3   Implementation of Emotiv EPOC Attention Monitor

Emotiv Systems, manufacturer of the EmotivEPOC headband, provides an SDK with different applications such as Emotiv Xavier Control Panel whose function is to monitor the sensors as shown in the Fig. 8. Another application is Emotiv Emobot whose function is the gesture recognition shown in the Fig. 9. The data acquisition implemented in Labview for this device is shown in the Fig. 10 [18].

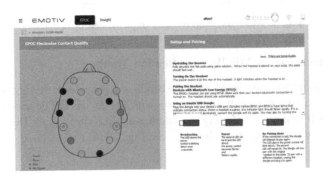

Fig. 8. SDK Xavier Control Panel (Sensors monitor).

Fig. 9. SDK Emotiv Emobot (Gesture recognizer).

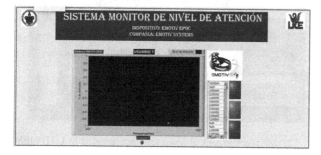

Fig. 10. Emotiv EPOC attention monitor implemented in Labview.

7   Experimental Tests and Results

Experimental tests were performed using the MindWave commercial device of the Neurosky company, to detect the level of attention in first semester students of the computer degree of the BUAP.

A sample of 22 students whose ages are between 17 and 22 years old was used.

The test consisted in a test to identify colors, which was obtained from the demos of the company Brain HQ (https://www.brainhq.com/why-brainhq/about-the-brainhq-exercises/attention), whose interface it is illustrated in the Fig. 11.

To obtain the data of brain signals, a graphical interface was implemented, using the software LABVIEW, in the Fig. 12 illustrates the graphic interface where you can observe the behavior of brain signals, a traffic light as feedback, a vector where the sampled data is stored and the variation of the user's level of attention.

The test was carried out in two modalities: with tablet and desktop computer. The practical development is shown in the Fig. 13.

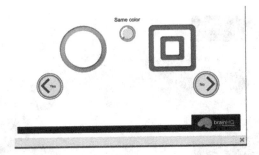

Fig. 11. Interface of the "same color" test of the company Brain HQ. (Color figure online)

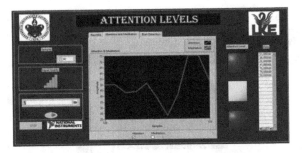

Fig. 12. Interface graphical interface implemented in LABVIEW.

Fig. 13. Practical development of the experimental test.

In the development of the experiment 60 samples are taken for each test and the level of attention of each student is obtained both in the tablet and in the computer. With the obtained data an analysis is made reflected in the graphs of the Figs. 14, 15 and 16; which show the percentage of attention per device, the percentage of individual attention and the percentage of attention per hits respectively.

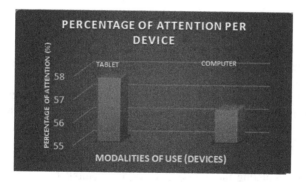

Fig. 14. Percentage of attention per DEVICE.

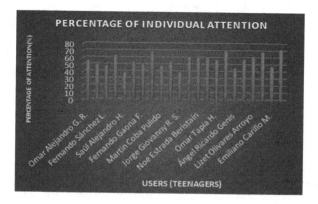

Fig. 15. Percentage of attention per USER.

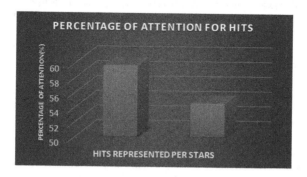

Fig. 16. Percentage of attention per HITS.

8   Conclusions

When the experimentation was developed, the MindWave device required a synchronization time of approximately 5 min, which delayed the application of the "same color" test.

When the headset was placed, the user had difficulties to recognize his brain signals, since sometimes, not making good contact with the sensors, the communication with the graphic interface slipped or lost, which caused a restart of the entire system of acquisition of the brain data.

The results obtained reflect greater concentration reached by users when handling a tablet than by manipulating the mouse of a desktop computer, which indicates that it influences as a distractor when executing a specific task.

In the present work we seek to generate a more efficient device in terms of response time, easy handling, and with greater robustness in its performance.

The analyzed headbands have specific characteristics, the performance of each depends on the application that you want to perform. Minwave is the most versatile headband even if it only has one sensor, Muse is the headband with the longest sampling time despite having four sensors and Emotive Epoc is the most complete headband.

References

1. Ravichandran, S., Huang, J.: Motivating children with attention deficiency disorder using certain behavior modification strategies. In: Lim, C.T., Goh, J.C.H. (eds.) 13th International Conference on Biomedical Engineering. IFMBE Proceedings, vol. 23, pp. 1057–1062. Springer, Heidelberg (2009). https://doi.org/10.1007/978-3-540-92841-6_260
2. Huh, J., Ackerman, M.S.: Exploring social dimensions of personal information management with adults with AD/HD. In: CHI EA 2010 CHI 2010 Extended Abstracts on Human Factors in Computing Systems, Atlanta, Georgia, USA, vol. 1, pp. 3715–3720 (2010). https://doi.org/10.1145/1753846.1754044
3. Regan, L.M., et al.: Games as neurofeedback training for children with FASD. In: IDC 2013 Proceedings of the 12th International Conference on Interaction Design and Children, New York, USA, vol. 1, pp. 165–172 (2013). https://doi.org/10.1145/2485760.2485762
4. Pascual, M.F., Begoña, Z., Buldian, K.M.: Adaptive cognitive rehabilitation interventions based on serious games for children with ADHD using biofeedback techniques: assessment and evaluation. In: COMPUTE 2010 Proceedings of the Third Annual ACM Bangalore Conference, Article 29, Bilbao, España, pp. 1–4 (2014). https://doi.org/10.4108/icst.pervasivehealth.2014.255249
5. Divia, V.: A smartwatch application for individuals with ADHD and mental health challenges. In: ASSETS 2016 Proceedings of the 18th International ACM SIGACCESS Conference on Computers and Accessibility, Nevada, USA, vol. 1, pp. 311–312 (2016). https://doi.org/10.1145/2982142.2982207
6. García, A.E.: Análisis de ondas cerebrales para determinar emociones a partir de estímulos visuales. Tesis Universidad Veracruzana Facultad de Estadística e Informática, México (2015)

7. Girouard, A.: Adaptive brain-computer interface. In: Proceedings of the 27th International Conference on Human Factors in Computing Systems, CHI 2009, USA, vol. 1, pp. 3097–3100 (2009). https://doi.org/10.1145/1520340.1520436

8. Campazzo, E., Martínez, M., Guzmán, A., Agüero, A.: Desarrollo de interface de detección de emociones para su utilización en redes sociales y entornos virtuales de aprendizaje. In: XV Workshop de Investigadores en Ciencias de la Computación, Paraná (2013)

9. Hernández, A., Vásquez, R., Olivares, B.A., Cortes, G., López, I.: Sistema de detección de emociones para la recomendación de recursos educativos. In: Programación Matemática y Software, México, pp. 58–66 (2016). ISSN 2007-3283

10. Marín, E.J.: Detección de emociones del usuario. Tesis Pontificia Universidad, Chile (2014)

11. Torres, F., Sánchez, C., Palacio, B.: Adquisición y análisis de señales cerebrales utilizando el dispositivo MindWave. In: MASKANA, I+D+ingeniería 2014, vol. 5, pp. 83–93. (2014). ISSN 1390-6143

12. Rojas, S., Garzón, J., Martínez, D., Escobar, M., Robayo, C.: Lector de ondas cerebrales para implementar un sistema alternativo y aumentativo de comunicación. In: 10th Latin American and Caribbean Conference for Engineering and Technology, Panamá, vol. 10, pp. 1–9 (2012)

13. Perakakis, M., Potamianos, A.: An affective evaluation tool using brain signals. In: IUI 2013 Companion, USA, vol. 1, pp. 105–106 (2013). https://doi.org/10.1145/2451176.2451222

14. Pinto, R.D., Ferreira, H.A.: Development of a non-invasive brain computer interface for neurorehabilitation. In: REHAB 2015, Portugal, vol. 1, pp. 1–5 (2015). https://doi.org/10.1145/2838944.2838975

15. Zuckerman, O., et al.: KIP3: robotic companion as an external cue to students with ADHD. In: TEI 2016 Proceedings of the TEI 2016: Tenth International Conference on Tangible, Embedded, and Embodied Interaction, USA, vol. 1, pp. 621–626 (2016). https://doi.org/10.1145/2839462.2856535

16. Horii, T., Nagai, Y., Asada, M.: Active perception based on energy minimization in multimodal human-robot interaction. In: HAI 2017, Alemania, vol. 1, pp. 103–110 (2017). https://doi.org/10.1145/3125739.3125757

17. Alvarez, C.L., Hernández, M.A., Hernández, H.M.: Automatic evaluation of learning objects based on cross-entropy of eye fixations minimization. In: Interaccion 2017, México, vol. 1, pp. 1–4 (2017). https://doi.org/10.1145/3123818.3123872

18. Gomez, J.E., Marcé, A.M.: Brain Sensors Aplicats a la Tecnologia Mecánica. Tesis TFG Universitat Politécnica de Catalunya, Barcelona (2016)

Debugging Block-Based Programs

Marilyn Tenorio Melenje María[1,2](✉) [iD],
María Alejandra Trujillo[1,2] [iD], Julio Ariel Hurtado Alegría[1,2] [iD],
and Cesar Collazos[1,2] [iD]

[1] Semillero IRIS Universidad del Cauca, Popayán, Cauca, Colombia
[2] Grupo IDIS, Universidad del Cauca, Popayán, Cauca, Colombia
{mtenorio,mariatrujillo,ahurtado,
ccollazo}@unicauca.edu.co

Abstract. The learning programming is an arduous and complex process, which is why many individuals leave it quickly. One of the most frustrating tasks in this process is the debugging of the programs, which consists of understanding, locating and solving a bug. In this work two studies are carried out to extract the main strategies and resources used by teams of children to debug programs based on the block paradigm. The first study, from secondary sources, is a review of the literature from which it is conceptualized about the purification, its strategies and resources used. The second study, based on primary sources, is a case study in which the debugging strategies that a group of children implicitly use to understand, locate, and solve bugs are explored of programs not made by them. The studies have allowed to establish a set of strategies and resources, as well as a life cycle for the debugging of block-based programs.

Keywords: Errors · Bugs · Reviews · Debugging · Quality · Unreachable code
Fail · Failure · Testing · Test · Test case · Oracle · Early childhood

1 Introduction

Today, computer programming has become a very important area of knowledge, in which several initiatives have been launched to learn the sciences and computer engineering in schools and colleges, where children are expected to develop their skills. computational thinking [1], which is a fundamental skill for all, not only for computer scientists and that involves problem solving, system design and understanding of human behavior, based on the fundamental concepts of computer science, with the premise that this type of thinking allows people to be trained in aspects of organization, decisions and new learning, not only in the area of computing as such, but in any other area of interest that the adult then develops.

Since the beginning of programming, debugging software has been a key but complex activity [2], due to the difficulty involved in identifying, locating and correcting a bug. Ahmadzadeh et al. [3], carried out an investigation to improve the didactic methods of teaching, observing the errors of the compiler and those of logic of the students, arriving at the conclusion that the majority of the good debuggers,

© Springer Nature Switzerland AG 2019
V. Agredo-Delgado and P. H. Ruiz (Eds.): HCI-COLLAB 2018, CCIS 847, pp. 98–112, 2019.
https://doi.org/10.1007/978-3-030-05270-6_8

are good programmers, whereas less of half the good programmers are good debuggers. The above allows to see the debugging, as an activity that requires as much skill as the programming itself. Therefore, it is of great value in the development of children's computational thinking, that they acquire software development and testing skills, particularly to address aspects related to debugging.

This article presents the results of two studies, a review of the literature and a primary case study conducted at the Técnico Industrial School in the city of Popayán, with 35 7th grade students. Both studies are aimed at identifying the main strategies and resources for debugging programs. Both studies were designed to answer the following question: What are the computational thinking strategies and resources that school-age children use to purge their programs? Among the main findings is that the most commonly used strategies are trial-error, teamwork, compare with similar code and functionally correct and understand the program well before looking for the bug.

The rest of the article has been organized as follows. Section 2 presents the background of the literature and related works. Section 3 presents the case study from its planning to its results. Section 4 presents the debug life cycle. Finally, Sect. 5 presents the conclusions, limitations and future work.

2 Background and Study of Literature

2.1 Background

The debugging is to eliminate all faults of a software product, which makes it a key task to achieve its quality. Therefore, it is a key task to train children in terms of total quality, to do things well and to do them well from the beginning [4]. For this it is necessary to contextualize the debugging as part of a larger context such as software quality. Software quality has as its main objective the fulfillment of the needs and expectations of customers about the software products or services offered to the market [5].

In general terms, quality includes three types of activities within the software process [5]:

Quality control: refers to the activities that every company must follow to control that its products maintain a minimum level of quality, oriented to the fulfillment of the requirements of the quality of the product evaluating the defects in the final and intermediate artifacts.

Quality assurance: refers to planning and follow-up activities aimed at providing confidence that the quality requirements will be met.

Quality management: refers to the management activities that are carried out before, during and after the construction of a software to achieve the quality of it. Coordinated activities to direct and control an organization in relation to quality. It includes quality policy, quality objectives, quality planning, quality control, quality assurance and quality improvement.

In the software development itself, one of the most complex tasks related to quality control is the debugging of programs, which is an implicit activity, whose relevance is ignored when teaching or learning to program, diminishing importance to learning through the same mistakes [6]. Many programming books teach programming in different programming languages, but there is very little content aimed at debugging bugs. This causes that the students develop very little the skills for the debugging of the programs. In most programming books, they teach how to use compiler tools, but they do not explain the different kinds of errors that can be committed [7].

Bugs, Faults, Failures, Errors, Defaults, and Mistakes

According to the IEEE a (error, mistake) is a "Human action that produces an incorrect result", that is to say a "Human action that generates a fault in the software" [8, 9]. A fault (fault, bug) according to the IEEE is "a problem that, if not corrected, could cause a failure in an application or produce incorrect results" [8, 9]. A failure (failure, default) according to the IEEE is "the termination of the capacity of a functional unit to perform its determined function within the specified limits" [8, 9].

Software Debug

The detection and elimination of bugs in a program receives the generic name of debugging. Debugging a program is usually done in two essential steps:

- First you have to fail the system and detect its failure.
- From this point it is usually necessary to go back to find what has produced the fault, that is, find the bug or fault [6].

You should verify what functionality is being evaluated at the time of the bug. For this the compilers and interpreters has a call stack [6], which can be used to locate the bug. Debugging is initiated through a step-by-step execution and can be invoked from within any function. That is, if it is known at what point the bug can occur, a resource can be inserted (for example, a program breakpoint) before this point. A common debugging resource is to use step-by-step execution, in order to evaluate the change of the variables at each step of the instruction [6]. A debugging process can be divided into four main steps [10]: location, classification, understanding and repair a bug.

Locating a Bug

This task is misleading because detecting a bug can be very difficult [10]. A typical attitude of inexperienced programmers with regard to bugs, is to consider their location, an easy task: they notice that their code does not do what they expected, and they feel confident knowing what their code should do.

Classification of an Error

Classifying an error is a difficult and risky task, but it is very useful. The list presented below is organized in order of increasing difficulty (which fortunately has a decreasing frequency order, that is, the most difficult errors are the least frequent) [10]:

Syntactic errors are those that refer to the structure of programming expressions and that should be easily captured by the compiler.

Construction errors arise from the linking of "object" or "binary" files that were not rebuilt after a change in some source files. These problems can be easily avoided by using tools to drive the creation of software, such as more mature software development environments.

The basic semantic errors derive from the lack of understanding of the use of variables: for example, uninitialized variables, the dead code (code that will never be executed) and the problems with typing [11]. A compiler can highlight their attention to them through flags.

Complex semantic errors: includes the use of variables or operators in the wrong way. No tool can capture these problems, because they are syntactically correct statements, although logically wrong with respect to the expected execution objective. To detect them, it must be done through a semantic checker or software tests.

Understanding a Bug

A bug must be completely understood before trying to solve it. Trying to fix a bug before fully understanding it could end up causing more damage to the code, since the problem could change shape and manifest itself somewhere else [10]. The following is a useful checklist to ensure a correct approach to understanding the bug:

- Do not confuse the observation of symptoms with the search for the true source of the problem.
- Check if similar errors (especially erroneous assumptions) have occurred in other parts of the code.
- Verify that only one programming error was found, and not a more fundamental problem (for example, an incorrect algorithm).

Repair a Bug

The final step in the debugging process is the correction of a bug. Repair a bug is more than modifying the code. Any correction must be documented in the code and tested correctly. More importantly, learning from mistakes is an effective attitude: it is good practice to fill out a small file with detailed explanations about how the bug was discovered and corrected. A checklist can be a useful aid [10]. There are several points worth recording:

- How the bug was detected, to help write a test case.
- As it was tracked, to give you a better insight on the approach to choose in similar circumstances.
- What kind of bug was found?
- If this bug has been found frequently, a strategy could be established to prevent it from being repeated according to the related error.

Resources for Debugging

Normally, debugging resources come as features of debuggers. According to Adragna [6] we have the resources of breakpoints which interrupts the execution of the program and allows to visualize the status of certain variables. Breakpoints are necessary resources in an interactive debug context. Another resource is the step by step execution, with two possibilities step on (step over, in the calls it jumps to the next instruction) or next step in (step into, when it is also executed in the function called the Step by Step). A valuable resource are watchpoints, which are a special class of breakpoints, which stop the program when the variable under surveillance changes.

2.2 Related Works

The new national curriculum for computer science in England [12] has been developed to train young people in this country with the fundamental skills, knowledge and understanding of computing that is needed for the rest of their lives [12]. This will develop in the students the computational thinking that will allow them to solve problems of daily life. It takes into account three aspects of computer science: Computer Science (CS), Information Technology (IT) and Digital Literacy (DL).

Particularly, in Computer Science two stages are proposed in the curriculum. In the first stage, we work with simple codes, focused on the compression of the algorithm concept, where low difficulty programs are created and debugged. To do this, they are asked to create an algorithm for a daily situation such as preparing a sandwich. It is necessary that the topic is clear in order to be able to capture the algorithm well and identify if it has bugs. In the classroom, this shows the need to incorporate aspects of debugging as an instrument for the development of computational thinking. At level 2, the proposal, like that of the present research work, is related to the teaching of youth programming and code debugging. Therefore, this research questions the strategies that students can follow to correct their code. These could include aspects related to the identification of the failure, find out what part of the code is creating the problem, the bug that causes it, and then work towards a solution.

McCoy et al. [13] Prepare 18 sixth grade students of the Montessori school in the United States in software debugging, during a period of four months. Through a cyclical process of development-debugging, students began to acquire effective debugging skills. It was observed that, after the first debugging lesson, the students spent less time finding a bug and fewer cycles. The authors define a procedure and identify search strategies for the bug during debugging, which lesser to more effective are: random search, brute force, brute force ending in bug and selective search.

Yen et al. [14] Makes a study regarding the understanding of bug by expert and novice programmers. For this, they classify the bug into 3 types: syntax errors, semantics errors and logic errors. Three C language experts and three novice were invited to participate in an evaluation by thinking out loud. Each of the programmers was assigned two programs with the three types of errors and the results showed that the experts have a better understanding of those things that the compiler shows, on the other hand the experts and novices showed similar results regarding the errors of syntax. Regarding the logic errors, the experts showed greater understanding. As this is an experimental work, you can contribute to the present work the idea that there are different types of errors that can be found and by having them clear we can evaluate children in the context of programming. The big difference between these works, is that while this work is applied to young novices and experts and the present work was applied to children between 11 and 13 years old. In addition, findings on the understanding of errors should be incorporated as part of the ChildProgramming methodology.

3   Exploratory Case Study

This paper seeks to identify the strategies of computational thinking that children use implicitly to refine their programs following the methodology of the case study [15] in a context of block-based development. The objective of the case is to be able to empirically complement the ChildProgramming model with specific program debugging practices. The exploratory case study included the debugging of two programs performed in the environment based on MIT Scratch blocks. The experience included three sessions, in the first session we worked on debugging the ping-pong game by teams of 6 ± 1 children between 10 and 12 years of the Técnico Industrial School. Two criteria were taken into account for the selection of the case: the school and the group of children typify the study's target population (public institution, children with knowledge of Scratch and in the stipulated age range), the school has a computer workshop that supports the activities and therefore offers a rich space to develop the research. Another criterion for its selection has been the proximity and availability of the school to carry out this type of studies. In the second session they debugged the game Captain versus Lantern, organizing the children now in teams of three participants. In the third, a discussion was held with the children through a round table. Therefore this is a holistic case study in the same context, with multiple units of analysis.

3.1   Planning and Design of the Case Study

In the context of ChildProgramming and to learn how teams implicitly perform debugging tasks, analyzing their own projects and the projects of their colleagues, this first case study aims to answer the following research question: What are the computational thinking strategies that Do children between 10 and 13 years of age of the Técnico Industrial college apply to debug their projects?

The objective of the study is to identify and analyze the computational thinking strategies used by teams of children between 10 and 14 years of age, from the Técnico Industrial Educational Institution, debugging Scratch programs from the researcher's point of view during two work sessions. This case study is characterized by being of a holistic type, where children's teams (6 in the first session and 13 in the second) with ages between 11 and 13 years, seventh grade "B" are considered as the unit of analysis., which for the purposes of this case, together with the debugged programs, and the registration form, constitute as the main sources of information, in total 35 children of the Seventh B course and 19 debug programs. This case study has an exploratory approach since it seeks to demonstrate the purification strategies used implicitly by the work teams. To obtain the necessary information for this case study and to answer the research question, it was necessary to design a set of metrics, indicators and instruments following the approach of Victor Basili [16]. Table 1 shows the summary of the indicators, metrics and instruments defined.

Table 1. Indicators, metric and case study instruments.

Research question	Indicators	Metric	Instruments
What are the strategies of computational thinking and Scratch resources used by children between 10 and 13 years of Técnico Industrial School?	PU	Frequency of Use (FU)	Observation form
		Total Teams (TE)	Observation form
	NE	Total Number of Bugs in the Original Program (NTB)	Scratch Program
		Total Number of Corrected Bugs (NTBC)	Scratch Program
	NEF, EF	Total Correction Time (TTC)	Observation form
		Total Number of Corrected Bugs (NTBC)	Observation form
		Number of Participants (NI)	Observation form
	Identified strategies	Descriptions of the strategies described by the children	Registration form /Poll
		Descriptions of the strategies described by the researchers	Observation form
	Identified Scratch Resources	Resource identified in the Scratch code	Project Repository
		Description of the resource by children	Poll
		Description of the resource by the researchers	Observation form
	Types of error, Understanding Error	Descriptions of the errors described by the children	Registration form /Poll
		Descriptions of the errors described by the researchers	Observation form

Indicators:

- Percentage of use of the Strategy (PU): this indicator refers to the percentage of use of each identified strategy used by the children and found in the case study and its formula is as follows:

$$PU = FU * 100/TE \tag{1}$$

Where FU is the frequency of use of each strategy and TE is the total of teams.

- Level of effectiveness of the equipment (NE): refers to the level of effectiveness of the work performed in each session as a percentage between bugs that are corrected (NTBC) with respect to the total number of bugs (NTB). Its formula is the following:

$$NE = NTBC * 100/NTB \qquad (2)$$

- Debug Effort (ED): refers to the effort required during debugging based on the total correction time (TCC) and the number of team members (NI). Its formula is the following:

$$ED = TTC * NI \qquad (3)$$

- Level of efficiency (NEF): measures the level of efficiency to solve problems based on the total number of bugs corrected (NTBC) and debugging effort (ED) and its formula is as follows:

$$NEF = NTBC/ED \qquad (4)$$

3.2   Case Development

Taking into account the dynamics that children apply in their academic courses at the Técnico Industrial Institution of the city of Popayán, this case study was designed with 3 work sessions in the seventh course B, which in the first session was divided into teams of 6 people, in the second session groups of 3 people, which were developed between October 31, 2017 and November 14, 2017, as follows:

First Work Session: This session was held on November 03, 2017, the group of 38 children was divided into teams of 6 as seen in Fig. 1. Where each group worked on a computer and interacted with each other. In this case they were placed a program in Scratch ping-pong which contained five bugs that should be found and solved by them. Once the activity was started, they were given one hour for the debugging activity. They were given a debug template where they should register each bug found, describe it, and correct the bug. Followed by this and once the activity was finished or the time that was given to them finished, they were given a survey to know their appreciations.

Second Work Session: It took place on November 10, 2017, the group of 38 children was divided into teams of three people, in order to improve the work in class. In this case they were placed a game "Captain Vs Lantern", which contained 4 bugs. Once the activity was started, they were given 40 min to solve this program. They were given as in the first session, a debug template and a survey.

Round table session: it was held on November 17, 2017 and unlike the first two sessions, in this session there was a round table where the two previous exercises were reviewed, and all the children were giving opinions about how I would solve every bug.

Fig. 1. Photography session 1 of work.

3.3   Results

The quantitative and qualitative results found from work done with children. These results allow identifying the strategies that represented the greatest value for the teams. The strategies found when reviewing the work material that was collected in each of the sessions with the children, were used by them implicitly to debug the proposed programs, which were delivered intentionally with some bugs:

- *By trial-error (EE)* is the strategy used by most teams. The children suppose where the bug is, they try a solution and if it does not work they change it.
- *Teamwork (TE)* is a strategy in which children communicate with each other and together they propose an adequate solution.
- *For example (PE)* is to look for similar code, compare and test.
- *By analysis (PA)* is to review, understand and use the program before looking for bugs.

3.4   Analysis of Results

Considering that a team with good performance, such as those with a level of effectiveness of more than 70% and an efficiency level of more than 1.5, the following can be analyzed:

- The most used strategies were: Trial-Error and Analysis.
- The *For Example* strategy was the only strategy used by the team that managed to find and correct the most bugs.

Regarding the number of children per team, it could be observed that children working in a team perform better than those who individually, however small teams (3 members in session 2) showed better performance than large teams (7). Members in the first session). In large teams, most of the members ignored the debugging process, leaving one or two to work.

Regarding the way the children define and correct the error, it could be observed that simple errors can describe them better, for example a team describes an error like this: *"in Captain America instead of going down with s, it goes up"* (the key). However, the same team was not able to describe the error in which Captain America loses more than one life in a single shot, instead they directly describe the bug (locating the error in the code): *"when the bullet of the Captain touches Lantern takes 0.1 s to lower life but the flashlight bullet hits Captain takes 0.5 s"*. This last problem specified at the level of code was discovered and tried to solve using the *For Example* strategy, however due to the lack of clarity of the problem at the logic of the game, it led to a wrong solution. It was observed that children trying to solve a problem found and not know how to solve it, in the case of the game of Capitan and Lantern, the error was that the time of the bullet should be greater than 0.5 s to deduct a live, but one of them had the time in 0.1 s which caused that when the bullet arrived, it lost 2 lives. When not analyzing this well, what some children did was to put in the same conditions the 2 characters to lose 2 lives per bullet. This is a wrong solution. This shows that having an example is very useful, but it is not enough if the problem is not properly analyzed, so the analysis strategy is a necessary strategy in debugging.

Regarding the types of bugs that were raised in the sessions, it was evident that few children identified the Dead Code (code that is not called), in the first session, only 2 groups of the 6 that had, managed to find it and They described: "Some blocks are not met or do not join with the blocks, one bar appears and one For Always is separate and never fits with the controls", "When you go to the ball programs and you see that there are two that do not have utility ", in session 2, only 1 of the 12 groups, could identify the dead code.

4 Depuration Life Cycle

4.1 The Steps to Follow in ChildDebugging

Before defining the strategies and resources that will lead to the creation of ChildDebugging practices, it is important to bear in mind that a series of steps must be followed to resolve the errors that can occur in any type of system. These steps are based on the simplified model of Katz et al. [17] which says that in general, a person must first understand or have a representation of the device to be repaired, test it even if only to observe that is it produces incorrect behavior.

In the case of computing, the person must locate the error in some way and once it finds it, it repairs it. After repairing the program, you should test it to make sure that correct behavior now occurs. If the program continues to act incorrectly, a location and additional repair may be necessary. Therefore, according to this model, problem solving contains four steps: understanding, testing, location and repair, repeating the last three steps if necessary as can be seen in Fig. 2.

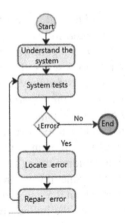

Fig. 2. Simplified model for solving general problems

4.2 Debugging in ChildDebugging

The main objective of the debugging in this model is to improve the quality of the resulting products and also to reduce the feeling of failure.

For this, we will define some debugging strategies which allow us to follow a series of steps to find flaws in the programs, to understand what is occurring, to find in which part of the code is the bug, which can be defined as what is causing the failure in the system and finally solution it.

This model coincides with that proposed by Adragna et al. [10] That defines four steps for optimal debugging, among which are locating the error, classifying, understanding and repairing an error.

4.3 Definition of the ChildDebugging Process

The new ChildDebugging process follows the same life cycle of ChildProgramming which is organized in three phases (pre-game, game and post-game) and in rounds of development. However ChildDebugging introduces the following alterations: The process adds to the phases of game pre-game and post-game, the debugging rounds as a global strategy that seeks to soften the process of incorporation of children in ChildProgramming and where children are expected to assimilate concepts of computational thinking to through the debugging of programs, as seen in Fig. 3.

The process links the debugging practices in the activities: plan strategy, apply strategy and review strategy within a round of the game phase in ChildProgramming.

Pre-game

The purpose of this phase is to establish the objective of the mission, that is, the delivery of the requirements that involve the activity to be carried out.

In the context of ChildProgramming, in this phase the Professor delivers the mission to the work team. This mission contains the detailed description where you can know the objective and the goals proposed for the activity, as well as the necessary material as support for the realization and fulfillment of the mission.

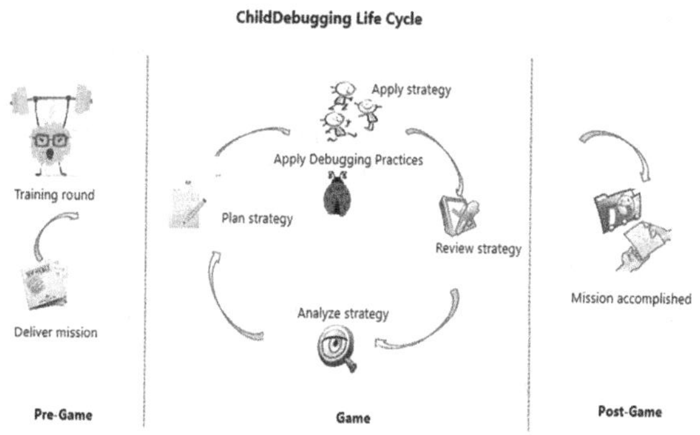

Fig. 3. ChildDebugging life cycle

In this station the work teams identify the tasks and give them a priority taking into account their personal criteria.

In this phase, as part of the ChildDebugging process, a debug module will be added, which consists of giving the team a program that contains bugs so that they can take ownership of all the concepts of debugging, before starting to work on your own creations to facilitate this process in the game phase.

Game

In this phase, iterations called rounds are carried out with the purpose of fulfilling the mission and leaving ready the deliverable that guarantees the fulfillment of the objectives of the activity.

Each round includes four game stations, which are: Plan the Strategy, Apply the strategy, review the strategy and analyze the strategy.

Plan the Strategy

This station consists of defining the tasks of each member of the team and prioritizing them. The teacher will give the team enough time for the members of the team to reach a consensus on the organization of the strategy or a way to tackle each task and its respective development. The team leader will be in charge of asking the members to make a sketch or initial design to help them define the tasks to face the mission.

Apply the Strategy

Once the planning of the strategy has been established, the work team enters the execution of its tasks. This station is the most important since they accumulate the greatest amount of contributions for its development and where the highest activity index will be shown evidencing commitment and active participation of each member of the work team. In addition, this station allows team members to take ownership of ChildProgramming concepts and practices such as agile and collaborative practices, and in this part of the process, debugging practices will be added that will allow locating and understanding bugs I was able to present this part of the process and finally repair them. Also a bug management practice that will allow you to register them to work on them in a next round. All this will help in the development process to execute tasks more easily and quickly to achieve better results when delivering the mission.

Review the Strategy

In this station, the work team along with the teacher verifies the tasks performed and the fulfillment of them in such a way that the result can be evidenced.

This station allows the work team to evaluate the progress of their mission, to know the work rhythm and to correct bugs, which will be useful for the planning of the strategy in the next round.

Analyze the Strategy

In this season the work team evaluates their work as a team, around the performance of the members, their contributions and their collaboration to determine whether the strategy used works or not. It is possible that they must rethink the way they are approaching the task to give a better solution and obtain better results at the end of the mission, either because it was successful or because it did not give an expected result and immediately the way of working for the next round. This station allows analyzing possible future situations and taking timely decisions to mitigate errors.

Post-game

In this phase delivery of the completed mission and the registration of the bugs is done, that is, the completely implemented solution accompanied by all the material associated with the activity and the repository of bugs. The teacher at the close of this mission, must evaluate that the work of the team reflects a learning process and that it has allowed, in an effective way, to fulfill the proposed learning objectives.

5 Conclusions

When starting the exploratory case study with students in their real environment, it is important to conclude that teamwork is the basis for obtaining better results. We worked with groups of 6 people in session 1 and with groups of 3 people in session 2 and it was observed that in small groups there was a better performance.

It is concluded that more than one strategy is necessary to obtain good results, where the analysis strategy is of great importance when it comes to debugging, that is, it is necessary to understand the bug very well in order to solve it properly.

Due to lack of analysis at the time of the debugging, it was evidenced that the children did not find dead code (blocks without function), which evidences the need to have a strategy based on analysis to identify the problems of the code.

Regarding the review of the literature, the debugging process based on the steps of locating, classifying, understanding and repairing a bug can be highlighted, which would allow to organize the identified debugging strategies and define the debug life cycle. This is the case of the analysis strategy, which would allow to locate and understand a bug, while the strategy of the example would facilitate the classification and repair. In addition, the main debugging resources are identified: the breakpoints, the step-by-step execution (on or entering the internal functionalities), the surveillance points and the execution trace. For example, a breaking point could be defined and used in Scratch, which stops the program and allows it to continue executing after pressing and releasing the c key. In the same way it is possible to define these resources in the Scratch environment and in general in the paradigm of block-based programming.

Life cycle that was incorporated in the three phases of ChildProgramming (pre-game, game and post-game) and in rounds of development. To be finally applied the confirmatory case study.

It is also concluded that children have great interest in learning and understanding about this area, however a sense of failure was evidenced, when they fail to solve the bugs they found, so the debugging of programs should be given great importance at the moment to develop children's computational thinking through software programming.

Gratefulness. This work was carried out thanks to the financing of the project ID 4625 Semilleros de Investigación Convocatoria 07-2018 of Innovation Cauca and to the collaboration of the Técnico Industrial School of the City of Popayán.

References

1. Wing, J.M.: Computational thinking. Mag. Commun. ACM **49**(3), 33–35 (2006). https://doi.org/10.1145/1118178.1118215
2. Lee, M.J., Bahmani, F., Kwan, I., et al.: Principles of a debugging-first puzzle game for computing education. In: Proceedings of IEEE Symposium on Visual Languages Human-Centric Computing, VL/HCC, pp. 57–64 (2014). https://doi.org/10.1109/vlhcc.2014.6883023
3. Ahmadzadeh, M., Elliman, D., Higgins, C.: An analysis of patterns of debugging among novice Computer Science students. In: Proceedings of 10th Annual SIGCSE Conference on Innovation and Technology in Computer Science Education (ITiCSE 2005), vol. 37, no. 3, pp. 84–88 (2005). https://doi.org/10.1145/1151954.1067472
4. Deming, E.W.: "Fuera de la crisis," Cambridge Massachusetts Inst. Technol. Cent. Adv. Eng. Study (1986)
5. Cabrera, C., Maria Lopez, A., Valencia, L.E.: Introduction to software quality, no. 39, pp. 326–331 (2008)
6. Sanchez, A.: Depuración y Optimización de Programas, pp. 1–13 (2008)
7. Luján Mora, S.: Un enfoque para la enseñanza de la depuración de errores en las asignaturas de programación, IX Jornadas Enseñanza Univ. la Informática, pp. 473–480 (2003)
8. Narváez Barrera, M.X.: Guía Metodológica para el proceso de validación y verificació de requerimientos de usuario final, Pontif. Univ. Javeriana, pp. 0–117 (2015). http://pegasus.javeriana.edu.co/~CIS1430IS08/docs/V2SoftGuiaMetodologica.pdf
9. International Standard: International Standard ISO/IEC/IEEE, ISO 2011, vol. 2010 (2010)
10. Adragna, P.: Software debugging techniques. In: Inverted CERN School of Computering, pp. 71–86 (1999). https://doi.org/10.5170/cern-2008-002.71
11. Liskov, B.: Data abstraction and hierarchy. In: Proceedings of OOPSLA 1987 Add. to Proceedings of Object-Oriented Programming Systems, Languages and Applications, October 1987. https://doi.org/10.1145/62138.62141
12. Berry, M.: Computing in the national curriculum A guide for primary teachers. Learning Matters (2013). http://www.computingatschool.org.uk/data/uploads/CASPrimaryComputing.pdf
13. Klahr, D., Carver, S.: Cognitive objectives in a LOGO debugging curriculum: instruction, learning, and transfer. Cogn. Psychol. 362–404 (1988). https://doi.org/10.1016/0010-0285(88)90004-7

14. Ching-Zon, Y., Ping-Huang, W., Ching-fang, L.: Analysis of experts and novices thinking process in program debugging. Psychol. Rev. **25**, 495–508 (2004). https://doi.org/10.1007/978-3-642-31398-1_12
15. Runeson, P., Host, M., Rainer, A., Regnell, B.: Case Study Research in Software Engineering, p. 216. Wiley (2012). http://www.egov.ee/media/1267/case-study-research-in-software-engineering.pdf
16. Basili, V.: Goal question metric parading. Encycl. Softw. Eng. (1994). http://www.cs.umd.edu/users/basili/publications/technical/T87.pdf
17. Katz, I.R., Anderson, J.R.: Human – Computer Interaction Debugging : An Analysis of Bug-Location Strategies Debugging, vol. 24, pp. 37–41, November 2016. https://doi.org/10.1207/s15327051hci0304_2

Design of Interactive Toy as Support Tool in STEM Education for Children with Special Needs

Sandra Cano$^{(\boxtimes)}$, Sandra P. Mosquera , Victor M. Peñeñory ,
and Pablo A. Bejarano

Universidad San Buenaventura Cali, Cali, Colombia
sandra.cano@gmail.com,
{spmosquera, vmpeneno, pabhoz}@usbcali.edu.co

Abstract. STEM education relates to a set of disciplines relevant as: Science, Technology, Engineering and Mathematics. Children with special needs (CSN) face many challenges in the classroom, since their learning may change depending on their disability or disorder. Teachers must use communication strategies and learning methods that can be adapted to their needs. The proposal is based on building a principal character, with one or several missions to fulfill, with whom the child can interact in areas of knowledge such as mathematics, literacy and computational thinking. The interactive toy called "Learning with Tobi" has the advantage of offering a rich playable environment in terms of use of multimedia and interactive usability, integrating the digital with traditional dolls. Nowadays, with the technology growth all the things tend to be connected. IoT offers a platform for sensors and devices to communicate seamlessly within smart environment and enables information sharing across platforms in a appropriate manner. Therefore, designing the Tobi interactive teddy bear, low-cost with electronic components and sensors as RFID, Gyroscope and Bluetooth to communicate through a mobile application and interacting with physical elements.

Keywords: Interactive toy · Internet of Things · Children with special needs
STEM education

1 Introduction

STEM education relates to a set of disciplines relevant to a rounded formation in modern society – namely the areas of Science, Technology, Engineering and Mathematics. STEM is increasingly being included in the educational agenda of the European Union with the aim of encouraging children at an early age in areas of knowledge important in society today. In Colombia, STEM education was first promoted in 2000 in the *Pequeños Científicos* (Little Scientists) project [1], an initiative backed by the University of the Andes, focusing attention on scientific literacy in children and adolescents.

© Springer Nature Switzerland AG 2019
V. Agredo-Delgado and P. H. Ruiz (Eds.): HCI-COLLAB 2018, CCIS 847, pp. 113–127, 2019.
https://doi.org/10.1007/978-3-030-05270-6_9

STEM works with active learning and is therefore related to the design and implementation of projects that encourage the student to acquire a set of aspects such as dialogue, collaboration, development and knowledge construction. To work with STEM in the classroom, it is necessary for the teacher to relate two or more areas connected to a real-life problem [2]. It is very often selected for use in primary education, since a single teacher is responsible for teaching the same students most or all of their subjects, meaning that it can be integrated within a multidisciplinary treatment. It also has a greater impact in primary since many high school students have already lost interest in science, a situation even more the case among female students [3].

Tsupros et al. [4] define STEM education as an interdisciplinary approach to learning, in which complex concepts applied to real-life problems are taught, where science, technology, engineering and mathematics is applied, and which occurs in contexts that manage to connect school, community, work and business in order to foster STEM competencies. STEM education can furthermore impact jobs, productivity and skills in different sectors such as health, technology, innovation and production.

In Colombia, ever-decreasing numbers of enrollments in scientific careers remains cause for concern. One difficulty lies in the lack of popularity of areas such as mathematics, physics, programming and chemistry. A report by the Ministry of Education shows that less than 30% of people graduate from technical or engineering subjects [5], which today generates a lack of interest among students enrolling in different areas of knowledge related to engineering, more so if these relate to electronics or systems.

Disinterest is currently perceived not only nationally but in the international arena and the term STEM education therefore began to be used as an option for promoting scientific literacy and encouraging a greater interest in the young. A study conducted in 2006, meanwhile, showed a strong positive relationship between students taking science subjects and choosing higher education study to continue in STEM-related disciplines [6].

As regards the evolution of education, another aspect to bear in mind is that children use technology daily to communicate, play or learn. Technology in this context would refer not only to a Tablet, for example, but also to books, games, toys and dolls that involve digital and electronic elements. Nowadays, children are growing up with interactive technologies. The ways in which they learn and interact with others is changing [7]. It is therefore important to understand the child in order to know how to design and integrate all of these technologies.

In this article we present a number of ways in which interactive systems applied to STEM education aimed at children with special needs can be designed. Section 2 describes a set of related work that has been done based on STEM education; Sect. 3 briefly describes concepts related to this work, such as interactive systems and STEM education; Sect. 3.1 outlines the problems that children with special needs face and how technology and interaction may change depending on their need; Sect. 3.5 describes the procedure of this work and the methodology that used in designing this proposal; and finally, Sect. 4 presents some conclusions and anticipated future work.

2 Background

2.1 STEM Education

The principle of STEM education aimed at children may be considered to be the initiation of Logo Turtles in 1967 by Seymour Papert [8], who brought out a high-level programming language aimed at children in normal conditions. Papert developed an approach based on Piaget's cognitive constructivism [9, 10], involving different areas of knowledge such as philosophy, educational theory, artificial intelligence, cognitive science, neuroscience, robotic programming and computer science. Another work proposed by Mitch Resnick and MIT [11] developed a visual programming language built by blocks, called Scratch [12]. This language is designed especially for ages between 8 and 16 years, but is used by people of all ages.

This is also the case of research carried out by Tufts University, which presented a robot called KIBO for children's education from 4 to 7 years old [13]. The KIBO robot features light, sound and movement sensors by which the child can develop programming skills using ten wooden cubes, which he must order according to the instructions he wants the robot to carry out. Another work, by the MIT laboratory, is called LittleBits [14]. In LittleBits, electronics is offered as learning material, using interactive objects such as electronic components (switches, batteries, buttons and sensors, etc.) and electrical circuits with which different science experiments can be built. This electronic system enables projects to be built using modular blocks. It features four types of blocks, each identified with a specific color: Source (blue), Inputs (pink), Wired (orange) and Outputs (green).

Piaget meanwhile has had a great influence on STEM education, since he indicates in his studies the way to conceive development in children [9], stating that they are typically extremely curious in their behavior because they are trying to discover and interpret their world. Children seek knowledge through the different interactions they conduct with the environment. Piaget was thus very interested in how they think about problems and their solution.

STEM education involves several areas of knowledge and is beginning to be included in primary education in different research topics such as educational robotics and computational thinking. The main interest in involving STEM education in the classrooms from the very youngest children is so that when they become teenagers they understand the different roles of engineering within society and how they can participate in it, to motivate them and to solve the problem of contextualizing areas such as mathematics or science [15]. It can currently be seen that computer classes in schools are taught by teachers with knowledge in the area of technology, and they usually limit themselves to teaching routines or development instructions. However, programming can be applied to other areas of knowledge and must not necessarily only be within the subject of computer science. Carnevale et al. [16] have proposed a set of cognitive competencies related with STEM, shown in Table 1.

Table 1. STEM cognitive competencies [16].

Knowledge	Skills	Abilities
Production and processing	Mathematics	Problem sensitivity
Computers and electronics	Science	Deductive reasoning
Engineering and technology	Critical thinking	Inductive reasoning
Design	Active learning	Mathematical reasoning
Building and construction	Complex problem-solving	Number facility

Nowadays, when forming relationships between STEM education and learning experiences, teachers express concerns as to how to conceptualize, interpret and relate STEM content to the impact of engineering with today's society, and how to relate concepts of science, mathematics and engineering to solve real-world problems. It is true that the growth of Information and Communication Technologies (ICT) has driven the creation of a range of interactive systems able to support the learning process in children. However, inclusion of technologies within the classroom and the importance of their use is a subject that is still debated among teachers. The following questions thus arise: Are teachers being trained to use ICT in the classroom?. In other learning environments? What are the roles of teachers when incorporating ICT as support material in the classroom?

2.2 Children with Special Needs

Children with special needs (CSN) face many challenges in the classroom, since their learning may change depending on their disability or disorder. Teachers must use communication strategies and learning methods that can be adapted to their needs. Research undertaken by Cano et al. [17] in teaching literacy skills to children with cochlear implants can therefore be taken into account, in which children are in the process of learning to recognize the sounds of words in order to speak: in the early stages of childhood it is very difficult to communicate verbally with the children and so teachers here must use visual strategies by means of color codes in order to structure a word.

Moreover, a child with intellectual disability or mental retardation has a slower, limited learning. It is necessary to use sensory channels with them to achieve communication and motivate them during their learning, because they require activities to be repetitive so as to memorize them [18]. These activities mostly are so repetitive that they can bore a child during the learning process, which reinforces the importance of designing interactive systems using real objects, vital to motivating children during their learning process.

It should be noted that the number of children in a special needs classroom is smaller because they need special guidance and personalized learning methods customized to their needs. However, it is a reality that education tends to be more inclusive every day and teachers must prepare themselves to understand that in their classrooms students are different and learn at different rhythms and by different methods.

2.3   Internet of Things (IoT)

Nowadays, with the technology growth all the things tend to be connected. Traditional things, such as windows, clothes, toys, dolls, bikes, cars are modified for communicate and send information. IoT offers a platform for sensors and devices to communicate seamlessly within smart environment and enables information sharing across platforms in an appropriate manner [19].

The IoT is an incoming paradigm that is quickly acquiring a foundation in a scenario of new wireless telecommunications. There has been a massive growth of IoT, the concept is not only implement in smart homes, it is widely used in manufacturing and industries that because it has helped people and process to be more efficient and to do task and to gather information.

In addition, IoT has been attractive to schools, which are working with new technologies in the classroom. To involve the children with more interactive learning strategies is a challenge for teachers. The use of sensor-activated objects and wearable devices should provide them with the tools to create and manage task-based scenarios including everyday objects and friendly Interfaces [20].

Actually, the ways in which children are able to interact with technology are intuitive. Traditional interfaces as mouse, keyboard, are typically excluded in the design of an interactive system, and are being replaced by other mechanisms that allow interacting with the body or a real environment. The IoT helps the ways in which digital technology can be embedded in the physical environment [20].

Wearable and IoT devices should be seen as the building blocks of novel intuitive interaction technologies. Furthermore, the execution of each action should be followed by the proper feedback message this will encourage the student to proceed until the successful completion of the task [20].

Therefore, designing interactive systems based on real scenarios where interaction techniques with IoT are applied to children is becoming in a very helpful tool for teachers. And teachers must be a guide and support for every interaction of the children, noting the learning and improvement of the student.

The IoT is an incoming paradigm that is quickly acquiring a foundation in a scenario of new wireless telecommunications. There has been a massive growth of IoT the concept is not only implement in smart homes, it is widely used in manufacturing and industries that because it has helped people and process to be more efficient and to do task and to gather information.

3   Proposal

The proposal is based on building a principal character, with one or several missions to fulfill, with whom the child can interact in areas of knowledge such as mathematics, literacy and computational thinking. The methodology chosen, Design Thinking [21], involves five stages: Empathize, Define, Devise, Prototype and Test. Below we describe what each stage consists of and what was done in each stage.

3.1 Empathize

In this stage it is important to understand the needs and the way in which the children interact with other children and the teacher in the classroom. It is also vital to understand more about the methods and learning strategies teachers use with their students (Invariant method, among others); we therefore attended various classes, in literacy and mathematics.

The participants were children with a cochlear implant (11 children between 7 and 11 years, from the Institute of Blind and Deaf Children in the Valle del Cauca, Colombia) and children with intellectual disability (7 children between 8 and 16 years, from the Tobias Emanuel Institute, Cali, Colombia). The analysis consists of identifying different variables that can affect interaction and these should be indicated according to the needs of the child, according to his/her disability. The characteristics analyzed are: level of disability, learning styles, age, academic level, gender, interests and behaviors. Therefore, the children with cochlear implants have to rely on the visual channel, as they are in the process of acquiring the language.

The children with intellectual disabilities on the other hand can rely on both visual and auditory channels to memorize concepts. Profile analysis of the child with special needs has been analyzed in prior research [22] in which different methods are used to evaluate the user experience in children with a cochlear implant, such as direct observation, Drawing Intervention [23], interviews, and Picture Card [24]. Direct observation and interviews were applied to children with intellectual disabilities. Some of these children were already 16-year-olds while others were 8-year-olds, so doing a single activity that involved everyone was difficult. It was therefore decided to apply only direct observation in the use of technologies and to conduct interviews with teachers.

In the interviews, questions addressed to the teachers included: What problems do the children have in developing basic skills (attention, perception, orientation, etc.)? What technological elements do you use in the classroom with the children? What are the biggest problems faced by the children in the areas of literacy and mathematics? Do the children have any didactic material to work with outside the classroom on specific problems? Do you use a particular learning method?.

Attention is a problem for children when given their cochlear implant, since they must learn to recognize each of the sounds. During that process the children use their visual channel to communicate, so teachers have a lot of visual material to explain the meaning of the words. Meanwhile, with the aim of analyzing the orientation of the children, a test was performed, consisted in them having to interact with a game through the movement of a snail climbing a tree with branches in different orientations (Fig. 1). None of the children could finish the first level of the game as it proved difficult for them to locate the snail in the positions of up, down, left or right.

Another question that gathered information was the use of technologies, where it was observed that most of the children, through belonging to a low or medium socio-economic level, do not have a Tablet or a PC. But they came to make good use of it in the classroom during their computer class, where the children interact with related applications in learning literacy through existing educational games. The Tablets that are available are iPads and Android, but in the IoT most of the applications are not free

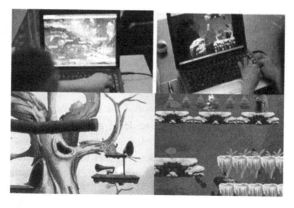

Fig. 1. Game for evaluating the child's spatial orientation.

and with Android they were not able to find an application that could be useful for their teaching strategy. In addition, the support material they have is either physical or digital, but not a combination of both.

The answers to another question, this time about the teaching method used, revealed that the Invariant method [25] was used for children with a cochlear implant, while for children with cognitive disabilities, the ABCD-Spanish method referred to in [18, 26] was favored. The focus of each of these methods is auditory and visual attention; auditory attention especially so for children with cochlear implant, while for children with cognitive disabilities, auditory and visual attention play equal roles. Another problem that children face is their poor acquisition of vocabulary when they want to express something and cannot find the words to do so. Furthermore, most of these activities work only in the classroom, because at home parents often fail to continue reinforcing this type of activity with them so that they can memorize vocabulary or identify each of the sounds aurally.

Fig. 2. Designing a character. Institute of Blind and Deaf Children of the Valle del Cauca.

Meanwhile, in work done with the evaluation methods applied to children with cochlear implant [22] we worked with the Drawing Intervention method, where an activity was carried out with the children, which consisted in constructing a character and giving each character a name. It was difficult, however, to assign names, because these students were only in the process of acquiring language and communicating with them was difficult (Fig. 2).

In the same work, the Picture Cards method was also employed. Emotion cards were used so that children could assign a scale of emotion to certain questions they were asked about technology or to relate a color with an emotion. However, although at the beginning a scale of five emotions was used, this had to be changed to only two emotions - happy and sad - since it proved difficult for them to recognize the other three emotions [28].

Teacher interviews were also conducted, in which a set of questions relating to the child's interaction within the classroom were formulated along with strategies and learning methods used in the classroom with the children. In addition, teachers were asked an open question, describing their experiences of the difficulties faced by children in the teaching of literacy and mathematics.

3.2   Define

Once the needs of the children and teachers are known, all the collected information obtained through the methods used in the previous stage is analyzed. The information collected is used to define the needs of the children [18, 29], which may vary depending on their disability, as well as their interaction.

Children with cochlear implants have greater difficulties in the area of literacy, because they are faced with first having to learn to listen so that they can then learn to speak and write. It is therefore a lengthy process that requires them to work not only within the classroom, but outside of it [29]. This problem can become greater, since some children receive their implants at a later age, which is reflected in a retarded learning and academic level.

Children with intellectual disabilities on the other hand face problems at the level of literacy. For them, the activities must be very repetitive to get to memorize the words [17]. Although they have visual and auditory memory they present intellectual retardation compared to a child in normal conditions.

3.3   Ideate

The objective in this stage is to have several alternative solutions and choose the one that best fits according to the needs identified in the children. The idea that was selected is that the child can interact with a physical and digital environment, which allows him to interact with the other children in his class according to his needs.

Therefore, as a design, an interactive physical system was proposed that might be an animal, since a toy animal would likely generate greater confidence in the child. A teddy bear was chosen, so that the children could adopt it as their pet or inseparable friend and have more confidence in themselves. It was decided to call the bear "Tobi". The advantage of offering smart toys is that they provide a rich playable environment in

terms of use of multimedia and interactive usability, integrating the digital with traditional dolls [30]. As indicated by Lampe & Hinske [31], adding multimedia content
to these traditional dolls can increase the fantasy quality of play and provide a more
creative environment for children.

Furthermore, interaction ought to be considered with real elements of interaction
with the physical character and suitable communication channels. Therefore, the
auditory and visual channel was taken into account, integrating mobile technology.

3.4   Prototype

In this stage, the purpose is to convert the proposed idea into a functional prototype, so
that an analysis was carried out of the different sensors and components that Tobi will
feature incorporated into his body.

An RC-522 RFID sensor, a GY-50 Gyroscope and an HC06 Bluetooth sensor were
incorporated in the body of the toy bear Tobi (Fig. 2) to establish communication
between the teddy bear and the mobile device. For visual feedback, a neopixel was
used that acts as the bear's heart. Its function is to exert positive feedback to the child if
it has done the activity correctly, so that all the LEDs turn red and the application
reproduces a spoken text, "My heart is happy now". Two feedback types are thus
received - visual and auditory. If feedback is negative, the LEDs flash on and off,
indicating a negative emotion of the bear. At the same time, it reproduces the text "That
is not correct", as the activity was not carried out correctly.

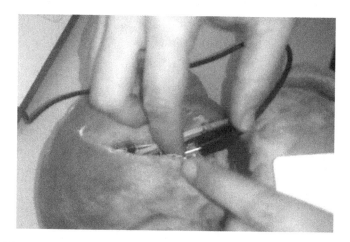

Fig. 3. Teddy bear adapted with Arduino and sensors (RFID, Gyroscope and Bluetooth) and a
Neopixel

In Fig. 3, the Neopixel is seen to be visible in the chest of the bear, while the RFID
(Radio-Frequency Identification) sensor located internally will allow the child to interact
by means of RFID cards and validate whether a card selection is correct or not. The
nano-Arduino, Gyroscope and Bluetooth sensors are also placed internally at the back.

Fig. 4. Tobi the bear with RFID cards and the neopixel with all LEDs lit.

The cards with which the child interacts are RFID cards as shown in Fig. 4. The cards represent the pictogram that must be associated according to the activity, either in the area of mathematics, literacy or basic programming instructions (start, up, right, left, down and finish). The cards feature a pictogram very similar to what children draw in their early stages of drawing, as it is intended that Toby act as any other child would act and that the child can thus have the confidence to perform their activities. Each card features the respective text in lowercase.

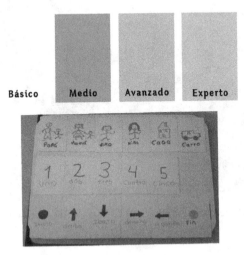

Fig. 5. Some Basic level cards for the areas of literacy, mathematics and programming. (Color figure online)

The cards are related to a level of difficulty (basic, medium, advanced and expert), so that each level corresponds to a card of different color. The white cards correspond to the basic level and basic activities are associated in the different areas of literacy, mathematics and programming (Fig. 5). The colors then for each level are: Basic, white; Medium, blue; Advanced, green, and Expert, orange.

The mobile application will connect through the Bluetooth device. In Fig. 6a, it can be seen that once the device has established a Bluetooth connection, it shows a main interface with the different areas (mathematics, reading, writing, location and programming) into which the player seeks to enter, accompanied by a voice message "Hi, I'm Toby. Let's play!" The mathematics and literacy areas (Fig. 6b, d) have the same operating structure, which by means of a voice instruction using the Google Text-toSpeech library, Toby asks the child to search for a certain word or determine a number of Elements. The child must select a card and place it on the chest of the bear to validate if it is correct. If the answer is correct, a pictogram appears and the text appears at the bottom, as shown in Fig. 6b and c. Pictograms are taken from ARASAAC [32]. These have been made for communication boards for people with special needs.

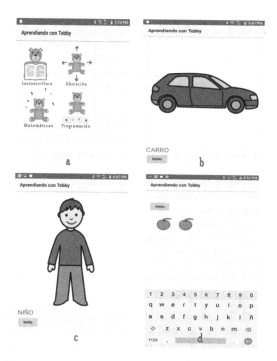

Fig. 6. Graphic interfaces of the mobile app "Learning with Tobi"

The area of location is worked using spatial orientation, where the child interacts with the application and the physical object. This is done in such a way that the child manages to make the movement, within his environment and real space, when the application indicates certain orders to be carried out with Toby, such as: "Turn him to the left", "Turn him to the right", "Lift him up" and "Put him down again". The Gyroscope consequently has limits of each position that have been configured with parameters in the application, and which serve to identify each position and work out whether or not it has been done correctly.

In the area of programming, the interaction is a digital maze in which Toby must find his way home. The child must therefore locate the set of RFID cards that make it possible to carry out this activity. In this first level we work with algorithmic thinking, where a set of RFID cards is selected in order to follow a correct sequence to find the way out.

3.5   Test

One evaluation technique is heuristic evaluation [33], which consists of a small group of evaluators who evaluate the system using a set of heuristics as guides for the inspection of the system. However, there is a dearth of research in which a heuristic evaluation has been applied for the design of interactive systems. The heuristics proposed by Nielsen and Molich [33] and Scholtz [34] were therefore used.

In the book "Psychology of Everyday Objects" describes the principle of visibility and information, which generates important questions to be taken into account in design and interaction when working with physical and digital elements, questions such as: Which parts are mobile and which are fixed? Which part should be handled? What kind of movement is possible? What information should be communicated? How should it be communicated? This set of questions should thus be taken into account to improve the design of the interactive system for children whose functional and cognitive conditions may affect the interaction and understanding of the system (Fig. 7).

The heuristics evaluated with the interactive system are:

1. Visibility and state of the system (Nielsen)
2. Coincidence between the system and the real world (Nielsen)
3. Control and freedom for the user (Nielsen)
4. Minimize the memory load (Nielsen)
5. Aesthetic and minimalist design (Nielsen)
6. Presence of the information and presentation (Scholtz)
7. Performance of the interaction (Scholtz)

The results obtained from the heuristic evaluation carried out with two people, where it was identified that in the visibility and state of the system, the feedback messages that are presented to the child should be improved. The same applies to the prevention of errors in the application, so that users are able to return to a previous state if they have made critical errors.

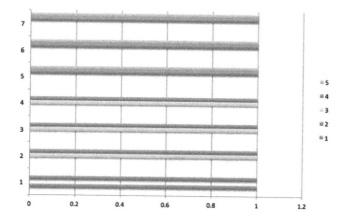

Fig. 7. Results of the heuristic evaluation, numbers from 1 to 5-evaluation scale.

4 Conclusions and Future Work

An interactive system design that simultaneously integrates a real and a digital environment is extremely useful in motivating children during their learning in different approaches related to STEM education. STEM education is today being employed only with children in regular conditions. It may also prove to be a very positive concept with which to work with special needs children, so that some thinking might be stimulated involving STEM education. Three important areas were worked on in the present research: literacy, mathematics and computational thinking, so that as the children progress through the levels they are able to acquire certain competences in each one. The idea is then that finally in the expert level, all of the areas worked independently in the earlier levels are integrated in one single activity.

In designing the Tobi interactive teddy bear, low-cost electronic components were used with the aim of making this educational product easily accessible to parents in the low and medium socio-economic brackets. As future work we would like to go a little deeper into each difficulty level. We would also expect to design the activities and ensure that it is entirely multi-modal, in order that any child with special needs is able to interact with Toby. We also hope to test each of the areas with a group of children with cochlear implants and children with cognitive disabilities. Finally, it is also planned to make adjustments to Toby as a system in which it is not only a bear, but a character that the child can condition as his or her classmate.

Acknowlegements. This work was part supported by the OCDS funded project OCDS-CUD2016/08 of the University of Balearic Islands, together with the Institute of Blind and Deaf Children of Valle del Cauca and Institute Tobias Emanuel, Cali – Colombia.

References

1. Pequeños Científicos (Little Scientists) STEM-Colombia. http://www.pequenoscientificos. org. Accessed 11 Dec 2017
2. Moore, T., Stohlmann, M., Wang, H., Roehrig, G.: Implementation and integration of engineering in K-12 STEM education. In: Purzer, S., Strobel, J., Cardella, M. (eds.) Engineering in Pre-College Settings: Research into Practice, pp. 35–60. Purdue Press, West Lafayette (2014)
3. Abell, S., Lederman, N.G.: Handbook of Research on Science Education. Lawrence Erlbaium Associates, New Jersey (2006)
4. Tsupros, N., Kohler, R., Hallinen, J.: STEM education: a project to identify the missing components, Intermediate Unit 1 and Carnegie Mellon, Pennsylvania (2009)
5. https://www.mineducacion.gov.co/sistemasinfo/Informacion-a-la-mano/212400:Estadisticas. Accessed 16 June 2018
6. Tai, R.H., Qi Liu, C., Maltese, A.V., Fan, X.: Planning early for careers in science. Science **312**, 1143–1145 (2006)
7. Hourcade, J.P.: Child-Computer Interaction. CreateSpace Independent Publishing Platform, North Charleston (2015)
8. Papert, S.: Teaching Children Thinking. Mathematics Teaching, no 58. Spring (1972)
9. Piaget, J., Bärbel, I.: The Psychology of Child. Basic Books, New York (1969)
10. Papert, S.: Mindstorms: Children, Computers, and Powerful Ideas. Basic Books, New York (1980)
11. Resnick, M., Kafai, Y., Maeda, J.: A Networked, Media-Rich. Programming Environment to Enhance Technological Fluency at After-School Centers in Economically Disadvantaged Communities. Proposal to National Science Foundation (2003)
12. Scratch. Programming language online. http://www.scratch.mit.edu. Accessed 16 June 2018
13. Sullivan, A., Elkin, M., Bers, M.U.: KIBO robot demo: engaging young children in programming and engineering. In: Proceedings of the 14th International Conference on Interaction Design and Children, pp. 418–421 (2015). http://dx.doi.org/10.1145/2771839. 2771868
14. Bdeir, A., Ullich, T.: Electronics as material: LittleBits. In: Proceedings of the Fifth International Conference on Tangible, Embedded and Embodied Interaction, pp. 341–344 (2010). https://doi.org/10.1145/1517664.1517743
15. Brophy, S., Klein, S., Portsmore, M., Rodger, C.: Advancing engineering education in P-12 classrooms. J. Eng. Educ. **97**(3), 369–387 (2008). https://doi.org/10.1002/j.2168-9830.2008. tb00985.x
16. Carnevale, A., Smith, N., Melton, M.: STEM, Georgetown University, Washington, D.C. (2011)
17. Cano, S., Collazos, C., Fardoun, H.M., Alghazzawi, D.M., Albarakati, A.: Model based on learning needs of children with auditory impairment. In: Meiselwitz, G. (ed.) SCSM 2016. LNCS, vol. 9742, pp. 324–334. Springer, Cham (2016). https://doi.org/10.1007/978-3-319-39910-2_30
18. Cano, S., Palta, A., Posso, F., Peñeñory, V.M.: Towards designing a serious game for literacy in children with moderate cognitive disability. In: Proceedings of the XVIII International Conference on Human Computer Interaction (Interacción 2017), Article 19, 5 pages. ACM, New York (2017). https://doi.org/10.1145/3123818.3123835
19. Pascual-Espada, J., Sanjuan-Martinez, O., G-Bustelo, B.C.P., Lovelle, J.M.C.: Virtual objects on the Internet of Things. Int. J. Interact. Multimed. Artif. Intell. **1**(4) (2011). https://doi.org/10.9781/ijimai.2011.144

20. de la Guia, E., Camacho, V.L., Orozco-Barbosa, L., Brea Lujan, V.M., Penichet, V.M.R., Perez, M.L.: Introducing IoT and wearable technologies into task-based language learning for young children. IEEE Trans. Learn. Technol. **9**(4) (2016). https://doi.org/10.1109/tlt.2016.2557333

21. Brown, T.: Change by Design: How Design Thinking Transforms Organizations and Inspires Innovation. Harper Collins, New York (2009)

22. Florez-Aristizabal, L., Cano, S., Collazos, C., Moreira, F., Alghazzawi, D., Fardoun, H.: Tools and methods applied in interactive systems to evaluate the user experience with deaf/hard of hearing children. In: Conference: Technological Ecosystems for Enhancing Multiculturality, TEEM (2017). https://doi.org/10.1145/3144826.3145365

23. Barendregt, W., Bekker, T.: Exploring the potential of the drawing intervention method for design and evaluation by young children. In: CHI '13 Extended Abstracts on Human Factors in Computing Systems (CHI EA 2013), pp. 193–198 (2013). https://doi.org/10.1145/2468356.2468392

24. Barendregt, W., Bekker, M.M., Baauw, E.: Development and evaluation of the problem identification picture cards method. Cogn. Technol. Work **10**(2), 95–105 (2008). https://doi.org/10.1007/s10111-007-0066-z

25. Solovieva, Y., Rojas, L.Q.: Método de formación de lectura para la corrección de dificultades en el desarrollo. Tesis de maestría en diagnóstico y rehabilitación neuropsicológica, Universidad Autónoma de Puebla, México (2012)

26. Cano, S., Alghazzawi, D.M., Arteaga, J.M., Fardoun, H.M., Collazos, C.A., Amador, V.B.: Applying the information search process model to analyze aspects in the design of serious games for children with hearing impairment. Univ. Access Inf. Soc. **17**(1), 83–95 (2018). https://doi.org/10.1007/s10209-016-0520-x

27. Cano, S., Collazos, C.A., Aristizábal, L.F., Gonzalez, C.S., Moreira, F.: Towards a methodology for user experience assessment of serious games with children with cochlear implants. Telematics Inform. **35**(4), 993–1004 (2018). https://doi.org/10.1016/j.tele.2017.09.011

28. Flórez Aristizábal, L., Cano, S., Collazos, C.A., Moreira, F., Alghazzawi, D.M., Fardoun, H.: Tools and methods applied in interactive system to evaluate the user experience with deaf/hard of hearing children. In: Proceedings of the 5th International Conference on Technological Ecosystem for Enhancing Multiculturality (2017). https://doi.org/10.1145/3144826.3145365

29. MBOT, Robótica Educativa. http://www.makeblock.com/. Accessed 16 June 2018

30. Kara, N., Aydin, C.C., Cagiltay, K.: Investigating the activities of children toward a smart storytelling toy. Educ. Technol. Soc. **16**(1), 28–43 (2013)

31. Lampe, M., Hinske, S.: Integrating interactive learning experiences into augmented toy environments. In: Proceedings of the Workshop on Pervasive Learning 2007, Toronto, pp. 1–9 (2007)

32. Portal Aragonés de la Comunicación Aumentativa y Alternativa, ARASAAC. www.arasaac.org. Accessed 16 June 2018

33. Nielsen, J., Molich, R.: Heuristic evaluation of user interfaces. In: Proceedings of the ACM CH 1990, pp. 249–256 (1990)

34. Scholtz, J.: Evaluation methods for human-system performance of intelligent systems. In: Proceedings of PERMIS 2002 (2002)

Determination of the Appropriation Level in the Collaborative Work, a Challenge in Distance Education Focused on E-learning

Concepción Barreda Ramírez$^{(\boxtimes)}$ ⓘ,
Claudia Elena González Cárdenas ⓘ,
Gustavo Eduardo Constain Moreno$^{(\boxtimes)}$ ⓘ,
and Paula Andrea Mora Pedreros$^{(\boxtimes)}$ ⓘ

CEAD, Open and Distance National University, Popayán, Colombia
{concepcion.barreda, claudiae.gonzalez,
gustavo.constain, paula.mora}@unad.edu.co

Abstract. This article inquires about the appropriation level of the collaborative learning strategy that the students have of distance university programs. It is based on the elements of university work condensed in the Academic Pedagogical Solidarity Project (APSP) (2011) of the Open and Distance National University - UNAD of Colombia, which is the didactic pedagogical element and the pillars of collaborative work described by Puentes (2002) such as: communication; organization of activities and tasks; exchange of ideas; Contributions and responses in collaborative work and consensus and consolidation. This research is of a quantitative, non-experimental exploratory cross-sectional nature made to 315 students of the Western Zone of the University under investigation, to whom a questionnaire of 32 questions was applied, which after the process of descriptive analysis applying statistical techniques, concluded that The perception of the students regarding the level of appropriation of the collaborative work they have is "high"% without linking to the fulfillment of the components already described, which leaves in a critical position the development of the collaborative work in the institution and the open way to the approach of support actions from the computer sciences that guide and motivate in the virtual classroom the dynamics of the components of this learning strategy so important for distance education.

Keywords: Learning strategy · Collaborative work · Appropriation
Collaborative engineering

1 Introduction

Distance education, as defined [1], is a bidirectional technological communication system, in which the face-to-face interaction between teacher and student is replaced by the systematic action of several discourses organized in didactic resources that favor learning autonomous and flexible students. The characteristic of this learning modality is the physical separation between the student and the teacher, referring to the spaces and times of interaction. The traditional academic and pedagogical model of distance education has been collaborative work; supported by work guides with routes to follow

© Springer Nature Switzerland AG 2019
V. Agredo-Delgado and P. H. Ruiz (Eds.): HCI-COLLAB 2018, CCIS 847, pp. 128–142, 2019.
https://doi.org/10.1007/978-3-030-05270-6_10

for teachers and students. Over time, ICT have incorporated support tools in the learning and development of this strategy adapting new forms of mediated interaction, but always with a pedagogy and a didactic of support that allows the generation of new knowledge. According to Jacobs 1995, cited in [2], working collaboratively requires structuring activities to achieve learning; this becomes a permanent challenge since, as it says [3], it is necessary to adapt technology to improve the interactive processes in online training as a key element in the quality of learning. The National Open and Distance University - UNAD, describes in its Pedagogical and Solidarity Academic Project (PAPS) [4], the detail of the university work components in the Organizational Administrative aspects; Cultural scholar; Textual technology; Regional community; Productive and Pedagogical Didactic Business; the latter being the one that develops the pedagogical and learning core.

Collaborative engineering according to [5] also defines collaborative work and its dynamics in the same general terms, but also highlights [6] the benefits and difficulties of teamwork, which shows the complexity of compliance with the collaborative work strategy. Investigating how these dynamics are developed in collaborative groups and being able to suggest actions and recommendations of the computer science to improve the yield, has been the purpose of this investigation, nevertheless, for this work to be effective it is necessary that within the group effective mechanisms are developed of interaction and communication, which achieve the desired learning, although there is no total guarantee that such interactions occur and the established objectives are achieved. This research, according to [6], is of a quantitative nature, not experimental, of an exploratory nature of a transversal nature. The variables to be analyzed are given by the concept of the pillars of collaborative work described by Puente (2002), cited in [6], such as: communication, organization, exchange or exhibition of ideas and consensus. From now on, a description of the theoretical context of the collaborative work and its components in the UNAD, its methodology, the identification of variables, the processing of the information and the interpretation of the results is presented, to finally suggest actions to follow from the point of view vision of the science of computing and the interactive pedagogy of virtual education that help to improve the development of the components of collaborative work in digital environments.

2   Theoretical Context and Components of Collaborative Work in a Distance University

We review evidence of research carried out in the last five years related to the subject at the University, where several questions related to the use of this learning strategy have been investigated: in [7], the causes of low participation in the work forums collaborative, finding flaws in both students and teachers for their lack of adaptation to virtual environments and tele-informatics tools and due to their low level of accompaniment and monitoring of collaborative activities. In [8], the research refers to the social competences required by students to develop collaborative work, identifying non-appropriation of collaborative work. Also in [9] the same results are obtained although communication technologies have become important resources for the strengthening of learning processes. Likewise, [10] they inquire about the potential of collaborative work and the expectations of ICT to improve this type of learning. Likewise, [11] they experience how, from an educational perspective, personal learning environments and networks (PLE and PLN) can be linked to institutional virtual learning environments (VLE), to promote collaborative work in autonomous learners working to achieve objectives. Common through the execution of group activities, obtaining the integration of environments and personal learning networks with the development of a training course.

3 Collaborative Work Components

The distance university object of this research determines in its governing document: Pedagogical Academic Solidarity Project (PAPS) [4], the components of collaborative work already mentioned. Taking into account what was presented by Puente (2002), cited in [6], in this research the components of the collaborative learning strategy are grouped into four (4) components that are described below and will be the basis for the construction of the instrument and the conclusions of this project:

The communication. This component groups together the different means and forms of communication established by the groups for the development of tasks, synchronous or asynchronous (emails, social networks, text messages, forums and chats in virtual classrooms. **The organization of tasks and activities.** It is related to the assignment or distribution of roles within the group and the development of activities. Also in collaborative work, as mentioned in [12], the teacher must change the role of facilitator of learning and the student to become the builder of their own knowledge. **The interaction between the members of the group.** For this, each member must make an individual contribution to the learning situation. Interactions among group members generate learning for others [13]. The degree of interactivity is not necessarily defined by the frequency of interactions between peers or group members, but by the way in which they can influence the cognitive process [2]. **The consensus of the ideas worked by the group**, after a process of creation, discussion, maturation and concretion and that corresponds to the final group work that creates in itself the learning and the social construction of the new knowledge. The essence of a collaborative group is to maintain a positive interdependence among the members of the group, which is evident in the sense that no one can achieve success if others do not [2]. The research carried out addressed the application of each of these components by students from the Western area of the Distance University subject of this research and according to the form and frequency with which they carried out their collaborative actions, it was registered, consolidated and analyzed the information. The variables used are the same components of the collaborative work already explained, whose application detailed the questionnaire applied in the questions posed.

4   Methodology

4.1   Research Classification

The research carried out according to [6] is of a quantitative nature, since it uses data collection to carry out the research, based on statistical analysis to establish patterns of behavior. It is a non-experimental research of transversal exploratory type. It also has a descriptive scope, because, with this type of studies it is intended to collect information independently or jointly on the concepts or variables to which it refers, without looking for how they relate to each other. In addition, in this studies, the researcher must be able to define what is going to be measured (variable concepts, components).

4.2   Variables

The variables to be analyzed are given by the concept of the pillars of collaborative work described by Puente (2002), cited in [6] and presented in Table 1, which are:

Table 1. Variables for the study (self-made)

Variable	Conceptual variable def.	Operational variable def.
Communication	Relationships between colleagues Synchronous and asynchronous communication	Questionnaire as synchronous and asynchronous communication through different means of telecommunication: Skype, WhatsApp, social networks, collaborative work forum
Task and activities organization	Assignment of roles and tasks Compliance with the schedule of activities	Questions that measure the planning, the fulfillment of the role and the fulfillment of the tasks
Exchange of Ideas	Exchange of ideas Productive discussion Progress and progress in activities	Ask if there is response and discussion of the group. Ask if there is progress in the activities
Consensus	If agreements are reached If the consolidation occurs	Ask how agreements are reached and consolidation of the final group work

4.3   Population and Sample

The students who settled for this research are the students of the distance university enrolled in the western zone during the 08-03 period. The population of this area to date is 1718 students. The West Zone is composed of five regional centers of distance education located in the cities of Medellín, Dosquebradas, Quibdó, Turbo and La Dorada. As explained in [14], the sample was calculated by applying the statistical formula and obtaining a sample size of 315, with a sampling error of 5% and a confidence level of 95% (see Table 2). The 315 students were selected by applying a stratified proportional sampling in which the fraction of the sample is calculated with the following formula:

$$\text{Sample fraction} = n/N = 315/1718 = 0.1834$$

Table 2. Statistics sample fraction

Regional center	Students enrolled	Sample size form formula	Sample size by regional center
Quibdó	113	113 × 0,1834	21
Dosquebradas	462	462 × 0,1834	85
Medellín	887	887 × 0,1834	162
Turbo	94	94 × 0,1834	17
La Dorada	162	162 × 0,1834	30
Totals	1718		315

4.4 Information Gathering

The instrument used for data collection was a questionnaire with closed questions designed to investigate the determining variables. In what refers [15], when the stages of descriptive research are related, the validation of the instrument was carried out, which was considered by a group of experts who evaluated the instrument and after the adjustments issued its favorable concept to apply it. The questionnaire consists of 32 questions distributed as follows: seven questions of general information of the respondent; four of the communication component; eleven of the component of organization of activities and tasks; three of the component of exchange of ideas, contributions and responses in the collaborative work; eight questions on the consensus component and the consolidation of collaborative work.

4.5 Processing and Data Analysis

For data collection, it was supported by the administration of UNAD that authorized the application of the instrument to the selected sample, clarifying that data management would be done internally and exclusively for academic purposes. The steps followed to obtain:

First, the database was obtained and the students to whom the instrument would be applied were selected at random. Second, the research was socialized among the selected students by sending an email requesting their collaboration. Third, they were sent a link to access the instrument and complete it according to the indications given in the socialization of the research. Fourth, the tabulation of the data was done gradually, as well as the statistical distribution of the variables in a frequency distribution table to have it ready for the analysis of the information. Fifth, the tabulation of the data and the statistical distribution of the variables in a frequency distribution table. Sixth, a descriptive analysis of the data was carried out that allowed us to use statistical techniques to identify the frequency of the data, significant trends and identify the variables with the greatest impact on the collaborative work strategy. The information obtained from the data analysis was presented in graphs and tables for the presentation of reports. Seventh, the conclusions and recommendations of the investigation were prepared.

5 Results and Analysis of Investigation

5.1 Respondent Profile

According to the answers obtained in this item, it was found that the majority of the respondents were female (60%), aged between 26 and 35 years (51%), employed (67%) and with marital status between single (53%) and married (34%) for the most part. Likewise, the respondents have a level of professional training (72%); most of them are former students (74%), who are familiar with the collaborative work strategy, belonging to the offices of Medellín (54%) and Dosquebradas (30%) of the distance university.

5.2 Analysis of the Components of the Learning Collaborative Work Strategy

Component Communication. Taking into account that the degree of this component is measured according to the frequency (number of times) with which the student respondent uses the digital means and synchronous communication tools such as: Skype, b-learning, CIPAS, Facebook, twitter, Instagram, to interact and communicate around the collaborative activities, it is highlighted that the average 56% of respondents have frequency zero (zero times) of use and 30% average of respondents have low frequency (1 to 2 times) of use; likewise, the chat of the course according to 26.5% of the respondents, is in medium level (3 to 4 times) of use; However, WhatsApp according to 61.8% of the respondents stands out for presenting a high frequency (5 or more times) in its use for collaborative activities, even though it is not a synchronous tool offered by the University remotely in its virtual classroom. This result is supported by similar ones found, for example, in [11], in which it was also observed that students increasingly involve the use of social networks to communicate, but more to the handling of information in general, but not so much for the construction of significant learning processes, being in this point where the teacher must assume a role of greater importance involving these tools, pedagogical elements to effectively take advantage of social networks in the learning processes. Likewise, asynchronous digital tools placed at the respondent's disposal such as the internal mail of the course, personal mail and institutional mail, are used on average (3 to 4 times) and low (1 to 2 times) according to the 30% average of the respondents, contrasting this result with that of the forum, which according to 81.4% of respondents has a high (5 or more times) frequency of use. It is confirmed with this, the result of the work of Cebrián-de la Serna (2011), cited in [16], in which the forum in the collaborative works, was used with high (5 times or more) frequency, which could lead to conclude the use of this tool as a communication element of greater use among the students of the collaborative group. In [8], they affirm that one of the causes of the lack of integration and participation of students in collaborative work is the lack of mastery of new technologies and the virtual platform. Likewise [16], states that one of the key elements to generate quality processes in virtual mediation, is that previously both teachers and students take ownership of the same tools of information and communication, since the use of they are a means and not an end in learning, that is why it is possible that in this research respondents more frequently use what they are familiar with and know how to use, but not knowing the potential of the other tools, nor being oriented in their use, do not use them and limit themselves only to the frequent and known.

Component Organization of Tasks and Activities. Continuing with the analysis of the results, in this component it is highlighted that the roles most used by the students according to the 36.3% of respondents are the compiler with measurement of high utilization (5 times or more) and the one of deliveries according to 34.3% of the respondents with an average measurement (3 to 4 times); On the other hand, the roles of reviewer, monitor and evaluator show a frequency of use that is Low (1 to 2 times) or Null (zero times) depending on the average 35% of the respondents. These results contrast with the importance that the same respondents give to the roles, since the roles that they do not perform are rated as very important by the average 68% of the respondents (with the exception of the compiler who considers it very important and if they perform it). Here it stands out that the respondents agree with the roles established in the collaborative work, because they qualify all the roles as very important for the development of the collaborative work, but they do not perform them. It also shows the acceptance of the roles when 41.2% confirm that always and 38.2% that almost always select their role, they know what it means and the responsibilities they imply and that always and almost always play their role from the beginning of the collaborative activity until the end, changing it only sometimes when few members of the collaborative group participate and must assume more than one role. The high frequency (5 times or more) with which 78% average respondents use the role of compiler and deliveries and the zero frequency (zero times) with which they perform the other roles, leads to reflect that they are working only to meet with the content of an activity and take a note when the activity is about to end and there is no time for reviews, evaluations or alerts, but only to compile and deliver. This same result is observed in the research of [7], in which the majority of the students consider that their performance in the collaborative work is efficient, but there are frequent changes of roles, concluding that not all the members assume their chosen role, generating dissatisfaction among the members of the group and that the learning goals are not reached adequately.

The respondents state that they carry out the activities within the times and under the conditions established in the activity guide always 56.9% and almost always 37.3%, which denotes appropriation of the time organization and fulfillment of the tasks, but when he asks them if at the beginning of the activities they plan individual and group tasks, 33.3% respond little and 36.3% fairly frequently; it is reflected that although they comply with the delivery of the task, they do not schedule times for discussion review and group consolidation of knowledge, that is, they do everything when the date indicates that the activity will end, adding to this that when asked if they consider it pertinent to deliver the individual contributions with three days left until the end of the activity and that this time is relevant for the fulfillment of the learning objectives, responding in high measure for 28.4% and moderately pertinent for 29.4%. So things, it is clear that they meet the agenda, play a role, meet the delivery times, but in the last week of activities, with only 3 days to close the collaborative activity and what is worse, most consider that this time is enough to meet the learning objectives. This result leads us to reflect on the true appropriation of the students of this strategy, since, as stated by Panit (2001), cited in [17], "in collaborative learning students are the ones who design their interaction structures and maintain control over the decisions (…) in this one share the authority and between all they accept the responsibility of the actions of the group". With this statement it is deduced that they are the ones who should organize the times and activities, but in the last three days it is not possible to develop in a relevant way a significant learning task.

Component Exchange of Ideas. Regarding this component, 65.7% of the respondents are almost always aware of the observations of their tutor or group colleagues to their individual contribution, making the requested adjustments 47.5% almost always and 30%. 7% always, also they make observations to their classmates and clarifying questions to the tutor; at the end of the work, almost always 51% is reflected in the exchange of ideas and analysis and the final work. Taking into account the organizational component, this dynamic occurs in the last week of collaborative work, which blurs and accelerates in order to comply with a note and on a date and not for the true learning process.

Consensus Component. With regard to this last component, the results show how the respondents contribute in a concrete way to the consolidation of the final work, always in 61.8% and almost always in 32.4%, while the delivery of the collaborative work is the product of the analysis, consensus and negotiation on the part of the members of the group in a 61.8%, whose most significant way of contributing to the group is reviewing the proposal consolidated by the compiler and making suggestions and improvements before delivery. The collaborative work is carried out in such a way that the respondent considers that the contributions of their peers contribute positively to their learning and enriches the construction of new knowledge in their training process with the support of a motivating, guidance and participative tutor a 42.2% almost always and 41.2% always. These results could confirm what was said by Jhonson et al. (1993), cited in [2], "the essence of a collaborative group is to maintain positive interdependence among the members of the group, which is evident in that nobody can achieve success if others do not succeed." However, it is pertinent to bear in mind that when analyzing the answers to the question about the aspects that favor collaborative work, there are two important points to be taken into account with very similar percentages as they were that effective communication is not favored, nor are that the collaborative work has a differentiating contribution. These two points lead to ratify what has been said by [8], "the formation of collaborative groups by themselves, is not a guarantee of interaction and collaborative construction of knowledge. Likewise, in [2] they conclude that "in collaborative learning it is expected that particular forms of interaction will occur that lead to the achievement of learning, but there is no total guarantee that these conditions are presented effectively" (p. 4).

In summary, taking into account the results of this research, in the students surveyed it could be said that there is a high level of appropriation of the synchronous WhatsApp tool and the asynchronous, collaborative forum; however, this does not guarantee that the communication will be totally effective for the achievement of the learning objectives. Likewise, it is also identified in the component of organization of activities, that although the respondents assure the appropriation of the roles, the planning of the tasks, these results are contradictory to the fact that the majority considers that it is possible to carry out the work in the last 3 days before the closing date of the collaborative activity. Likewise, in the component of the interaction and exchange of ideas, it was observed that there is an active participation on the part of those who participate in the process, but when analyzing this point in front of the roles and participation in synchronous and asynchronous communications, it could be conclude that possibly this interaction is not as complete as it seems. Finally, in the component of consensus and that has to do with the final construction of the task, it is recognized that collaborative work contributes to the enrichment of the construction of new knowledge; it is also a point to reinforce effective communication and thereby also improve the perception that this strategy generates differentiating and significant contributions for learning.

6 Pedagogical and Computational Actions to Support Collaborative Work

6.1 Learning Management Systems

When we talk about knowledge management, it is fundamental to think about the importance of the use of information and how each aspect adapts to the needs of the user; In the case of e-learning systems, one of the main advantages of its constitution is the ability to filter the excess information that exists when giving an account of the level of relevance [18], therefore, a specific appropriate definition for learning management systems that is to say that they are computer and telematics tools that are organized according to the objectives of the integral training, so that they can reach the ideal of their functioning and interaction [19], then it is understandable that computer science has become in the perfect ally between software, communication, mobility, adaptability and a computer, therefore, the great challenge lies in the pedagogical quality that must be present in its design and implementation so that the student has resources and a much more valid learning and cash. From the LMS, learning management systems are built in software that has the function of supporting the development or service in the appropriation and administration of knowledge (Sotelo andSolarte 2014 [25]). Figure 1 represents the main functions that allow LMS to promote appropriate courses [20], always supported by the pedagogical and didactic resources that give it quality, so its implementation requires thinking about the following characteristics exposed by Sotelo and Solarte [21].

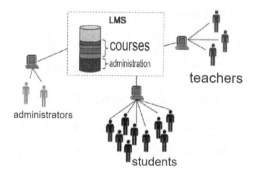

Fig. 1. LMS functions

- Administrative roles, teachers and students: which allow defining the functionality of each actor and the structures associated with their role
- Content structure, its form and its dialectic: the instructional design, defined later, is framed in quality, coherence and contextualization that develops from this role
- Virtual spaces, scenarios and tools for user action: in addition to the previous one here, learning spaces are a priority, because not only do they care about meaningful interaction, but also due to the appropriate use of technological resources that allow a balance to exist in the task of the user through a dynamic interface and on the contrary to avoid a saturation that takes him away from the learning process
- Technological tools that allow management: all the above is possible thanks to current, mobile, adaptive technological tools; that is why, being aware of repositories, OVA and other software allows us to offer a much more current and technologically updated learning experience.

7 General Aspects of Engineering of Collaboration in Training Environments

In any organizational context that wants to obtain important results in their daily activities, it is very important to keep in mind that most of the important decisions are made by groups of people. This makes it possible, for example, to obtain a timelier and accurate solution to complex problems that require the expertise of several people [22]. From the theory of collaboration engineering we can consider as a working group two or more people acting as a single unit with the purpose of carrying out some common activity [23]. In general terms, a collaborative group must contain some characteristics to be cataloged as such in terms of its operation (Permanent/Temporary, In one place/Distributed, Concurrent meeting/At different times) and as to its constitution (Committee, panel, team, department, interaction circle, etc.). What is really important is the general capacity that is achieved to give accurate answers to the need that gives rise to the conformation of the collaborative aspect. In this sense, [5] affirms that working in a group brings benefits such as:

- Ease of understanding a problem regarding whether it is faced by a single person.
- Responsibility for solving the problem is shared.
- It facilitates the identification of errors on time and the search for complete solutions.
- A group has more information (knowledge) than a single person, so it is part of the same team.
- The effectiveness and quality of the production is in team is greater than what each of its members can produce individually, this due to the synergy generated by the collective interaction.
- Greater commitment to making decisions and executing them.

This is how from the Computer Sciences has been deepening the concept of collaborative work supported by computer (CSCW) as the theory that studies the way people work in groups, and how this work can be supported with computational technology [23]. CSCW coined the concept of collaborative systems to refer to computer systems that lend some support to work groups, which are also called collaborative applications or simply groupware). Now, when applying CSCW in clearly formative environments we find great advantages that facilitate learning such as:

- Current facility for both trainers and apprentices to establish connections to the network and thus access the sources of information and communication arranged by the person offering the training program.
- Increase in bandwidths in most places in Colombia and ease of acquisition of web connection services.
- Reduced costs related to mobility to attend a training center.
- Greater computational potential in current equipment, this is related to the management of graphics, multimedia, speed and storage capacity of commercial equipment today.

The above has actually meant great advantages for those who decide to appropriate and take advantage of these advantages, but it has also meant enormous challenges for organizations that design and offer training programs due to the need to migrate their applications to distributed systems, permanent improvement of communications, application of social theory to an environment where previously it was not so common

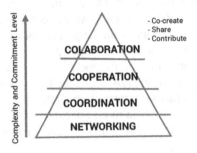

Fig. 2. Design levels for CSCW

and the design of interfaces based on the Human-Computer and Human-Computer-Human interaction that determine how the learning environment should be presented in online environments (Fig. 2).

In this sense of collaborative work for training scenarios, it is equally imperative to apply classification and design taxonomies of the activities (tasks) that have to be carried out in terms of Time and Space of the same, as follows (Fig. 3):

This allows us to define the tools that would be most effective for carrying out

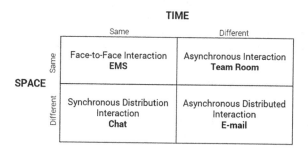

Fig. 3. Time-Space taxonomy

certain tasks in accordance with the learning expectations and development of specific competences that we want to develop in the group of students considered. For this, you can use, for example, electronic communication tools (e-mail, forums, blogs, wikis, shared documents), conference tools (web conferences, audioconferences, electronic whiteboards, shared desktops, chats) or collaborative management tools (electronic event calendars, project management systems, knowledge management systems, activity flow control systems, social media support systems, collaborative information management systems, content management systems and platform type - CMS).

8 Recommendations

Below are some recommendations to apply and motivate students to develop a meaningful collaborative work.

As they affirm [2], "working collaboratively is not easy, it is necessary to learn to do it, since it is not enough simply to place a group of people face to face and indicate that they must work to perform a task" (p. 6). Training is then required, not only for students but also for teachers. Taking into account the results of this research, it is important to develop positive interdependence among students, because as it is presented [2], positive interdependence seeks that the members of the collaborative groups understand that they have a common goal and objectives, and that everyone as a team must reach them, creating a commitment of each member with the goal to achieve. The authors consider that one way to achieve this positive interdependence is to motivate the students so that from the beginning of their collaborative activity establish their own work plan, a kind of micro-agendas, with dates agreed by the group, with commitments that they establish themselves according to the activity guide presented by the course director. This also reflects that there is a change in the traditional role of the teacher, who was in charge of directing all the student's activities from planning to the execution of the work, but in the new pedagogical tendencies, as expressed [25], the teacher has a communicative and interactive vocation with the students, becomes a facilitator and recreates real situations that foster interaction and cooperation among their students.

The fact that the same group establishes its commitments will favor the development of autonomy and self-regulation skills.

With regard to the inconsistencies found in terms of the importance of the roles and those that really assume, it is suggested to the University to review the relevance and relevance of the roles, of deliveries, evaluator and alerts. González [25], has developed a role proposal based on her experience as a director of the Pharmaceutical Care course at the remote University under investigation, which is described below:

Moderator or Coordinator: is the one in charge of organizing everyone's work. It is pending that each participant makes their individual contributions and assumes the roles for participation in the group construction of the final task. In case any of the members does not participate then reassign the pending role or failing to assume the missing role.

Rapporteur: is the one who gives shape to the final work, compiles the group contributions to which, after the academic discussion, the collaborative group arrives in consensus. Share the draft with the rest of the members to evaluate it and then upload it to the forum on the established date.

Reviewers of the Work: they are the ones in charge to elaborate the introduction, the objectives and the conclusions. In addition to review the consistency of the final work, the spelling and the application of technical standards to quote the references consulted. (There may be 3 reviewers).

Finally, it is recommended that as the development of collaborative work requires the intervention of two actors, the student and the teacher, it is necessary to complement this study on the appropriation of the collaborative work from the teacher's role in order to present conclusions and integral solution alternatives.

Another key aspect is the retention strategies that the institution can generate by implementing technological tools, one of the most significant is the system of early alerts that through the performance reported by the platform specifies the alert value in its evaluation quantification.

Technological platforms and virtual learning objects are dynamic resources favorable for the development of meaningful learning [19], since they not only combine novelty and innovation, but also respond to specific training needs, including the existence of special educational needs, with the use of dynamic and attractive hypertext resources for the participant.

References

1. García, A.: Educación a distancia hoy. UNE, Madrid (1994)
2. Collazos, C.A., Mendoza, J.: How to take advantage of "collaborative learning" in the classroom. Educ. educ. **9**(2), 61–76 (2006).http://educacionyeducadores.unisabana.edu.co/index.php/eye/article/download/663/748
3. Gros, B., García, I., Lara, P.: El desarrollo de Herramientas de Apoyo para el Trabajo Colaborativo en Entornos Virtuales de Aprendizaje. Universitat Oberta de Catalunya (España) RIED **12**(2), 115–138 (2009). http://e-spacio.uned.es/fez/eserv.php?pid=bibliuned:revistaRied-2009-12-2-2060&dsID=Documento.pdf. ISSN 1138-2783
4. UNAD, U. : Solidary Pedagogical Academic Project (2011). https://academia.unad.edu.co/images/pap-solidario/PAP%20solidario%20v3.pdf
5. Collazos, C.: Ingeniería de la Colaboración. Material de estudio para el curso de Ingeniería de la Colaboración. Universidad del Cauca (2018)
6. Baptista, P., Fernández, C., Hernández, R.: Metodología de la investigación. McGraw-Hill, México (2010)
7. Fandos, M., González, A.: Estrategias de Aprendizaje Ante las Nuevas Posibilidades Educativas de las TIC. Universidad de Rovira i Virgili (2005). http://dspace.uces.edu.ar:8180/jspui/bitstream/123456789/592/1/Estrategias_de_aprendizaje_Fandos.pdf
8. Ovalle, D., Betancur, C.: Integración y Participación del Estudiante Virtual en Foros de Trabajo Colaborativo de la Universidad Nacional Abierta y a Distancia (2015). http://repository.unad.edu.co/bitstream/10596/3721/1/40797128.pdf
9. Abadía, Gómez, L.: Las competencias sociales dinamizadoras de la interacción y aprendizaje Colaborativo (2013)
10. Cardona, J.J.C.: Collaborative learning as a strategy for knowledge construction processes. Educ. Soc. Dev. **4**(2), 87–103 (2010).https://dialnet.unirioja.es/servlet/articulo?codigo=5386312
11. García, A., Hernández, A., Recamán, A.: La metodología del aprendizaje colaborativo a través de las TIC: una aproximación a las opiniones de profesores y alumnos. Universidad de Salamanca Revista Complutense de Educación **23**(1), 161–188 (2012). https://doi.org/10.5209/rev_RCED.2012.v23.n1.39108. http://revistas.ucm.es/index.php/RCED/article/view/39108/37721
12. Cabero-Almenara, J., Díaz, V.M.: Educational possibilities of social networks and group work .: perceptions of university students. Comunicar: Ibero-American Sci. J. Commun. Educ. (42), 165–172 (2014). http://dx.doi.org/10.3916/C42-2014-16
13. Scagnoli, N.I.: Estrategias para motivar el aprendizaje colaborativo en cursos a distancia. https://www.ideals.illinois.edu/bitstream/handle/2142/10681/aprendizaje-colaborativoscagnoli.pdf?sequence=4
14. González, P.: Curso de Cátedra Unadista. UNAD. Lección 56 (2011)
15. Marín, V., Negre, F., Pérez, A .: Personal learning environments and networks (PLE-PLN) for the collaborative learning. Palma de Majorca. Sci. J. Educommun. **21**(42), 35–43 (2014). http://dx.doi.org/10.3916/C42-2014-03
16. Reynés, M.R.M., Bertos, J.E., Vila, M.C., Ramón, M.I.: Seguimiento, tutorización y evaluación de prácticas externas mediante plataforma virtual de trabajo colaborativo: la experiencia en el Grado de Geografía. Revista de investigación en educación **2**(12), 254–267 (2014). https://dialnet.unirioja.es/servlet/articulo?codigo=4890007
17. Meneses, T.: La colaboración en las pedagogías de la Cibercultura (2011). http://www.umng.edu.co/documents/63968/80124/2.pdf

18. Turban, E., Jay, E.A.: Decision Support Systems and Intelligent Systems, 6th edn, pp. 3–30. Prentice Hall, Upper Saddle River (1993)
19. Zapata, M.: Sistemas de gestión del aprendizaje–Plataformas de teleformación. Revista de educación a distancia **9**, 1–48 (2003). http://dx.doi.org/10.6018/red/50/5
20. Merlo, J.A.: La evaluación de la calidad de la información web: aportaciones teóricas y experiencias prácticas. Recursos informativos: creación, descripción y evaluación. Sociedad de la Información **8**, 101–110 (2003)
21. Morgado, E.M.M.: Gestión del conocimiento en sistemas e-learning, basado en objetos de aprendizaje, cualitativa y pedagógicamente definidos (2007)
22. González, C.: Guía Integrada de Actividades Curso Atención Farmacéutica UNAD, 13 p. (2015)
23. Werner, S., Horton, G.: Changing the Perspective: Improving Generate thinkLets for Ideation. Faculty of Computer Science. University of Magdeburg, Germany, 10 p. (2015)
24. Pérez, L.B.: El rol del docente en el aprendizaje autónomo: la perspectiva del estudiante y la relación con su rendimiento académico. ISSN 1996-1642, Editorial Universidad Don Bosco, año 7, No. 11, Enero-Junio de 2013, pp. 45–62 (2013)
25. Sotelo, F., Solarte, M.F.: Incorporation of web resources as e-learning services into the learning management system. LRN: a review. Tecnura: Technol. Cult. Affirming the Knowl. **18**(39), 165–180 (2014). https://dialnet.unirioja.es/servlet/articulo?codigo=4778487

Gesture-Based Interaction for Virtual Reality Environments Through User-Defined Commands

David Céspedes-Hernández[1]([⊠]) [iD],
Juan Manuel González-Calleros[1] [iD], Josefina Guerrero-García[1] [iD],
and Liliana Rodríguez-Vizzuett[2] [iD]

[1] Facultad de Ciencias de la Computación,
Benemérita Universidad Autónoma de Puebla, Puebla, Mexico
dcespedesh@gmail.com,
{juan.gonzalez, jguerrero}@cs.buap.mx
[2] Facultad de Ciencias de la Electrónica,
Benemérita Universidad Autónoma de Puebla, Puebla, Mexico
liliana.rodriguezviz@alumno.buap.mx

Abstract. Natural user interaction has been recently identified as a field of interest of computer sciences, mainly due to the development of hardware devices that enable fast identification and recognition of gestures within a diversity of contexts. In this paper, the investigation of body gestures that users naturally perform to navigate virtual reality environments is reported. For this purpose, users were asked to show the commands they would perform when realizing basic navigation tasks within a virtual world, and they were observed following the Wizard of Oz approach. The performance gesture-based interaction is evaluated in terms of usability, contrasted with traditional desktop interaction, and analyzed. Finally, as result of this work, a set of gestures (language) to navigate virtual reality environments is defined, along with insights regarding this interaction modality, and comments on the future direction of natural user interfaces using full-body movement as input.

Keywords: Virtual reality environment · Gesture-based interaction
Natural user interfaces · Body gestures · Usability evaluation

1 Introduction

Multimodality is a powerful paradigm aimed to elevate the level of realism and ease of interaction in Virtual Reality (VR) environments. The development of systems that allow multimodal input and specifically the creation of virtual worlds and its navigation involves several challenges, including finding techniques that support 3D interaction, and for satisfying functional requirements and meet desired levels of efficiency, accessibility, and other dimensions of usability and user experience [1].

When following a Model-Driven Approach (MDA), for better understanding the requirements of the User Interface (UI), it is important to start by identifying the frequent and significant tasks to be carried out in the application. These tasks are defined as

V. Agredo-Delgado and P. H. Ruiz (Eds.): HCI-COLLAB 2018, CCIS 847, pp. 143–157, 2019.
https://doi.org/10.1007/978-3-030-05270-6_11

coordinated or logical sequences of actions, and can share different applications; then, the identified tasks can be broken down into elementary actions. For example, Constantine identified twelve functions enclosing all the operations that can be performed within interactive applications: action, start, stop, select, create, delete, modify, move, duplicate, perform, toggle, and view [2]; while Wüthrich summarizes interaction in virtual environments to three atomic actions: selecting, positioning, and deforming [3].

The usefulness of a 3D application is, in fact, proportional to the ability of its users to interact with the information that it contains, and that may be positioned in multiple locations within the virtual environment, and reachable from different angles, making it necessary that users are able to navigate efficiently in the environment, obtaining different views of the stage and objects of study. Thus, this work is focused on the navigation within VR environments, which is the most commonly used task in such type of applications [4], while secondary tasks such as selection and manipulation are out of the scope of this work.

Despite the fact that navigation is a primary activity to be done in virtual environments, and that the equivalent task in real contexts is achieved through movement and positioning of the full-body, in a state of the art review that was carried out prior to the realization of this project involving 60 works on gesture recognition, it was noticed that 6 of the works were focused on full-body gestures recognition, and that of them, 3 were aimed at controlling robots, 2 were dedicated to determining user characteristics, and only 1 addressed navigation in virtual worlds.

Through the effective design of navigation for VR environments, users are given the feeling of an easy and intuitive motion within a virtual world. A good 3D navigation design typically results in two products: research to understand the cognitive principles within the navigation, and tailored design to create navigation for tasks and application-specific techniques. While experimenting with the use of Natural User Interfaces (NUI) such as gesture-based interfaces and vocal interfaces among others, we have observed that they are not as natural as their name promotes, as the mental model of the interaction in each individual is different. Furthermore, if users define their own natural language, then the problem is on the workload, and on the complexity of remembering the number of commands that they had just created.

In this order of ideas, the research question that inspired this work is: Is natural interaction, achieved through the definition of a body-gesture user-defined language, more effective than traditional GUI based interaction? For approaching the solution to this question, we designed an experiment, in which users are asked to perform a specific task on a VR environment using gesture-based interaction, and on a traditional GUI based application using the Wizard of Oz technique. The performance of users interacting with both alternatives is contrasted in order to get conclusions regarding ease of use and preference of users with respect to one type of interaction or the other.

The remainder of the article is structured as follows, next section introduces concepts on the model-based development of gesture-based interactive systems as a general, defining how it may be applied on the design of a VR environment navigation application. Section 3 is aimed at presenting the gesture vocabulary that was obtained through the conduction of the experiment, and on describing the setup of such exercise. Then chapter four discusses the results that were obtained, and finally, conclusions of this work and the future labor to be done, are addressed in Sect. 5.

2   Design of a Navigation Application Following a Model-Based Development Approach

UsiXML [5] is a methodology to generate UI following a model-based approach. It describes the UI for multiple contexts of use, such as Graphical User Interfaces (GUI), Auditory User Interfaces, and Multimodal User Interfaces. The conceptual framework of UsiXML relies on the Cameleon Reference Framework [6].

UsiXML proposes four steps to define the user interface (Fig. 1). The *Tasks & Concepts* level describes the interactive system specifications in terms of the user tasks to be carried out, and the domain objects of these tasks. An *Abstract User Interface* (AUI), abstracts a *Concrete User Interface* (CUI) into a definition that is independent of any interaction modality (such as graphical, vocal or tactile). A CUI abstracts a *Final User Interface* (FUI), into a description independent of any programming or markup language in terms of concrete interaction objects, layout, navigation, and behavior. Finally, an FUI refers to an actual UI rendered either by interpretation (e.g., HTML) or by code compilation (e.g., Java). By reusing this mechanism, the UI of a workflow model, that includes task models, can be generated.

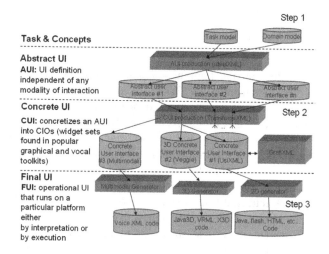

Fig. 1. UI generation framework based on UsiXML [5].

A model-based approach is intended to assist in designing UI with a more formal computer supported methodology rather than the more traditional paper-based design methods, such as storyboarding. It describes the application model as an executable specification, yet at an abstraction level that is higher than that of the code. It attempts to explicitly represent knowledge that is often hidden in the application code.

The first step of the approach is to create a task model. Task models do not impose any particular implementation so that user tasks can be better analyzed without implementation constraints. This kind of analysis is made possible because user tasks are considered from the point of view of the users need for the application, and not on how to represent the user activity with a particular system. This layer, called task model, is thus user-centered. For the expression of this model, we get the following tree representation, Fig. 2, using the CTTE editor [7]. Task models are complemented with domain models [5], this is typically forgotten when adopting a model-based UI design strategy, but to fully understand the context of use, it is recommended in the W3C initiative [8]. Domain models can be represented in different ways, and they are intended to display the data that is related to the model, along with its relationship to the task to be executed.

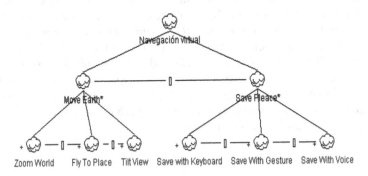

Navegación virtual

Move Earth*   Save Pleace*

Zoom World   Fly To Place   Tilt View   Save with Keyboard   Save With Gesture   Save With Voice

Fig. 2. Task model of the navigation system using CTTE [7].

For our specific domain, the minimum necessary tasks for interacting with an interactive virtual world application, are: Zoom (in and out), fly to place, tilt view, and save location. We use the interface notation to depict the functionality and the strategy pattern to show the overriding of the interactive abstract methods: Zoom behavior, fly to place behavior, tilt view behavior, and save location behavior. The domain model includes the definition of places, coordinates, markers, and everything is encapsulated in the navigation concept. The complementary domain and dialog model for this task model is presented in Fig. 3.

The abstract model, retrieved from the W3C recommendation [8], of the UI model is independent of any device, technology or interactive art. This AUI model consists of abstract units of interaction which are composed of abstract iterative objects (*AUIObjects*), abstract interactive behaviors (*AbstractBehavior*), and other abstract interaction units. An *AUIObject* is the basis of a hierarchy of abstract interactive objects. The *AUIObjects* are described as a set of attributes: first, a "*label*" which is a way to access content in an understandable way and using natural language; second, the "*longlabel*" which is a more complete version of the description of the object; third, the "*shortlabel*" which is a concise description of the object; in fourth place, the "*help*" attribute is a text string the can be used to help users understanding the meaning and purpose of the interaction object; next, "*contextCondition*", which is an attribute for describing the context conditions (user variables, work environment characteristics, devices); and finally, the "*role*", this attribute allows to assign the behavior or relevance of the object within the interactive system.

There are two types of *AUIObjects*: abstract interactors (*AUIInteractor*) and abstract containers (*AUIContainer*). An AUIContainer allows to organize and to bring elements together. It denotes the grouping of tasks that have to be presented in the same space-time, for example, in a window within a GUI, or within a vocal container for vocal interfaces. *AUIContainers* can be composed of *AUIInteractors*, or of other *AUIContainers*.

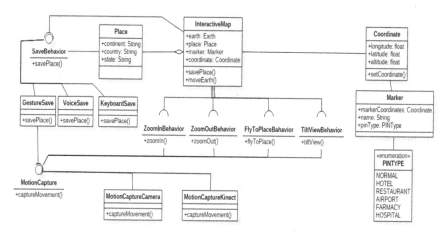

Fig. 3. Domain and dialog model for interactive maps with different interaction techniques.

Furthermore, the *AUIInteractors* are individual elements that populate *AUIContainers*. These interactors are specialized in two different types: *DataInteractors*, and *TriggerInteractors*.

The *AUIInteractors* are described with the attributes: reference (*ref*) indicating that a data model or domain is associated with the interactor; the maximum cardinality (*maxCardinality*) representing the maximum number of data elements (*DataItem*) to use, or to present in the interactor; minimum cardinality (*minCardinality*) represents the minimum number of *DataItems* to use, or to present in the interactor.

On one hand, a *DataInteractor* may be composed of one or more interactive elements representing the three abstract types of data manipulation, i.e. data output (*output*), data input (*input*), and selection of an option (*selection*). It is considered also that *DataInteractors* may be composed of a number of *DataItems*. *DataItems* can either be provided by the system (*systemProvided*) or by users (*userProvided*). This means, that these two entities are responsible for providing data to the *DataInteractors*.

An *input* represents data that is fed to a *DataInteractor*. An *output* represents information that was generated and presented to the user. Finally, a *selection* is a representation of a *DataInteractor* which has the purpose of presenting options to the user and getting information in return. This type of interactor is described by the following attributes:

- *orderCriteria*: defines the sort order in case the *DataItems* within it need to be ordered.
- *isContinuous*: defines whether *DataItems* are continuous or not.
- *start*: indicates the initial value for a set of *DataItems*.

- *end*: indicates the final value of a set of *DataItems*.
- *step*: indicates the distance or difference between two adjacent values in the set of *DataItems*.
- *isExpandable*: indicates whether it is possible to expand the current set of *DataItems* with new values or not.

On the other hand, *TriggerInteractors* allow users to execute commands or navigate in a system based on the features that are available at any given time. Therefore, they have two facets, the execution of commands (*Command*), and execution of transitions between windows or navigation (*Navigation*). *Commands* have the purpose of performing a determined operation with existing information, while a *Navigator* is responsible for loading items into the current display unit, providing the user with the ability to work on different sets of tasks that may be presented on different display units, or *AUIContainers*.

In the abstract level of the UI model, relationships (*AUIRelationship*) between *AUIContainers* and *AUIInteractors* are defined. *AUIRelationships* are classes for explicitly explaining how *AUIContainers* and *AUIInteractors* are associated. In this sense, *AUIContainers* indicate if they contain *AUIInteractors* as a *hierarchy AUIRelationship*. Likewise, *grouping AUIRelationships* may be defined between two or more *AUIInteractors* within *AUIContainers*.

Finally, for describing the behavior (*AbstractBehavior*) of the abstract interaction units, an aggregate of listeners is used. A *listener* is associated with at least one *AUIObject* which was waiting to execute an operation. Listeners are modeled through the definition of *rules* (i.e. when an event occurs, if-condition-then-action). At this level of abstraction, we must refer to a canonical set of events (*AbstractEvents*) and actions (*AbstractActions*). Such events, belong to one of the following types (*AbstractEventTypes*): *onDataInput*, *onDataOutput*, *onErroneousDataInput*, *onDataSelection*, *onDataUnSelection*, *onCommandTrigger*, *onNavigationTrigger*, *onObjectFocusIn*, *onObjectFocusOut*, *onObjectRelevant*, *onObjectIrrelevant*, and *onModelUpdate*. While the referred *AbstractActions* may be of the following types: *modelSearch*, *modelCreate*, *modelRead*, *modelUpdate*, *modelDelete*, *modelInvoke*, *modelReset*, *modelCopy*, *objectActivate*, *objectDeactivate*, *objectSetFocus*, *objectCreate*, *objectDelete*, *objectUpdate*, *listenerCreate*, *listenerDelete*, and *eventDispatch*. It is important to point out that these lists are not restrictive, and that other values may be added to suit any need. Also, notice that the condition to be evaluated in the *rule* is just an expression in natural language.

Based on the before mentioned tasks for interactive virtual world navigation applications, and in compliance with UsiXML, it is possible to generate an AUI model for describing them. Within this AUI model, the main *AUIContainer* called "Navigation GE" is included, inside of it two other *AUIContainers* were added: "Save place", shown in Fig. 4, and "Move in map"; and inside of these *AUIContainers*, the necessary components are placed.

As can be seen, the "Save Place" *AUIContainer* holds the components: "Indicate Save", "Identify Command", "Execute Command", and "System Feedback". Up to this point, no programming language nor interaction modality has been defined, so it is possible that some of the modeled features when implemented, belong to different modalities, or are executed using different devices or platforms.

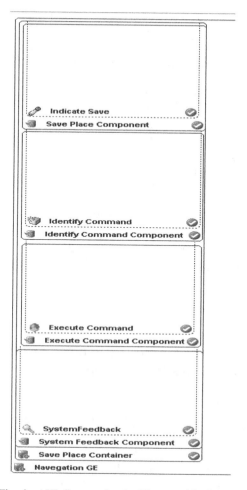

Fig. 4. AUI diagram for the "Save position" task.

The notation that was used on the AUI model in Fig. 4, is described in Fig. 5, and is consistent with the interactive elements within *DataInteractors* that were introduced earlier in this section.

For our domain of application, an *input* element is added to the "Indicate save" *AUIContainer*, as it represents the user's intention to save a location within the virtual world. Into this *AUIContainer*, a *Navigation*, and a *Command* interactive elements are included, in order to represent the action of execution and process of the given input. Finally, as feedback to the user is required, an *output* element is also incorporated.

Concept	Description	Icon
AUI Container	It is an abstract interactive object like can group one or more abstract interactive components	
AUI Interactor	An abstract interactive component, an object is independent interaction of the interface used and may have one or more facets	
Input	Facet interactive component responsible for the inputs regardless of the technology used in our interface	
Navigation	Facet Navigation of the component provides the required code to acknowledge the order, it will depend on our interface and language	
Command	Facet Command work with the indicated orders depending on our entry and recognized order	
Output	The last facet, this is responsible for displaying information outlets, again independent of our technologies of data output, either visual, mechanical or another	

Fig. 5. Graphical notation to represent an AUI.

3 A User-Defined Body Gesture Language for Navigating Interactive Virtual Reality Environments

According to the UsiXML approach introduced in the previous section, the third transformation step towards the implementation of a system consists of applying a set of transformation rules in order to achieve the transition from the AUI model to the CUI model. A CUI is defined as the abstraction of any FUI with respect to computing platforms, but with the interaction modality given. This type of UI is made up of Concrete Interaction Objects (CIO), which are abstractions of widgets that may be found in a platform. A CIO may be associated with multiple behaviors.

Nevertheless, as explained in the introduction, the scope of this paper is to define a body gesture language to interact with a VR environment. In this sense, we decided to analyze the problem using a Wizard of Oz technique [9] for the gesture-based interaction and continue a normal development process for a desktop version. The Wizard of Oz method has been used throughout the history of the development of interactive systems, and in particular, in the field of natural interfaces development as it is a way to collect data for mixed reality environments [10] or movement commands for interaction with kids [11] among other application domains. The selection of this strategy was based on the desire to prevent the development of an expensive system, in terms of time and effort. As a consequence, we decided to execute experiments using a real GUI based interactive virtual world system, asking users to define their own body gestures to navigate through the virtual world and giving them the feeling that those commands actually worked on the application, but actually providing the input via keyboard commands.

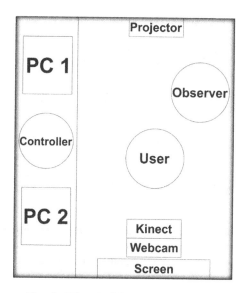

Fig. 6. Wizard of OZ experiment setup.

The setup of the experiment, as shown in Fig. 6, included two computers (PC1 and PC2), the first one for controlling a Microsoft Kinect[1] sensor and a webcam in order to retrieve users' movement information, and allowing to document the experiment; while the second one was connected to a projector for providing the user with feedback and simulating users' interaction with the system. The test subjects who took part on the experiment, were responsible in a first stage, for participating in an interview, in order to understand their appreciation towards Natural User Interfaces (NUI), in a second stage, of providing gestures for a simulated platform configuration, and for interacting with the application following a set of instructions, and in a third stage, of evaluating the usability of both interactions by answering a survey. An observer of the experiment was also designated and located next to the user in order to provide support in case any doubt arises. The experiment controller, managed the devices to document the experiment and to explain how each user performed the activity.

In the experiment, eight undergraduate students participated. Each of them was asked to indicate what body gesture would he/she do to perform a series of tasks, repeating this process until users were satisfied with the gestures they gave. Thus, a set of 64 body gestures was obtained. Those 64 gestures were compared, grouped and analyzed, resulting in the body-gesture language for interacting with VR environment navigation applications presented in Fig. 7.

---

[1] https://developer.microsoft.com/en-us/windows/kinect.

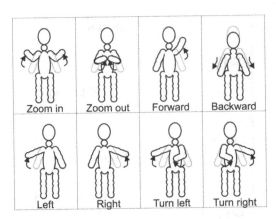

Fig. 7. Proposed body-gesture language for interacting with virtual reality environments. From left to right and top to bottom, the gestures for zooming in, zooming out, moving forward, moving backward, moving to the left, moving to the right, turning left, and turning right.

During the experiment, it was observed that tasks, such as, save place, move to marker, and add marker, were discarded as there was a lot of confusion on how to move the body to communicate that functionality to the system. Therefore, vocal communication was the solution when users required to use those functionalities. The results of the performed experiment are discussed with more detail in next section.

The "zoom in" task was most commonly achieved by moving both arms up and away from the body. In a reciprocal way, "zoom out" was achieved by enclosing both arms. "Moving forward" was represented as raising the left arm up while "moving backward" was characterized as crouching and throwing both arms front. For "moving to the left" and "moving to the right", users chose to either move left arm to the left, or right arm to the right. Finally, for "turning to the left" and "turning to the right", users moved both arms to one side or the other.

4   Evaluation and Discussion

During the experiment, performance measures were collected and complemented with qualitative responses that were gathered at the end of the experiment. Although the number of participants in the experiment (eight) is not statistically significant, 68% of related research works, reported having fewer users involved [12].

On the evaluation process, students from the Computer Science Faculty of the Benemérita Universidad Autónoma de Puebla were involved. They were instructed on the use of the tool and received a brief description and examples of how to use the platform, as well as on how Wizard of Oz technique is applied. Later, they were asked to go through faculties within the university asking for volunteers. For both experiments, one using the keyboard and mouse interaction, and one using the body gesture simulation as described in the previous section, seven males and one female showed up.

Interesting information was gathered during interviews prior to the experiment, as the eight users agreed that they would prefer the use of the body-gesture based application, over the GUI application, most of them mentioned that is was just simply because it seemed funnier to them. Moreover, one respondent mentioned that he would prefer it, as he would like to exercise with it.

While the experiment was taking place, users' performance and preference were compared while interacting with the navigation application. In the GUI experiment, all users were able to complete the activities, and the response times did not exceed a minute long. On the contrary, the use of body gestures lasted an average of more than four minutes. Clearly, user performance was worse in the second scenario. A summary of the problems that users faced is presented in the following list; the number corresponds to the user:

1. Problems to find the target place. The user was constantly lost in the virtual world.
2. No problem detected.
3. No problem detected.
4. Failed to accomplish the task. Very confused, most common problem was related to wayfinding, a lot of errors while trying to remember defined vocabulary. The user does not know where to go. Frustration pushed the user to abandon the experiment.
5. A lot of doubts, frustration, and desperation while trying to navigate the virtual environment. Constantly getting lost, at some point, the user tried to talk to the system for receiving assistance.
6. Pleased with the technique. The user wanted to use the application longer.
7. Minor frustration. The user only used one-hand gestures to manipulate the application.
8. Some problems with wayfinding, memory, doubts about the user-defined language.

After each test, participants were asked to answer the IBM CSUQ [13] in order to get data regarding their appreciation towards the system in terms of usability. The IBM CSUQ instrument is composed of 19 questions, with a 7-point Likert scales concerning system use (Q1–Q8), information quality (Q9–Q15), UI quality (Q16–Q18), and general feedback to the system (Q19).

These results along with the evaluation of average time, errors, and unfinished tasks are reported in Fig. 8. It is possible to notice from those results, that even when users took longer to perform the tasks, committed more mistakes during the interaction, and were not able to complete some tasks, the appreciation of them towards the system was not significantly affected. Specifically, when asking users if they would use the gesture-based system afterward, on a Likert-scale of 7, a 6.6 value was gotten, which suggest a high interest to use the interactive map with body gestures. The feedback was really encouraging despite the terrible performance of users.

Comparing the here proposed work to other related projects in the literature, the requirement of interacting with applications using body gestures has been addressed by a number of authors, moreover, there are a number of works dedicated to the development of techniques for navigation through maps, although they are highly dependent of interfaces of hardware. These techniques are efficient for isolated navigation tasks, but if the global actions in VR environments (including tasks of navigation, selection, and manipulation) are considered, where the interoperability of several devices or modalities may be necessary, in addition to the need to switch between them according to the characteristics of the task, they may not work properly.

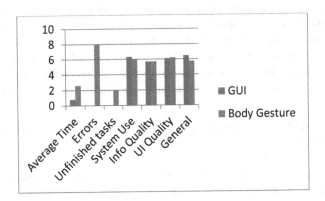

Fig. 8. Overall evaluation of the system in terms of average time for each task, errors, unfinished tasks, and the usability dimensions covered in the IBM CSUQ [13].

Furthermore, there are other alternatives with which the results that were obtained and reported in this paper must be contrasted, for instance, there is a proposal for a model of 3D interaction which facilitates and takes into account previous observations is the Fly Over technique [1], which is aimed on maintaining the same logic of use through devices, making interaction intuitive for users. Another interaction technique in the literature is the Visual Interaction Platform [14] with its respective hardware including a projector to provide the idea of having a computer with a larger workspace on a flat surface which contains a digitizing tablet. Most of the work in the field includes the analysis of NUI [12], 3D UI [15], guidelines for the creation of VR environments [16], among other related topics, but there are no other proposals regarding the definition of a body gesture language to interact with maps.

Be worthwhile to highlight the work in [17], in which taxonomy is created for categorizing already existing navigation techniques along with using complaints to create structures related to navigation tasks, enabling and inspiring the creation of new techniques. Finally, even though many works have studied user-defined languages for mobile phone interaction [18, 19], tablets [20], augmented reality [21], active tokens [22], in a similar way as it was done in this paper, there is a need to formalize user-defined languages by adopting a more formal strategy such as the one proposed in [23].

5 Conclusions and Future Work

In this paper, the process that was followed to define a body-gesture language for navigating VR environments, by using the Wizard of Oz technique, is reported. For the elaboration of such vocabulary, it was necessary to conduct a three-stage experiment in which eight users participated. The first stage of the experiment was an interview for user stereotyping, and for understanding users' prior appreciation of NUI.

The second stage of the experiment was dedicated to first defining a body-gesture language for the navigation tasks (zoom in, zoom out, go forward, go back, go left, go right, turn left, and turn right), for later using it in order to complete a set of instructions. Users were then asked to perform a similar set of instructions using the keyboard, mouse, and a traditional GUI.

Finally, the third stage was aimed at evaluating usability on both NUI and GUI. For this purpose, users were asked to answer an evaluation instrument covering dimensions of usability such as ease of use, information quality, UI quality, and general appreciation. It was interesting that even though through observation, it was possible to notice that the interaction with body gestures was more complicated and frustrating than with the GUI, the usability dimensions that were evaluated did not show significant differences when comparing NUI and GUI.

Our conclusion is about emphasizing that even though a solution is built expecting to have specific results, it is necessary to look at users' actual needs, proposed guidelines, learned lessons, and recommendations from an impartial perspective. This is a double-edged blade, as it may lead to complex projects or to multimodal/multi-device design, but at the same time is meant to be of help to any NUI designer or HCI researcher towards a more effective user-centered design.

Two interesting aspects were also noticed in the gestures set that was obtained. The first one with regard to opposite movements (zoom in/zoom out, forward/backward, move left/move right, and turn left/turn right) that do not always have opposite gestures associated, consider, for instance, the movement which was obtained for moving forward and the one for moving backward. The second insight is about mirroring movements, as users were located in front of the projector, it was observed that depending on the direction to which avatars were pointed, the gestures varied. This is the reason for which same gestures were received when asking users to move to one side or the other.

Regarding universal access, which is one of the goals pursued with the implementation of NUI, some interaction modalities have a more evident contribution to assistive technologies. This last remark is especially true if we consider that in our experiment, users found it easier to interact with the application using voice commands rather than body-gestures, for a number of tasks. Providing different modes of operation with distinct information carriers implies offering not only multiple forms of communication but also different types of feedback that can each be suitable for a kind of disability and use contexts.

As future work, it will be necessary to express in a more formal way the vocabulary for navigating on VR environments, as well as actually implementing body-gesture interaction to the developed VR environment navigation application, in order to allow testing in a more precise manner and incorporating more metrics.

Acknowledgment. This work has been funded by PRODEP, CONACYT and BUAP-VIEP projects. We truly appreciate the work of students of the computer science and architecture schools of the Autonomous University of Puebla (BUAP) for their tremendous contribution on the creation of the VR environment. Particularly to the students: Cortés García Raymundo, Rodríguez Hernández Fredy, Tlapaya Tepech Ismael, Roberto Pérez Hernández, Daniel Romero Dominguez, and Manuel Juarez.

References

1. Boudoin, P., Otmane, S., Mallem, M.: Design of a 3d navigation technique supporting vr interaction. In: Arioui, H., Merzouki, R., Abbassi, H.A. (eds.) AIP Conference Proceedings, vol. 1019, no. 1, pp. 149–153 (2008). https://doi.org/10.1063/1.2952967
2. Constantine, L.L.: Canonical abstract prototypes for abstract visual and interaction design. In: Jorge, J.A., Jardim Nunes, N., Falcão e Cunha, J. (eds.) DSV-IS 2003. LNCS, vol. 2844, pp. 1–15. Springer, Heidelberg (2003). https://doi.org/10.1007/978-3-540-39929-2_1
3. Wüthrich, C.A.: An analysis and a model of 3d interaction methods and devices for virtual reality. In: Duke, D., Puerta, A. (eds.) Design, Specification and Verification of Interactive Systems 1999, pp. 18–29. Springer, Vienna (1999). https://doi.org/10.1007/978-3-7091-6815-8_3
4. Bowman, D.A., Koller, D., Hodges, L.F.: Travel in immersive virtual environments: an evaluation of viewpoint motion control techniques. In: Virtual Reality Annual International Symposium 1997, pp. 45–52. IEEE (1997). https://doi.org/10.1109/VRAIS.1997.583043
5. Vanderdonckt, J.: A MDA-compliant environment for developing user interfaces of information systems. In: Pastor, O., Falcão e Cunha, J. (eds.) CAiSE 2005. LNCS, vol. 3520, pp. 16–31. Springer, Heidelberg (2005). https://doi.org/10.1007/11431855_2
6. Calvary, G., Coutaz, J., Thevenin, D., Limbourg, Q., Bouillon, L., Vanderdonckt, J.: A unifying reference framework for multi-target user interfaces. Interact. Comput. **15**(3), 289–308 (2003). https://doi.org/10.1016/S0953-5438(03)00010-9
7. Paterno, F., Mancini, C., Meniconi, S.: ConcurTaskTrees: a diagrammatic notation for specifying task models. In: Howard, S., Hammond, J., Lindgaard, G. (eds.) Human-Computer Interaction INTERACT 1997. ITIFIP, pp. 362–369. Springer, Boston, MA (1997). https://doi.org/10.1007/978-0-387-35175-9_58
8. Fonseca, J.M.C., et al.: Model-based ui xg final report. W3C Incubator Group Report, May, p. 32 (2010)
9. Kelley, J.F.: An iterative design methodology for user-friendly natural language office information applications. ACM Trans. Inf. Syst. (TOIS) **2**(1), 26–41 (1984). https://doi.org/10.1145/357417.357420
10. Dow, S., Lee, J., Oezbek, C., MacIntyre, B., Bolter, J.D., Gandy, M.: Wizard of Oz interfaces for mixed reality applications. In: CHI 2005. ACM, April 2005 (2005). https://doi.org/10.1145/1056808.1056911

11. Höysniemi, J., Hämäläinen, P., Turkki, L.: Wizard of Oz prototyping of computer vision-based action games for children. In: Proceedings of the 2004 Conference on Interaction Design and Children: Building a Community, pp. 27–34. ACM (2004). https://doi.org/10.1145/1017833.1017837

12. Maike, V.R.M.L., de Sousa Britto Neto, L., Baranauskas, M.C.C., Goldenstein, S.K.: Seeing through the kinect: a survey on heuristics for building natural user interfaces environments. In: Stephanidis, C., Antona, M. (eds.) UAHCI 2014. LNCS, vol. 8513, pp. 407–418. Springer, Cham (2014). https://doi.org/10.1007/978-3-319-07437-5_39

13. Lewis, J.R.: IBM computer usability satisfaction questionnaires: psychometric evaluation and instructions for use. Int. J. Hum. Comput. Interact. 7(1), 57–78 (1995). https://doi.org/10.1080/10447319509526110

14. Aliakseyeu, D., Subramanian, S., Martens, J.B., Rauterberg, M.: Interaction techniques for navigation through and manipulation of 2 D and 3 D data. In: ACM International Conference Proceeding Series, vol. 23, pp. 179–188 (2002)

15. González-Calleros, J.M., Vanderdonckt, J., Muñoz-Arteaga, J.: A structured methodology for developing 3D web applications. In: Integrating Usability Engineering for Designing the Web Experience: Methodologies and Principles, pp. 15–43 (2010). https://doi.org/10.4018/978-1-60566-896-3.ch002

16. Kaur, K.: Designing virtual environments for usability. In: Howard, S., Hammond, J., Lindgaard, G. (eds.) Human-Computer Interaction INTERACT 1997. ITIFIP, pp. 636–639. Springer, Boston, MA (1997). https://doi.org/10.1007/978-0-387-35175-9_112

17. Tan, D.S., Robertson, G.G., Czerwinski, M.: Exploring 3D navigation: combining speed-coupled flying with orbiting. In: Proceedings of the SIGCHI Conference on Human Factors in Computing Systems, pp. 418–425. ACM (2001). https://doi.org/10.1145/365024.365307

18. Kray, C., Nesbitt, D., Dawson, J., Rohs, M.: User-defined gestures for connecting mobile phones, public displays, and tabletops. In: Proceedings of the 12th International Conference on Human Computer Interaction with Mobile Devices and Services, pp. 239–248. ACM (2010). https://doi.org/10.1145/1851600.1851640

19. Ruiz, J., Li, Y., Lank, E.: User-defined motion gestures for mobile interaction. In: Proceedings of the SIGCHI Conference on Human Factors in Computing Systems, pp. 197–206. ACM (2011). https://doi.org/10.1145/1978942.1978971

20. Kurdyukova, E., Redlin, M., André, E.: Studying user-defined iPad gestures for interaction in multi-display environment. In: Proceedings of the 2012 ACM International Conference on Intelligent User Interfaces, pp. 93–96. ACM (2012). https://doi.org/10.1145/2166966.2166984

21. Piumsomboon, T., Clark, A., Billinghurst, M., Cockburn, A.: User-defined gestures for augmented reality. In: Kotzé, P., Marsden, G., Lindgaard, G., Wesson, J., Winckler, M. (eds.) INTERACT 2013. LNCS, vol. 8118, pp. 282–299. Springer, Heidelberg (2013). https://doi.org/10.1007/978-3-642-40480-1_18

22. Valdes, C., et al.: Exploring the design space of gestural interaction with active tokens through user-defined gestures. In: Proceedings of the SIGCHI Conference on Human Factors in Computing Systems, pp. 4107–4116. ACM (2014). https://doi.org/10.1145/2556288.2557373

23. Vatavu, R.D., Wobbrock, J.O.: Between-subjects elicitation studies: formalization and tool support. In: Proceedings of the 2016 CHI Conference on Human Factors in Computing Systems, pp. 3390–3402. ACM (2016). https://doi.org/10.1145/2858036.2858228

High-Level Libraries for Emotion Recognition in Music: A Review

Yesid Ospitia Medina[1](✉) ⓘ, Sandra Baldassarri[2](✉) ⓘ, and José Ramón Beltrán[2](✉) ⓘ

[1] ICESI University, Cali, Colombia
yesid.ospitia@gmail.com
[2] University of Zaragoza, Zaragoza, Spain
{sandra, jrbelbla}@unizar.es

Abstract. This article presents a review of high-level libraries that enable to recognize emotions in digital files of music. The main objective of the work is to study and compare different high-level content-analyzer libraries, showing their main functionalities, focused on the extraction of low and high level relevant features to classify musical pieces through an affective classification model. In addition, there has been a review of different works in which those libraries have been used to emotionally classify the musical pieces, through rhythmic and tonal features reconstruction, and the automatic annotation strategies applied, which generally incorporate machine learning techniques. For the comparative evaluation of the different high-level libraries, in addition to the common attributes in the chosen libraries, the most representative attributes in music emotion recognition field (MER) were selected. The comparative evaluation enables to identify the current development in MER regarding high-level libraries and to analyze the musical parameters that are related with emotions.

Keywords: MER (Music Emotion Recognition)
MIR (Music Information Retrieval) · API (Application Programming Interface)
Music features

1 Introduction

Psychology experts have found that music can be considered an emotional transformer [1]. Some studies suggest, in a general way, that musical features as rhythm and harmony have a direct relationship with the listener's emotional perception. The fast rhythms usually generate emotions perceived as positive, meanwhile slow rhythms tend to generate emotions closer to neutral and relaxing ones. In the case of harmony regarding chords progression, the major modes are usually related with a happiness perception, and the minor modes with a sadness perception [2].

That relationship between music and emotions has awakened interest in emotional recognition in music from computational sciences. This task has been addressed from different approaches, such as: labeling processes, application of affective classification models, content analyzers, cultural information gathering and integration and/or physiological signals analysis [3]. Among all these approaches, in this work we will focus on content analyzers due to their direct relationship with the analysis and treatment of sound features.

© Springer Nature Switzerland AG 2019
V. Agredo-Delgado and P. H. Ruiz (Eds.): HCI-COLLAB 2018, CCIS 847, pp. 158–168, 2019.
https://doi.org/10.1007/978-3-030-05270-6_12

With respect to content analyzers, the depth of study that is performed must be specified. On the one hand, there is a study of internal functioning, where one wants to understand, analyze, improve or even propose new techniques, directly related to the processing of the signal or to some later signal processing phases. On the other hand, there are high-level libraries that offer a series of music features extraction functionalities, for which classifying models can be applied, like emotional classification of music.

A content analyzer must rebuild the intrinsic features of music from an initial step of a signal processing block. To make it, various techniques are implemented in the signal, extraction, selection and classification processing algorithm [4]. In Fig. 1 the process that typically follows a content analyzer is shown, from the digital signal processing stage, followed by the extraction of low-level features, and the reconstruction of high-level features, to finally apply classification models to obtain classified musical pieces.

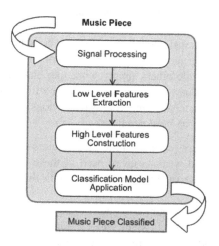

Fig. 1. General process of a content analyzer.

First, content analyzers have the main objective of extracting the sound features. In some cases, some analyzers include additional functionalities, where they have already implemented models that allow classifications by criteria such as musical genre, style, artist, composer, emotions and more [5]. High-level libraries can be considered as those user-friendly content analyzers, which do not require advanced knowledge in topics related to digital signals processing, and which also offer additional classification functionalities.

In this article a selection of high-level libraries, that are part of the content analyzer, is presented. Initially, Sect. 2 presents a basic description of the features of high-level libraries, for later describing, with more detail, the most used ones: *Spotify API* (Sect. 2.1), *jMIR/jAudio* (Sect. 2.2) and *AcousticBrainz* (Sect. 2.3). For each one, the musical features that allow obtaining and reconstructing the emotions that can be recognized are identified, and some works based on those libraries are also presented.

Section 3 establishes a comparative framework between these libraries, evaluating some of the most common and important attributes inside this field of study. Finally, Sect. 4 highlights the conclusions obtained from this study and the proposed future work.

2 High-Level Libraries: Description

The high-level libraries for music features recognition are presented as APIs (*Application Programming Interface*) and are oriented to give a set of functionalities for extraction and classification of intrinsic musical features.

Usually, this type of tools is directed to an end user profile. The reliability and effectiveness of each of these libraries will depend to a large extent on its internal technical definition, which is part of the various techniques developed in the MIR (*Music Information Retrieval*) systems.

Some general features of the different libraries are:

- They have a limit on the variety of intrinsic features of music that can be analyzed.
- They have a certain reliability, in terms of the effective reconstruction of some intrinsic features of the music and their respective classification.
- Regarding their licensing model, they can be free or for commercial use.
- Some are open code, while others simply work like black boxes.
- Some are available as cloud services and require the Internet for their use.
- For the cloud services, there are some access restrictions, for example the number of times a web service can be used per hour.

The use of musical features extraction libraries requires a rigorous selection process to identify the strengths and weaknesses of each of these solutions. It could even be considered the combined use of different libraries, with the purpose of achieving the best possible results.

The sound features that a library can detect are generally classified into two categories: high-level and low-level. In some cases the highest level features of music as rhythm, harmony and mode, are classified inside the tonal and rhythm categories [6]. It is important to understand the type of sound features that each library uses and their direct relationship with musical concepts.

There are different libraries and tools that allow us to work with audio signals for feature extraction: *Spotify API* [7], *jAudio* [8], *AcousticBrainz* [9], *Psysound toolbox from Matlab* [10], *MIR toolbox from Matlab* [11], *Marsyas* [12] and *MediaEval* [13].

In this work, the *Spotify API*, *jMIR* and *AcousticBrainz* libraries have been selected for analysis, taking into account their functional capabilities and the large reference documentation. These libraries can be considered as a starting point for the emotion recognition in music. For these libraries, those high-level features that allow direct identification of emotions in music have been selected. Low-level features have also been selected, which according to [1] can be used to infer emotions.

2.1   Spotify API

Spotify [7] is one of the main platforms for music reproduction. It has a large song repository in different genres and styles, which can be accessed online from a web environment, as from mobile applications. The *Spotify*'s recommender system and the way to classify music to facilitate access and searches are the most relevant features that have allowed the successful reception of users.

Among the various functionalities offered by *Spotify*, there is the possibility of using the services API [7]. This services API started with the *Echonest* project [14], that was absorbed by *Spotify* in 2014, changing some technical aspects of implementation and functionality, among the most significant, the functionality to load sound files disappeared. Nowadays, the *Spotify*'s API only allows to apply its services in songs that are in its repository, being this a big limitation for experimentation exercises.

Next, some of the more relevant functionalities are described:

- To facilitate the integration of web applications and mobile environments to *Spotify*'s services
- To access *Spotify*'s music catalog.
- To obtain information (*metadata*) in *JSON* format about artists, albums, and songs stored in *Spotify*'s catalog.
- Direct access to the playlist created by a user profile.

According to the reference manual presented in the *EndPointReference API* of *Spotify* [7], this library has defined an entity called *audio object features*, with a total of **18 features**. Among them, the most related to emotions in music, are presented in Table 1.

With respect to the recognition of music emotions, there is the possibility of extracting the *valence* and *energy* features. From the point of view of emotional models, this two features can be analyzed as a *arousal-valence* type coordinate [15], in such a way that the emotion can be located on a two dimensional plane, including its appreciation (positive or negative) and its intensity level.

Table 1. Some of the high level features extracted by *Spotify API.*

Feature	Description
Key	Song tonality identification
Mode	Song mode (major or minor) identification
Tempo	Associated with rhythm and song's speed. It allows to generate an estimate of beats per minute
Liveness	Allows to identify if it is a live song. Values closer to 1 indicate a higher chance the song is in live
Instrumentalness	Allows to identify if a song have vocal content. The closer its valor to 1 the higher the chance the song does not have vocal content
Energy	Represents intensity and activity level in the song. Values closer to 1 indicate higher intensity in the song
Valence	This feature is associated with the positive a song can be. Closer values to 1 determine positive emotions, meanwhile 0 indicate negative emotions

Regarding the application works, it stands out in [16] and [17] the use of the library *Echonest*, in its first development stages, for the recognition of emotions in audiovisual content, achieving the sound classification in a dimensional model (*arousal-valence*), with some particular adjustments that allow to recognize the following emotions: excited, happy, relaxed, sad, and angry. This model is used by a recommendation system, to facilitate the consumption of audiovisual content through an adaptive *streaming* strategy.

In [18] the library is used to extract audio features with which music is classified according to musical similarity between artists. This information is used by a recommendation system that also analyzes the context information and plots the location of each musical piece in a dimensional model of emotions (*arousal-valence*). In [19] the library is used to analyze the *beat synchronous* feature and generates an emotional classification of music, along with the processing of other features extracted with *Matlab*; the classification process involves the manual labeling of 1000 songs, and then each one of the songs is classified through a dimensional model (*arousal-valence*).

2.2 JMIR/JAUDIO

jMIR [20] is an open code software implemented in Java, that can be used for sound information recovery. It is integrated by a group of components that can be used together, if the experiment conditions allow it. Regarding the recovery of musical information, *jMIR* is constituted as a *framework*, considering its flexibility and the possibility of extension in its uses, in addition to the different components that integrate it an all its advanced functional capacity.

jAudio is one of the components that integrates *jMIR*, and it allows the extraction of sound features from a digital sound file. *jAudio* was designed to work directly with sound in a general way and, at the beginning, it did not implement any specific tool that would allow analyzing high-level musical features. Among the main advantages of *jAudio*, and its main functionalities, the following can be highlighted:

- It works as a local application, so there is no dependency on any type of communication medium.
- It allows to use extension and parameterization by the user. For example, it is possible to create additional sound features to those already defined by default, in order to expand the possibilities of experimentation.
- It is developed in *Java* and can be integrated with other applications.
- It allows to export the recognized features to an *XML* file with all the metadata associated to sound features. This format is interpreted by the different available modules in *jMIR*.
- It can be used together with *jSymbolic*, which is another module that integrates *jMIR*, and allows to analyze more specific features of the musical theory through symbolic information extracted from *MIDI* files.

To obtain emotional type classifications, musical genre and others, *jMIR* has the *ACE2* module that allows to define taxonomies and features, making possible to load in *ACE2* the results obtained with *jAudio* during the low-level features extraction process.

Each one of these results loaded in *ACE2* are considered as an instance, and subsequently various classification models can be applied, obtaining then high-level features that have been previously defined by the user.

jAudio allows the extraction of **26 main low-level features**, from which *metafeatures* can be defined. A *metafeature* is a feature designed by the user, that is calculated from the main features that *jAudio* can extract. In Table 2, some of the low-level features more related with the context of music and emotions are presented.

Table 2. Some of the low-level features extracted by *jAudio*

Feature	Description
Power spectrum	Allows to measure the song's intensity and activity. The signal magnitude is presented in decibels (Db). It is very related with the *energy* feature defined in other libraries
Beat histogram	From a histogram that represents rhythm regularity, the *tempo* of a song can be determined. Other features that allow to calculate the *beat Histogram* are: *Strongest Beat, Beat Sum, Strength of Strongest Beat* [8]. This feature allows to show the frequency with which a determined speed is presented in different moments of a song
Pitch	The frequency range obtained between song's *low pitch* and *high pitch* is a measure that serves as starting point to estimate the predominant note of the song, and with that the tonality and the mode are derived

jMIR also allows integrating classification models, which must be initially designed, and then proceed to load and train them through the *ACE2* component. For the specific case of *jAudio*, although it does not have an emotional classification model, the emotions can be analyzed from some of the low-level features, as the case of *Power spectrum* and *Beat histogram;* which allow to personalize the emotional classification of a song according to its speed and rhythm. There could also be proposed different *metafeatures* that relate *pitch* values, creating associations between tonal and rhythms features and emotions. The emotional classification model could be categorical or dimensional [15], depending largely of the annotation system that is selected to use. The model would need some mechanism to establish the emotional annotation process, and most likely, that mechanism should be implemented as an additional development with which *ACE2* must be integrated, or with any other extern library that allows classifications with predictive algorithms, as the ones used in machine learning techniques.

With respect to the application works, in [8] the *jMIR* functional capacity is described in great detail, in relation to *jAudio*, its broad scope in sound processing problems is a highlighted in a general way. In [2] *jSymbolic* is used to identify and interpret the timbre, rhythm, dynamic and melody. In this work, *jAudio* is used to recognize the *MFCC, Spectral Centroid, Spectral Flux* and *Zero Crossings* features. This work focuses on identifying the emotions in music from chords progression analysis, so that the tonality and mode of the song can be identified and, with that, the emotion can be inferred and placed inside a dimensional model (*arousal-valence*).

2.3 AcousticBrainz

AcousticBrainz [9] is a library whose main functionality is to facilitate the recovery of musical information about songs. *AcousticBrainz* is based on the functionalities offered by *Essentia toolkit* [21], generally include all the sound processing and analysis capacity. This project has been developed by the collaborative effort between the *Music Technology Group* from the *Universitat Pompeu Fabra* and the project *Music Brainz* [22].

AcousticBrainz have classified the features that can extract from a song in two fundamental categories: low-level and high-level. The low-level features include **31 acoustic, 9 rhythmic and 8 tonal descriptors**. In Table 3 shows of the most representative low-level features in the context of music.

Table 3. Some of the low-level features extracted by *AcousticBrainz*.

Feature	Description
Bpm	Associated to the song's rhythm and speed. It allows to generate an estimated of the beats per minute
chords_key	Song's tonality identification
chords_scale	Song's mode (major or minor) identification

AcousticBrainz works with computationally defined and trained models, so from low-level features these models can build high-level features that usually work as classifiers. In terms of high-level features, *AcousticBrainz* uses classification models that allow music to be classified according to various criteria, such as musical genre and emotions. Table 4 shows some of the most representative high-level features in the emotional context.

AcousticBrainz allows the identification of 4 basic emotions [24]: happy, aggressive, sad and relaxed. It is also possible to identify some additional features as with the acoustic, electronic and party case; which could be related with the emotions inside a classification and/or annotation process.

With regards to the *moods_mirex* features, the emotions included inside of each of the *clusters* [23] are detailed next:

- *Cluster 1*: passionate, enthusiastic, confident, bustling, noisy.
- *Cluster 2*: cheerful, animated, funny, sweet, kind/of good character.
- *Cluster 3*: Emotionally intelligent, touching, melancholic.
- *Cluster 4*: humorous, silly, corny, peculiar, capricious, ingenious, ironic.
- *Cluster 5*: aggressive, fervid, tense/anxious, intense, volatile, visceral.

Some works in which this library is applied are: in [25] for the classification of music by musical genre for a database of 120 songs, in [26] is used for the detection of 4 basic emotions through a categorical affective model that recognize emotions: happy, angry, sad, relaxed; additionally also the precision of the emotion recognition is validated, varying the features selection that are extracted and used in the classification model; and finally in [6] the library is used to detect the *valence* and *arousal* values in musical recordings, showing the importance of combining low-level features with high-level features to achieve better results in emotional classifications of music.

Table 4. Some of the high-level features extracted by *AcousticBrainz*.

Feature	Description
mood_happy	Classify the song by happiness emotion. The closer it is to 1 the higher the probability the song is classified with happy emotion
mood_aggressive	Classify the song by aggressiveness emotion. The closer it is to 1 the higher the probability the song is classified with aggressive emotion
mood_relaxed	Classify the song by relaxation emotion. The closer it is to 1 the higher the probability the song is classified with relaxed emotion
mood_sad	Classify the song by sadness emotion. The closer it is to 1 the higher the probability the song is classified with sad emotion
moods_mirex	Classify the song in one of the 5 predefined clusters for emotional state categories (mood) [23]
mood_acoustic	Classify the song in acoustic or not acoustic. The closer it is to 1 the higher the probability the song correspond an acoustic version
mood_electronic	Classify the song according its type of sound. The closer it is to 1 the higher the probability the song has an electronic type of sound
mood_party	Classify the song by type of activity: party. The closer it is to 1 the higher the probability the song classifies with party activity

3   Comparative Framework of Libraries

Table 5 presents a comparison between the three libraries selected in this article: *Spotify API*, *jAudio* and *AcousticBrainz*.

For this comparison, in addition to describing the general features indicated in Sect. 2, the most representative and common attributes in those libraries have been selected, as well as some additional attributes that are considered relevant in *MER* systems and that are mentioned in [27].

About the data presented in Table 5, it is important to highlight that:

- In a general way, high-level libraries have as main functionality the extraction of audio features, however, the quantity, diversity and level of classification (low-level or high-level) differ from one another.
- Some libraries work exclusively with low-level features, so that, they require prior knowledge about the analysis of digital signals, before design the high-level features to be calculated outside the library.
- Not all high-level libraries implement classification models. In some cases, the classifier system must be designed as extension of the libraries, as for example occurs with *jAudio*.
- Typically the high-level libraries use general emotional classification models (*GMER*) [27]. *GMER* consists in applied one same emotional classification of music for all users, and not a personalized classification for each user.
- The *fuzzy* type classification systems are used by some libraries, in some cases through *clusters*, indicating the level of belonging that a certain song has to each *cluster* [27]. Usually, a vector as [0.1, 0.3, 0.9, 0.1] is given as the classifier output, where each position in the vector is associated with a particular *cluster*, and each *cluster* contains a series of emotions.

Table 5. High-level libraries' comparative table

Attribute	Library		
	Spotify API	*jAudio*	*AcousticBrainz*
Type of recognized features	High-level (18)	Low-level (138)	Low-level (80) High-level (20)
Licensing model	Commercial	Free	Free
Results output format	JSON file	XML file	JSON file
Architecture	Cloud service	Local	Cloud service
Allows its extension and parameterization	✗	✓	✗
Allows to implement models for high-level features within the same library	✗	✓	✗
Easy to use (normal, intermediate, advanced)	Intermediate	Advanced	Intermediate
Classification affective model	Dimensional (1D)	✗	Dimensional (2D)
General emotional classification model (GMER)	✓	✓	✓
Recognized emotions	Energy, Valence	✗	Happy, relaxed, sad, aggressive 5 MIREX cluster
Emotional classification of music with fuzzy technique	✗	✗	✓
Recognize musical genre	✗	✗	✓
Recognize live songs	✓	✗	✗
Recognize instrumental songs	✓	✗	✓
Identify the voice by gender	✗	✗	✓
Identify the speed, Bpm	✓	✗	✓
Identify the tonality (Chord recognition)	✓	✗	✓
Identifies song's mode	✓	✗	✓

4 Conclusions and Future Work

The recovery of musical features from digital files implies a solution to the problem of extracting sound properties through libraries and content analyzers. The success of this extraction process depends largely on the effectivity of the internal techniques and the analysis of diverse low-level features combinations, to properly reconstruct high-level features. The high-level features are usually proposed as classification models, being the emotions classification in the music one of the model most used. This classification is complex, and in many cases it must be validated by experts who, through annotation or labeling, associate emotions with a determined song. Later, this manual classification is compared with the automatic classification from the high-level libraries, with the aim of analyzing the success rate, and then, trying to improve this rate using training and learning techniques.

This work has been focused on the classifications of emotions that can be detected through intrinsic music features, and not from the emotions perceived by the listener. For that, the functional capacity of some of the most used high-level libraries was described, and some works in which they have been applied were commented. In addition, a comparative study was carried out among those libraries that contrast their functionalities, including the intrinsic characteristics that they can recognize, the models used to obtain high level parameters and then, in particular, the relationship with the emotions that they can detect.

Based on the study performed, it could be said that although the *MER* libraries currently offer information of interest, *MER* systems are not yet sufficiently developed to offer a universal solution and provide a highly reliable entry for the recommendation systems.

The comparative study developed between the *Spotify API, jAudio* and *AcousticBrainz* libraries is a first step to analyze the musical parameters that are related with emotions. In the future, it is pretended to formulate a classification model that can be used by a recommender system to suggest the listener musical pieces according to the emotion that is intended to transmit. Additionally, it also is pretended to study some additional attributes to the ones verified in Table 5, and that also are not supported by any of the libraries included in this work. The objective of that revision will be to analyze how the attributes mentioned in [27] can improve the emotional classification of music.

Acknowledgment. This work has been partially financed by the Spain Government through the contract TIN2015-72241-EXP.

References

1. Sloboda, J.A.: La mente musical: La psicología cognitiva de la música., Madrid (2012)
2. Cho, Y.-H., Lim, H., Kim, D.-W., Lee, I.-K.: Music emotion recognition using chord progressions. In: 2016 IEEE International Conference on Systems, Man and Cybernetics (SMC), pp. 002588–002593. IEEE, Hungary (2016). https://doi.org/10.1109/SMC.2016.7844628
3. Kim, Y.E., et al.: Music emotion recognition : a state of the art review. In: Information Retrieval, pp. 255–266 (2010)
4. Pouyanfar, S., Sameti, H.: Music emotion recognition using two level classification. Proc. Intell. Syst. 1–6 (2014). https://doi.org/10.1109/iraniancis.2014.6802519
5. Mckay, C.: Automatic Music Classification with jMIR, jmir.sourceforge.net (2010)
6. Grekow, J.: Audio features dedicated to the detection of arousal and valence in music recordings. In: 2017 IEEE International Conference on Innovations in Intelligent Systems and Applications (INISTA), pp. 40–44. IEEE, Gdynia (2017). https://doi.org/10.1109/inista.2017.8001129
7. Spotify: Spotify Developer API. https://developer.spotify.com/

8. McEnnis, D., McKay, C., Fujinaga, I., Depalle, P.: JAUDIO: a feature extraction library. In: Proceedings of the International Conference on Music Information Retrieval, pp. 600–603 (2005)
9. Music Technology Group, U.P.F: AcousticBrainz. https://acousticbrainz.org/
10. Cabrera, D., Ferguson, S., Schubert, E.: PsySound3: software for acoustical and psychoacoustical analysis of sound recordings. In: Display, P. (ed.) Proceedings of the 13th International Conference on Auditory Display, pp. 356–363, Canada (2007)
11. Lartillot, O., Toiviainen, P., Eerola, T.: A matlab toolbox for music information retrieval. In: Preisach, C., Burkhardt, H., Schmidt-Thieme, L., Decker, R. (eds.) Data Analysis, Machine Learning and Applications, pp. 261–268. Springer, Heidelberg (2008). https://doi.org/10.1007/978-3-540-78246-9_31
12. Tzanetakis, G., Cook, P.: MARSYAS: a framework for audio analysis. Organised Sound **4**, S1355771800003071 (2000). https://doi.org/10.1017/S1355771800003071
13. Soleymani, M., Aljanaki, A., Yang, Y.-H.: DEAM: MediaEval Database for Emotional Analysis in Music, pp. 3–5 (2016)
14. Tristan, J., Brian, W.: Echonest. http://the.echonest.com/
15. Russell, J.A.: A circumplex model of affect. J. Pers. Soc. Psychol. **39**, 1161–1178 (1980). https://doi.org/10.1037/h0077714
16. Solarte, L., Sánches, M., Chanchí, G.E., Duran, D., Arciniegas, J.L.: Dataset de contenidos musicales de video basado en emociones Dataset of music video content based on emotions (2016)
17. Chanchí, G.E.: Arquitectura basada en contexto para el soporte del servicio de vod de iptv móvil, apoyada en sistemas de recomendaciones y streaming adaptativo (2016)
18. Andjelkovic, I., Parra, D., O'Donovan, J.: Moodplay. In: Proceedings of the 2016 Conference on User Modeling Adaptation and Personalization - UMAP 2016, pp. 275–279. ACM Press, Canada (2016). https://doi.org/10.1145/2930238.2930280
19. Soleymani, M., Caro, M.N., Schmidt, E.M., Sha, C.-Y., Yang, Y.-H.: 1000 songs for emotional analysis of music. In: York, A.N. (ed.) Proceedings of the 2nd ACM International Workshop on Crowdsourcing for Multimedia - CrowdMM 2013, pp. 1–6. ACM Press, Barcelona (2013). https://doi.org/10.1145/2506364.2506365
20. JMIR: JMIR Audio Utilities. http://jmir.sourceforge.net/index_jAudio.html
21. Music Technology Group U.P.F: Essentia. http://essentia.upf.edu/documentation/
22. Kaye, R.: Musicbrainz. https://musicbrainz.org/
23. Hu, X., Downie, J.S.: Exploring mood metadata: relationships with genre, artist and usage metadata. In: Proceedings of 8th International Conference on Music Information Retrieval ISMIR 2007, pp. 67–72 (2007)
24. Laurier, C., Meyers, O., Serra, J., Blech, M., Herrera, P.: Music mood annotator design and integration. In: 2009 Seventh International Workshop on Content-Based Multimedia Indexing, pp. 156–161. IEEE (2009). https://doi.org/10.1109/cbmi.2009.45
25. Martins de Sousa, J., Torres Pereira, E., Ribeiro Veloso, L.: A robust music genre classification approach for global and regional music datasets evaluation. In: 2016 IEEE International Conference on Digital Signal Processing (DSP), pp. 109–113. IEEE, Beijing (2016). https://doi.org/10.1109/icdsp.2016.7868526
26. Grekow, J.: Audio features dedicated to the detection of four basic emotions. In: Saeed, K., Homenda, W. (eds.) Computer Information Systems and Industrial Management CISIM 2015, vol. 9339. Springer, Cham. https://doi.org/10.1007/978-3-319-24369-6_49
27. Yang, Y.-H., Chen, H.H.: Music Emotion Recognition. Taylor & Francis Group, Boca Raton (2011)

Integrating Collaborative Aspects in the Design an Interactive System in Teaching of Literacy to Children with Moderate Cognitive Impairment

Catalina Ruiz Vergara$^{(\boxtimes)}$ ⓘ, Sandra Patricia Cano Mazuera ⓘ,
and Alvaro Felipe Bacca Maya ⓘ

Research Group LIDIS, Universidad San Buenaventura Cali, Cali, Colombia
catalinaruizv@gmail.com, sandra.cano@gmail.com,
afbaccam@usbcali.edu.co

Abstract. This research is presented to develop an interactive system integrating collaborative aspects, which can support in teaching of literacy as well as encouraging teamwork and enrichment of learning processes following a teaching method called ABCD-Spanish (in Spanish ABCD-Español) applied in children with moderate cognitive disabilities. The User Centered Design (UCD) methodology is applied to an interactive system that involves physical and digital elements in an interactive way, which can motivate to the child during the learning process, as well as provide constant feedback on the achievements obtained and the things that should be improved. This methodology guides the design according to the information obtained from the user, this makes the person the center of the design process. This project is presented like an inclusion opportunity for a group of people who deserve a quality education too. This research shows how the technology can be a tool to create new options and opportunities for everybody.

Keywords: Moderate cognitive impairment · Collaborative learning
ABCD-Español method · Literacy

1 Introduction

Disability refers to the existence of a limited condition due to some type of problem that the person may present, be it physical or mental. The disability is a deficiency that limits the ability to perform one or several activities that are considered part of everyday life [1]. The disability can be categorized in 4 levels, such as: mild, moderate, profound and severe. People with moderate cognitive impairment usually reflect an IQ between 35 to 50 [2], which are the ones that work for this research proposal.

There is a very wide range of people with different disabilities. However, the technology offers unlimited opportunities for these people with special needs in education, employment and social environments [3]. Children with moderate cognitive impairment that have intellectual disability present a slow and limited development in cognitive processes as, attention or memory both short and long term [4].

© Springer Nature Switzerland AG 2019
V. Agredo-Delgado and P. H. Ruiz (Eds.): HCI-COLLAB 2018, CCIS 847, pp. 169–183, 2019.
https://doi.org/10.1007/978-3-030-05270-6_13

These children are characterized in that the learning pace is slow in comparison to a child or under normal conditions. Therefore, they require accompaniment for the realization of certain activities; have difficulty in developing skills in relationship to language and social behavior in general, among other aspects. This calls for contemplating different strategies to improve their learning [5, 6]. Teachers seek methodology for children to access knowledge, just as work towards that as technology to suit their needs. Disabled people constitute the group that has history of exposure to the consequences of segregation and exclusion [6].

Intellectual disability in people has difficulties in developing activities both socially and educationally and staff. These people tend to benefit from low - skilled jobs and under the supervision of others. They can have autonomy to the self - care and travel, but their conceptual skills develop slowly. However their communication is efficient. People with this disability establish relationships with the environment and with outsiders, can take responsibility for their own decisions and participate in social life, although with help and with a prolonged period of learning.

On the other hand, an interactive system where integrates collaborative aspects implies to take into account concepts related with collaborative learning. Collaborative learning refers to the activity developed by small groups in the classroom. Within each team, students exchange information and work on a task until all members have understood and finished it, developing skills, attitudes and values, such as: ability to analyze and synthesize, communication skills, collaborative attitude, listen, tolerance, respect and order, among others [7]. Those systems that act as interconnection between people and favoring the realization of tasks and scope of the objectives it is what is called Interactive Systems [8].

The paper is structured as follows. Section 1 is described a set of related works with the research proposed. Section 2 describes main problems that have children with moderate cognitive impairment. Section 3 is briefly described some concepts related with this research. Section 4 a proposal presented following the user centered design methodology for the interactive system design. Finally, Sect. 5 a set of conclusions and future work.

2   Problem

Nowadays, the Institute Tobías Emanuel in Cali, Colombia has children with cognitive impairment (moderated and profound), which has been incorporated in a reading and writing methodology for almost two years called ABCD-Español, proposed by González [9].

Initially, this methodology was designed to alphabetize adults. However, has been implemented with children without disabilities with very good results. ABCD-Spanish (In Spanish ABCD-Español) is incorporated in a physical game, which is composed by a physical board, 49 cards and 10 templates, which the templates has color drawing and without color, and a set of words that it is learned by level.

The board game is guided by a teacher, who gives the respective instructions of what should be done. ABCD-Español [10] is worked in groups from three to four students, encouraging teamwork by supporting to realize the activities without competition and with respect between each one turns.

Institute Tobías Emanuel has decided to implement this game and apply the *teaching of reading and writing for children with moderate cognitive impairments* methodology. However, this implies that the different elements that compound this methodology are not designed directly to children with these conditions, which represents a problem for development, implementation and adaptation of it.

Initially, the problem begins from the fact that the game does not involves Information and Communication Technologies (ICTs), this represents the lack of different levels of interaction as automatic feedback. On the other hand, the demand of the game can sometimes exceed the abilities of children according to their condition, that is, if a game is not created and designed to meet the specific needs of a person. In this case a child with cognitive impairment, the game has not enough visual support, which makes it hard to be understand. Also the vocabulary that makes part of the teaching methodology involves words that children do not use commonly within the jargon they handle, so it can cause a greater difficulty to comprehension due complex explanations to make them understand words such as: hammer, flasks, tricycle, skulls among others.

For their condition, the dependence of the students' on a teacher who manage the activity and give them the instructions, are much greater than it would be for people who do not have cognitive disability. This is considered as part of the problem to be described because the methodology does not come with a tool that plays the role of the instructor. Is here when is necessary to bring a possible solution.

This project is proposed as a continuation of a project that was developed by a students group at Universidad San Buenaventura Cali, Colombia in the Multimedia Engineering program [11], whose contribution was to generate a mobile application for the physical game ABCD-Español. The recognized problem is about the development or implementation of the application specifically because the actual levels of the physical game present a degree of complexity greater than the real capacity of assimilation of learning those children with cognitive disabilities have.

The proposed application in the same way does not represent a tangible solution for the independence of children with respect to the person who gives the conditions of play. Also is considered necessary to improve the system of awards and recognition of children already existing in the application.

At the same time, it is necessary to find a complementary activity that allows preserving the collaborative learning methodology used in the physical game for the development and learning of others areas in the children educational context with interactive technologies. Therefore, it is wanted to provide a solution to the identified problems, and giving continuity to the improvement and compliance of the particular requirements and own needs at Institute Tobías Emanuel.

3 Background

3.1 Moderate Cognitive Impairment

Children with moderate cognitive impairment have specific educational objectives, but during his learning processes it suffers adaptations to meet specific needs that ensure an enable the best environment for their participation [12].

Nowadays, the technology has accepted the challenge to create or provide techniques necessary for children with special educational needs. Those children can have access to education and optimum learning. Some research has been done where information technologies (ICTs) can be an alternative of support in the education processes. A project called Divermates [13] is aimed at children with Down Syndrome and pretends to be a didactic tool that brings knowledge of mathematics to children and teachers. Divermates, consists of a blackboard that consists of a blackboard that allows to write numbers and contains an eraser that fulfills its function similar as over paper, helping children to have a better comprehension of what he is doing.

This project comes with an automatic diagnosis of errors, which allows to categorize them starting from a base table which contains the type of errors that can be committed by the child, allowing to formulate methods to eradicate them. Finally, it also includes a self-learning system where exist enough feedback to improve child autonomous learning and knowledge acquiring towards what needs to be improved.

In other research proposed by Durango et al. [14], uses real objects for the development of therapies. The methodology is made in such way that the child can interact with objects. The interactive system also is directed towards children with special needs, and is used for therapists for the association of various real elements with their respective graphic representation in favor of providing children a tool to learn a new and alternative communication system.

The interactive system was design in the "Center for child development and early care (CDIAT for their Spanish initials)" context, where a pilot program test was done with children with some type of cognitive disability such as: specific language impairment, autism spectrum disorder or attention deficit, giving favorable results regarding the agility with which the children achieve the learning objectives. Which in this case is the association between real and tangible fruits with their graphic representation through an interactive panel. For this, the child uses a basic bracelet made by aluminum foil and Velcro which provides a closed electrical circuit between fruit and Arduino.

On the other hand, Lozano et al. [15], involves two interaction techniques: Co-Brain *Training* and *TraInAb*. These techniques are based on tangible user interfaces, designed under NFC (Near Field Communication) technology. These two techniques of interaction involve giving physical form to digital information. This is why they are said to be a combination of hardware and software elements that provide a way allowing users to carry out a single task. The goal is to simulate the way in which users usually works in their casual environment, which is to concentrate on a particular task and interact with everyday objects within their space.

The system proposed by Lozano et al. [15] aims to provide simple and novel interaction mechanisms for distributed environments. The use of tangible interaction must be simple and intuitive, using common elements that could be easily assimilated by the users and without previous knowledge of the system or used devices to use it.

Co-Brain Training [16], is an interactive and collaborative game based on a distributed and tangible interface in order to support cognitive formation. In the other hand, **TraInAb** [17], is an interactive and collaborative game designed to stimulate people with intellectual disabilities. In both projects, users can interact with the system through everyday objects, such as: cards, toys, coins, among others. The only condition is to carry and move the tangible object or interface to the mobile device.

Finally, a project by Universidad de San Buenaventura students from Cali, Colombia called ABCD-Español [11] as degree work in the Multimedia engineering program. Based in a tangible game with the same name created by Javier González [9]. Integrates some of the original levels, this levels contains a set of images or words that the children must associate depending in their relationship: image to image, image to word or word to word. However, the interaction is completely digital and there isn't a collaborative work.

3.2   Collaborative Learning

Collaborative learning (CL) refers to the activity of small groups developed in the classroom. Although CL is more than just teamwork from students, the idea behind it is simple: students form "small teams" after receiving instructions from the teacher, within each students exchange information and work in a task until all its members have understood and finished it, learning through collaboration [18].

CL is not just a set of steps to work in an orderly manner in a group, is much more than that, is a philosophy of life in which participants are clear that the whole of the group is more than the sum of its parts. However this learning is characterized by the autonomy with which each student achieves the activities. At the same time, it allows the development of skills, attitudes and values. For example: capacity for analysis and synthesis, communication skills, collaborative attitude, willingness to listen, tolerance, respect and order. It is precisely in this aspect that lies the benefit that students receive from this learning methodology, because along with the academic knowledge they obtain, there are linked a series of elements that are also important in the training process.

Among the existing strategies for collaborative learning, the following should be mentioned: The solution of cases, method of work by projects, learning based on a problem, analysis and discussion in groups and debates [19]. However, what is still disturbing in collaborative learning is how to take into account two roles in the learning process, (1) learning outcomes that can be obtained, and (2) capacity of each activity.

Finally, it is important to have in mind that collaborative learning considers the Piaget [19] and Vygotsky [20] theories. Piaget is the interaction of the participants, since the participant says things that can be used for cognitive restructuring. While, Vygotsky is the interaction between the social and the cognitive development of the individual, sustaining in this aspect the theory on "Zone of Proximal Development".

Some aspects of learning collaborative proposed by [21] as:

(a) *Situation* is related with the level of collaboration
(b) *Interactions*, which there are strategies that can involve more collaboration into group
(c) *Mechanisms*, is related with learning mechanisms being more intrinsically collaborative
(d) *Learning Effects* concerning how to measure the effects of collaborative learning participate in the terminological wilderness of this field.

Actually, Institute Tobias Emanuel implements the methodology of collaborative learning. In classrooms, respect for peers, leadership, teamwork, maintaining discipline and order, tolerance, creativity and willingness of children and the constant support between them are essential.

4 Proposal

The design of this interactive system follows the User-Centered Design methodology. Following the phases, as: (1) definition of the user requirements/analysis of the user profile; (2) Design of physical and digital interaction; (3) Development and (4) Evaluation.

4.1 Participants

The participants are five (5) children from Institute Tobías Emanuel between ages of 9 to 16 years of age, diagnosed with moderate cognitive impairment. For the selection of these children, were taken three children who are in the learning process of the ABCD-Español method, therefore their level of literacy is very low, which one of them has Down syndrome. A fourth child whose level of literacy is high but learned with other method, so he does not know the physical game ABCD-Español. Finally, a fifth child with a high level of literacy who learned with the ABCD-Español method.

4.2 Requirements and Analysis

A first approach was made by attending a writing and reading class where children use the ABCD-Spanish physical game, as shown in Fig. 1. The interaction consists of 3 steps, these are: (1) children work collaborating with between them with the ABCD-Spanish game, where the teacher appoints a group leader, who will have the function of coordinating the turn of each child. (2) Once the whole board is constructed with the cards, the teacher begins to select a set of activities, which consists of looking for the formation of two-syllables that form in one of the cards. Finally, in (3) the children come to the board, where they must draw the word that the teacher says out loud.

It was observed that there is an active participation of all children, who work collaboratively in groups of four or five children. In addition, the teacher organizes the work tables according to the level of scope of each child, thus classifying the activities they must perform. Also, it is observed that sometimes, the game is performed

Fig. 1. Direct Observation of the ABCD-Español method into the classroom at the Institute Tobías Emanuel, Cali-Colombia.

mechanically; since the structural basis of the game is repetitive It is also observed that some children already know by heart the location of the cards or the drawings in the booklet.

The main objective of the board is that the student can develop the capacity to perceive iconic representations and assimilate reality. During the method, teacher use teaching strategies involving multimedia technologies, where is showed multimedia content to that child can relate with viewed word through of drawing and real environment. For example the xylophone is known because the teacher has shown them a multimedia content (video or image) of how the xylophone works. When they achieve to associate the image with the real object is when they memorize the meaning. They also reinforce it by drawing the object in their notebooks as a strategy to memorize the meaning of the word.

Also, it has been identified that age is not very important, since you can have children from 9 years up to 16 years old in the same room, but indistinctly the age, some may have a higher writing and reading proficiency level or lower than others. However, all have been diagnosed with moderate cognitive disability. Another important aspect is that the child or adolescent with moderate cognitive disability has a physical appearance similar to a child of seven years depending on age. Therefore, no analysis can be made considering age. In addition, each of the activities carried out between them, cannot compete, since not all have the same rhythm of learning, what is ultimately sought is for everyone to work regardless of the time it takes.

From the research made by Cano et al. [15], some adjustments are made in the amount of cards and game levels according to the physical board, and it is decided to perform a following evaluation with the children to observe their interaction (Fig. 2).

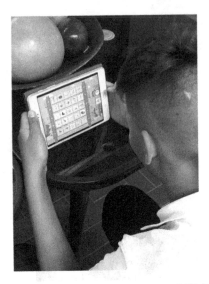

Fig. 2. Evaluation with the digital game ABCD-Español.

The evaluation applied to children consists of 6 questions, which are:

1. Have you understood the activity you did?
2. Was the activity clear? (In relation to how to execute the activity)
3. Do you feel that you have made a lot of effort to carry out the activity?
4. Did you enjoy the experience?
5. Did you have concentration when doing the activity?
6. Have you clearly understood the activity? (Global understanding of concepts)

Figure 3 shows results of evaluation applied, where it shows that the child one responding to questions 2 and 6 shows greater dissatisfaction. These questions correspond to the clarity and understanding of the activity. This case in particular concerns a child diagnosed with Down syndrome, his level of writing and reading proficiency is considerably low, which makes his answers consistent with the difficulties he expressed at the time of performing the activity.

The child two, as can be seen in the graph, shows greater dissatisfaction in question number 5. In this question it was evaluated how much concentration the child had when carrying out the activity. In this case it is a child who has a high level of writing and reading proficiency, which facilitated the execution of the game and did not require greater concentration.

In the Fig. 3 shows that the child three obtained a greater dissatisfaction in question 2. As mentioned previous corresponds to the understanding level of the activity. Within his response he expressed confusion in the way he should interact with the digital game. Therefore, the importance of adjusting the tutorial, where it shows an animation of the activity that the child must make. Finally the children four and five agree in expressing dissatisfaction in questions 2 and 6. The child four presents a low level of writing and reading proficiency, this justifies the difficulty he presented to perform the

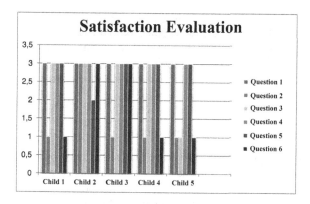

Fig. 3. Results of Evaluation with ABCD-Español digital game.

activity. However, the child five has a high level of reading and writing, which validated the expressed dissatisfaction. Within his answers and as you can see in the graph he states that he has made a very big effort for the development of the activity, this because he has vision problems and had a considerable visual exhaustion, here the importance of covering all the needs that these children manifest and how they influence the positive or negative performance and the child's understanding of the development of an activity.

In the evaluation applied to children was obtained the following observations:

1. The game has an animation at the beginning, where it explains how to interact with the Tablet. However, most of the children were confused with the interaction, since at the beginning they tried to click on the card before dragging it and taking it to the place where the other one was.
2. The drag event takes a lot of effort at the beginning.
3. The letters size and the board must be larger than the one presented since many of the children need glasses. The case was evidenced with two children who have vision problems and were visually exhausted when performing the evaluation since it was difficult for them to read.
4. To Improve feedback when doing the activity correctly or incorrectly.
5. For children with low literacy level, the third level took them more difficulty, so they did not finish it.

Observations obtained it is decided to adjust the degree of difficulty of each of the levels, so that it adapts to the real capacity of the children. The existing levels will be modified in such a way that they keep the same structure as the ABCD-Español physical game methodology. The levels are: (1) association image - image, (2) association image - image, where they are in random positions different from those of the physical board. (3) association text - text. Finally a level (4), where you must associate two syllables within a word.

To get better understanding and assimilation of information in children, the adjustments will be made in relation to colors and typography used, so that it is large and legible, the drawings on the other hand in a large and simple size, the vocabulary of easy association to everyday life, retaining the one used in the original game.

However, collaborative aspects aren't integrated into a purely digital application. Therefore, in the different observations that were made in the first stages of the methodology, it is detailed that children interact in a group with the physical ABCD-Spanish board, where one of them fulfills the role of leader, who is the person who must coordinate the turn for each child to interact with the physical board, and in turn approve if it has been done correctly.

4.3 Integrating the Collaborative Interaction

To involve the collaborative part, a physical interaction must be included that allows the child to supply the need for dependence on the teacher as a provider of the game instructions. Therefore, the proposal is aimed at proposing a physical device that randomly generates activities implemented with the bisyllabic method. These activities consist of the combination of vowels or consonants that the child must search within a word. This contribution is given after observing how the teacher must constantly generate instructions for the students about the activities to be carried out. Therefore, the design of a physical device is developed as an alternative support for the teacher, considering that the child who has the role of the leader can coordinate the management of this device. At the same time, the way in which this device is designed could be entrusted to the child who is the leader in the group of children who work collaboratively.

On the other hand, the electronic device showed in Fig. 4, has hardware elements, an Arduino UNO, red and green diodes, a display and two buttons. The child will be able to interact with this device through the buttons. The first button will be the one that allows the device to generate combinations of vowel or consonant and vowel letters. Following this, a red light bulb will be activated parallel to the moment in which the combination of the syllables appears on the display. The red light indicates that the child is in a position to look for the words that contain that syllable within the application and make their respective association.

Fig. 4. Electronic device that generates playing conditions. (Color figure online)

Once the child finishes the search, proceed to press the second button. This will activate the green light bulb on behalf of which the activity has been completed and will cause the device to emit an alarm that will serve as a reference for the teacher.

In the design of this device, the information is easy to perceive through the display that shows the respective combinations of the letters without generating any confusion. The other elements that make up the device, i.e. the bulbs, buttons and speaker are easy to use and intuitive and the information they generate is easily assimilated. At the same time, knowing the motor difficulties that children can present, a design is generated using a material resistant to falls and easy to handle. So, the box of the device is made of wood.

Considering the physical interaction, the aim is to strengthen the child's motivation and give him an accurate feedback by positively performing the collaborative activity. Therefore, it is decided to award scores when they correctly carry out the activity supported by an award system with tangible cards (Fig. 5), which will be given to each child once the activity has been realized correctly, and in this way is incentive his performance.

Fig. 5. "Good Work" Card, Physical award card to be included in the digital game ABCD-Español

As a complementary activity to integrate the collaborative aspects, a physical puzzle is proposed (Fig. 6), which can be assembled by children in the work group. In this way, it is possible to preserve the collaborative part by encouraging the achievement of a common objective. This puzzle contains an image that contextualizes each of the words of the game in a real common space, achieving a better association of the vocabulary learned in daily life.

4.4   Development

The process of interaction with all the physical and digital elements involved is as follows:

1. The electronic device must be started by each group leader.
2. The button must be pressed to generate the bisyllabic words to be made, at this point each child begins to search within the physical board the words that contain said bisyllabic.

3. Once the words are found, the child will press the button again to notify the teacher or the children of the same group that has finished their activity. Therefore, the leader child, who is responsible for this action, is who will coordinate with the teacher if the activity has been carried out correctly. The process continues until the teacher finishes the activity.

An activity is also done as a complement so that the children can interact collaboratively through a physical puzzle (Fig. 6), where the children must solve it. Each of the words that involve the game ABCD-Español, are inside the puzzle.

Fig. 6. Puzzle game ABCD-Español

In order for each child to work independently, the digital application is used, where some activities are carried out involving associations of the type: image-image, image-text and text-text. Figure 7 shows the elements that allow working the collaborative part with the children; the electronic device and the puzzle are observed.

5   Conclusions and Work Future

The design of the interactive system fulfills the stated objective by involving technology as a means by which the inclusion of people with moderate cognitive disabilities in the field of education can be made.

The possibility of continuous improvement in the application, and the possibilities of interaction with the game that the child may have, motivates their learning process and encourages their autonomy.

With the completion and design of the puzzle, the children achieve a common goal, which reflects the value of group work and the sum of individual contributions.

The proposed electronic device represents an opportunity for greater autonomy of children in the face of the need for a tutor who always considers the conditions of the game.

Fig. 7. Physical elements of interaction

The design of the proposed award cards is a tool that encourages and motivates the learning process of children, achieving healthy competition and a greater effort to achieve the objectives.

It is intended to continue in the process of constant improvement of the proposed collaborative interactive system, so that a more accurate approach to the original Spanish ABCD game is achieved. Likewise, as a contribution to the Tobias Emanuel institution, achieve all the proposed objectives to meet the needs and requirements of the methodology implemented for the teaching of reading and writing to children with moderate cognitive disabilities.

As future work, the functional prototype of the electronic device and the collaborative activity with the puzzle must be evaluated. Also, to identify some metrics that allow evaluating the collaborative aspects.

Acknowledgments. To the Tobias Emanuel Institution.

References

1. Licona Hernández, J.M.: Los derechos humanos de las personas con discapacidad. Revista Quórum legislativo **89**, 123 (2007)
2. Psicología y Mente. Tipos de discapacidad intelectual - Diferentes grados de discapacidad. https://psicologiaymente.net/clinica/tipos-discapacidad-intelectual. Accessed 20 Feb 2018
3. González, C.S., Bruno, A., Moreno, L., Noda, M., Aguilar, R., Muñoz, V.: Teaching mathematics to children with down's syndrome. In: Artificial Intelligence (2003)

4. Matices en educación especial. Características - Necesidades educativas especiales asociadas a discapacidad intelectual. http://maticesenee.blogspot.com.co/2013/04/necesidades-educativas-especiales.html. Accessed 20 Feb 2018
5. Definición ABC - Tu diccionario hecho fácil. Definición de lectoescritura. http://www.definicionabc.com/comunicacion/lectoescritura.php. Accessed 20 Feb 2018
6. Ministerio de Educación Gobierno de Chile, Unidad de Educación Especial. Orientaciones para dar respuestas educativas a la diversidad y las necesidades educativas especiales. Atenas Ltda., Santiago de Chile (2011)
7. Investigación e innovación educativa - Centro virtual de técnicas didácticas del instituto tecnológico y de estudios superiores de Monterrey. (México 2010). ¿Qué es aprendizaje colaborativo? http://sitios.itesm.mx/va/dide2/tecnicas_didacticas/ac/qes.htm. Accessed 20 Feb 2018
8. Asociación Interacción persona - ordenador (AIPO Blog). Sistemas Interactivos e Interacción Persona Ordenador. Sistemas interactivos e IPO. http://www.aipoblog.es/2013/01/sistemas-interactivos-e-interaccion.htm. Accessed 20 Feb 2018
9. Gonzalez, J.: ABCD-Español: el juego de la lectoescritura. Revista Semana (2002). http://www.semana.com/opinion/articulo/abcdespanol-juego-lectoescritura/49579-3. Accessed 15 Sept 2016
10. Cerebro, corazón y manos: Pensar, sentir y hacer. abcd Español el juego de la lectoescritura (2016). http://javiergonzalezquintero.blogspot.com.co/2016/01/abcdespanol-el-juego-de-la.html. Accessed 20 Sept 2016
11. Cano, S., Palta, A., Posso, F., Peñeñory, V., Collazos, C.: Towards designing a serious game for literacy learning in children with moderate cognitive impairment. In: Proceedings XVIII International Conference on Human Computer Interaction (2017)
12. Cegarra Andrés, F., García Vilar, G.: Intervención educativa en el alumnado con discapacidad intelectual (pdf). http://www.psie.cop.es/uploads/murcia/Intervención%20Discap%20Intelectual.pdf. Accessed 03 Apr 2017
13. González, C.S., Bruno, A., Moreno, L.: Learning mathematics in the diversity: play wit divermates. In: Post-proceedings of the International Conference on Technology, Training and Communication, vol. 361 (2007)
14. Durango, I, Carrascosa, A., Penichet, V.M.R., Gallut, J.A.: Tangible serious games with real objects to support therapies for children with special needs. In: Interaction 2015, Proceedings of the XVI International Conference on Human Computer Interaction, Article No. 41 (2015)
15. Lozano, M.D., de la Guia, E., Penichet, V.M.R.: Interacting with tangible objects in distributed settings. In: DUI 2014 Proceedings of the 2014 Workshop on Distributed User Interfaces and Multimodal Interaction, pp. 15–18 (2014). https://doi.org/10.1145/2677356.2677659
16. de la Guía, E., Lozano, M.D., Penichet, V.M.R.: Tangible and distributed user interfaces to improve cognitive abilities within people affected by Alzheimer's disease. In: DUI 2013: 3rd Workshop on Distributed User Interfaces: Models, Methods and Tools. In Conjunction with ACM EICS 2013, London, UK 24 June 2013. ISBN-10: 84- 616-4792-0, ISBN-13: 978-84-616-4792-7
17. de la Guía, E., Lozano, M.D., Penichet, V.M.R.: TrainAb: a solution based on tangible and distributed user interfaces to improve cognitive disabilities. In: Proceedings of CHI EA 2013, pp. 3039–3042. ACM (2013). ISBN: 978-1-4503-1952-2, https://doi.org/10.1145/2468356.2479605

18. Martha, V., Fidel, M.: PAIEP. Estrategias didácticas para el aprendizaje colaborativo (pdf) http://acreditacion.udistrital.edu.co/flexibilidad/estrategias_didacticas_aprendizaje_colaborativo.pdf. Accessed 25 Jan 2018

19. Piaget, J.: Play, dreams and imitation in childhood, New York (1962). https://doi.org/10.1002/1520-6807%28196604%293%3a2%3c189%3a%3aaidpits2310030222%3e3.0.co%3b2-z

20. Vygotsky, L.S.: Play and its role in the mental development of the child. In: Bruner, J.S., Jolly, A., Sylva, K. (eds.) Play: Its Role in Development and Evolution. Basic Books, New York (1997). https://doi.org/10.2753/rpo1061-040505036

21. Dillenbourg, P.: What do you mean by collaborative learning? In: Dillenbourg, P. (ed.) Collaborative learning: Cognitive and Computational Approaches, pp. 1–19. Elsevier, Oxford (1999)

Mobile Learning Applications: Exploring Location Sensing Mechanisms

Cecilia Challiol[1,2(✉)] ⓘ, Alejandra B. Lliteras[1,3] ⓘ,
and Silvia E. Gordillo[1,3] ⓘ

[1] UNLP, Facultad de Informática, LIFIA,
50 y 120 s/n, La Plata, Buenos Aires, Argentina
{ceciliac,lliteras,gordillo}@lifia.info.unlp.edu.ar
[2] CONICET, Buenos Aires, Argentina
[3] CICPBA, Buenos Aires, Argentina

Abstract. In this paper, we present an exploration of two location sensing mechanisms, such as QR codes and beacons, used in Location-based Learning Applications which are performed inside small indoor spaces (e.g. a classroom). The exploration of QR codes was carried out through an implementation of a Location-based Learning Application which was used by students between 7 and 11 years old inside of Primary Schools. Meanwhile, for the exploration of beacons, a functional prototype was made which was systematically tested by students of Faculty of Informatics of UNLP (Argentina). We analysed those characteristics that we have been learned related to how these mechanisms behave when they are used inside small indoor spaces because, in these cases, relevant places to provide learning contents are nearest from each other. We wish to create a discussion about the exploration of these two location sensing mechanisms. We expect that this discussion helps not only to design and develop Location-based Learning Applications, but also to improve authoring tools that are using to generate this kind of applications.

Keywords: Location-based Learning Applications · Sensing mechanisms
QR codes · Beacons · Learning content · Mobile learning · HCI

1 Introduction

Mobile Applications have been growing over the last years due to technological improvement [1]. Nowadays, there are different kinds of mobile applications, those that consider user's location to provide information or services according to his/her location are called Location-based Applications. In [2], this kind of applications is classified as: tour guides, learning tools, location-aware fiction and location-aware games. However, fictions or games also could be combined with learning (or educational) applications or tools. Different patterns to structure the content of these applications are described in [2]. Thus, each pattern provides to user different kind of interaction.

In Location-based Applications are defined relevant places (of a physical space) where users receive some kind of interaction [3]. In particular, Location-based Learning Applications provide, in these relevant places, learning content to students

V. Agredo-Delgado and P. H. Ruiz (Eds.): HCI-COLLAB 2018, CCIS 847, pp. 184–198, 2019.
https://doi.org/10.1007/978-3-030-05270-6_14

through their mobile devices. For example, a learning content could be a question [4]. Related to this kind of applications is involved location sensing mechanisms which allow to sense student's location. So, when a sensed location matches to a learning content, this content is provided to students.

Sensing mechanisms could be classified, for example, as direct or indirect [5], depending on whether they demand some sort of explicit users interaction. Direct mechanisms do not require any users interaction, for example GPS. However, indirect mechanisms require users interact in some way, as for example, QR codes [6] which need users read explicitly the code with their mobile devices. On the other hand, according to [1], contextual data (which include user's location) could be collected in different ways: physical sensors (e.g. GPS and QR code reader), digital sensors (as the calendar of mobile devices), social networks or be input manually by users. Note that, some of these ways of collect contextual data are direct while others are indirect (requiring some user interaction).

The goal of this paper is to present an exploration of two location sensing mechanisms, such as QR codes and beacons [7] (which make used of Bluetooth Low Energy -BLE- technology). These mechanisms in this exploration are used in Location-based Learning Applications which are performed inside small indoor spaces (e.g. a classroom). So, learning activities are carried out completely inside of a classroom. This means that relevant places to provide learning contents are nearest from each other. Note that, these activities are provided to students through Location-based Learning Applications. In this paper is analysed those characteristics that we have been learned related to how these mechanisms behave when they are used inside small indoor spaces. We wish to create a discussion about the exploration of these two location sensing mechanisms. We expects that this discussion helps not only to design and develop Location-based Learning Applications, but also to improve authoring tools that are using to generate this kind of applications.

The exploration of QR codes (indirect sensing mechanism) was carried out through an implementation of a Location-based Learning Application which was used by students between 7 and 11 years old inside of Primary Schools. We have considered that all learning tasks of this application are referred to curricular contents previously presented to students by their teachers. Meanwhile for the exploration of beacons (direct sensing mechanism), a functional prototype was made as part of *"Location-based Learning Activities"* project (in the context of *"Projects of Development and Innovation Applications with Students 2017"* of the Faculty of Informatics of UNLP, Argentina). This functional prototype was systematically tested by students who were participating of this project. In particular, this paper presents how these two sensing mechanisms behave when they are used inside a small indoor space, such as a classroom.

The paper is structured as follows. In Sect. 2, we describe some related works. In Sect. 3 is presented our exploration of two location sensing mechanisms when they are used inside small indoor spaces. Some discussion issues are described in Sect. 4. Conclusions and some future works are presented in Sect. 5.

2 Related Works

In this section some related works to the topic of this paper are presented. To help the reader, some specific characteristics of how location sensing mechanisms work are detailed below, especially when they are used from mobile applications. These mechanisms can be classified or grouped in different ways. According to [5], one way of grouping is if these are direct or indirect mechanisms. This kind of classification is related to interaction involved in each mechanism. Direct mechanisms do not require any users interaction, for example GPS. When a mobile application uses this kind of direct sensing mechanism to detect the user's location, it is "listening" for new sensing values; whenever a new value is detected, updated information is automatically provided to users (according to their new location). This kind of applications are known as context-aware mobile applications [2] which have to implement the behavior to react automatically to changes received by each sensing mechanism.

Indirect sensing mechanisms require users interaction in some way, as it is the case of QR codes [6] in which users read codes explicitly with their mobile devices. Mobile applications that use this kind of indirect sensing mechanism (to detect user's location) provide to users some way to interact with the application, in order to detect a new sensing value. For example, if QR codes are used to sense user's location, the mobile application should provide a way to access to a QR code reader (which should be previously installed on the mobile device). When a user reads a new code from this mobile application, a QR code reader opens; then the reader detects a new code, so, the application reacts by providing information or services. Thus, it can only be possible to detect a location changes when user reads a new QR code. Another example of indirect location sensing could be when users indicate where they are at each moment, for example, by choosing from a list of possible places. In this case, it can not be possible to detect location changes until user selects a new item from this list.

According to the description above, it can be notice how depending on the kind of sensing mechanism users receive different form of interaction from mobile applications. In direct mechanisms, there are not interventions required from users to sense their current location. This is one of the reasons why they are often more used due to facilitate how to users interact with the application. Below some location sensing mechanisms used in the area of learning are presented.

GPS massification has allowed emerging Location-based Learning Applications for outdoor spaces, for example, in the domain of natural sciences, some applications of this kind are described in [8]. In [9], augmented reality application is analysed in which locations are determined by printed symbols and natural markers. The authors mention some problems of these mechanisms, for example, how sunlight affects to detect natural markers. Another augmented reality application is presented in [10], but in this case inside of a museum where locations are determined by beacons. These beacons are strategically located in relevant places of the museum with considerable separation from each other to avoid signal overlapping. When this application detects that user is near to a one of these beacon, he/she receives augmented reality information related to that place. On the other hand, in [11] are shown Location-based Learning Applications for indoor and outdoor spaces. These applications use Google Map for outdoor spaces

[12] and GPS as a location sensing mechanism, while for indoor spaces are used static images and locations (for these spaces) are indicated manually by the students. That is to say, in [11] for the indoor spaces are using an indirect sensing mechanism; until students do not indicate where they are, the information related to their current location is not updated. So, the description mentioned above indicates Location-based Learning Applications could be use different types of sensing mechanisms to determine student's location, some direct and others indirect [5]. In fact, these applications could be evolve and change their sensing mechanisms over time. So, it depends on how they were initially designed, this evolution will have a minimal impact as mentioned in [13].

Teachers' participation [14] is fundamental for the design and creation of Location-based Learning Applications. According to this, in recent years has begun to be explored different approaches or tools to facilitate teachers' participation in this task. In [4], four phases related to Location-based Learning Applications are identified: conceptual design, development cycle, put into practice the development and put into practice's evaluation. For the conceptual design phase, in [4], a conceptual framework is proposed for co-design this kind of applications which is focused particularly on the reuse of both learning contents and relevant locations. This conceptual framework uses the vision of separation of concerns (used in Software Engineering) to address co-design, in which at least teachers and technology experts are involved. On the other hand, in [11] is proposed to design these applications using the puzzle metaphor. The pieces are built, and then there are converted to XML files [15] to generate functional applications. In [11] is describe how this metaphor is used and shown how to use the generated applications. The authors mention in [11] that metaphors, in general, are widely used in the area of Human-Computer Interaction (HCI) to be able to handle unknown contexts from known concepts. For this reason, the authors use puzzle metaphor.

Achieving teachers have total control to design and create this kind of applications requires having authoring tools (for example, applications or Web sites) which help them to integrate location sensing mechanisms [16] without demand technical knowledge thereof. That is to say, it would be desirable that these kind of authoring tools allow teachers to create a mobile learning application that uses, for example, GPS without needing to know technical details of it. In this case, authoring tools should handle all technical and packaging details to generate mobile applications. Thus, teachers should only focus on creating and defining relevant locations where they want students receive learning content. Then, this is taken by the authoring tool to generate mobile learning applications which students use later on their mobile devices.

In order to create authoring tools, in particular for Location-based Learning Applications, an exploration of sensing mechanisms is required to provide a solution that does not demand teachers to know technical details of these. In recent years different authoring tools have been emerging which give a high level of abstraction of technical details for different location sensing mechanisms. For example, in [16] an authoring tool is described which contains a catalogue of beacons. This make easier, for teachers, to associate learning content with them. Previously, beacons have been strategically placed in the physical space in order to avoid signals interfere with each other. Then, experts in technologies have measured all beacons' signal to achieve that the tool considers this information to facilitate teachers how to use them. So, authoring tool shows available beacons and teachers choose one of them to associate learning content. In this way learning contents are located. For this, teachers do not require to know any technical detail of the beacons. On the other hand, in [3] is presented SituAR which is a platform to create augmented reality content. Users are creators of their own stories and they do not require programming knowledge to generate them. This platform use GPS to associate location to each content. This association is not visible for the users. Every time user creates content, this is associated automatically with the current GPS location. Another authoring tool is SmartZoos [17] which allows designing content as modular open educational resource. Then, these resources are combined with location (latitude-longitude) which is obtained using a map. For this, SmartZoos provides Google maps which allow users to select relevant places in the physical space and associate them with content. This is used by SmartZoos to generate applications which make use of GPS as location sensing mechanism. On the other hand, in [18] an in-situ authoring tool for indoor-outdoor Location-based Learning Applications is presented. This tool defines learning contents and locations in a decoupled way, according to [4]. This information (learning contents and locations) are exported to XML files [15]. These files could be used to generate functional applications. The sensing mechanisms used by the tool defined in [18] are GPS and QR codes.

According to previous description about authoring tool, it could be appreciated that each of them focuses on some kind of sensing mechanisms. This is because of complexity of embedded sensing mechanisms (as part of tool) in a way that they do not require any type of technical expertise from users. To do that, these mechanisms should be explored enough, in order to understand how to use them in a simple way for any user. We hope that the exploration of sensing mechanisms presented in this paper would help to enhance authoring tools for this kind of applications.

3   Exploring Two Sensing Mechanisms in Location-Based Learning Activities Inside Small Indoor Spaces

In this section, we present an exploration of two location sensing mechanisms, such as QR codes and beacons. In particular, these mechanisms have been tested inside a small indoor space such as a classroom. The Learning Activity defined in [19] has been used for the exploration presented in this paper. This activity is composed of four tasks (three of collection and one of deposit) which have been designed for students between 7 and 11 years. Knowledge required to resolve these tasks are previously presented to students by their teachers because this knowledge is part of the curricular content of the course. So, one way to put this knowledge into practice was through these tasks. Each task presents some question to students. For collection tasks, students should pick concrete elements up that can be considered in response to a received question. Deposit tasks imply to put these collected elements on a container according to predominant type material with that each of them has been produced (e.g. paper, metal or plastic). In [19], this Learning Activity is defined to encourage reuse not only each task but also each location. In Fig. 1 is shown an example of collection task, its question, and its elements. Additionally, this task can be associated, in another layer, with a particular location of the physical space.

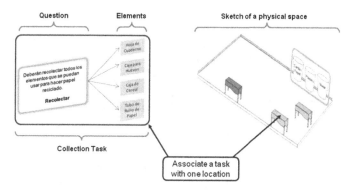

Fig. 1. A collection task associated with one location.

In the physical space visualized in Fig. 1, there are three relevant places related to collection tasks (tables). It also is shown a fourth relevant place related to a deposit task (containers). These places (locations) are defined independently of tasks which can be offered there. This allows reusing these places.

It should be noted that the Learning Activity presented in [19] is defined independently of the technological platform. So, it can be implemented using any sensing mechanism to determine student's location. That is, relevant places or locations are defined generically [13] in order to be combined with any location sensing mechanism. This allows that the same Learning Activity can be implemented with different sensing mechanisms. More details of how this Learning Activity was designed could be read in [19].

The Learning Activity mentioned above has been used as a base to implement a Location-based Learning Application and a functional prototype. The first one uses QR codes to sense the student's location while the second one uses beacons to do that.

Exploration performed related to these sensing mechanisms (QR codes and beacons) is described below. It should be noted that, in both cases, all relevant places (where questions of each task are provided) are inside a small indoor space. In particular, they are in the same classroom as is shown in Fig. 1.

3.1   Exploration of the Use of QR Codes in the Implementation of a Location-Based Learning Application

The exploration of QR codes (indirect sensing mechanism) was carried out through an implementation of a Location-based Learning Application which was used by students between 7 and 11 years old inside of Primary Schools. This application is called *"Aprendo Jugando"*. It should be noted that this application was implemented as a proof of concepts for validate a modeling approach proposed in [19]; this approach is for model location-based learning activities which consider concrete elements. Owing to *"Aprendo Jugando"* features, physical space requires to be configured previously because tables (with their elements) and containers need to be located in specific places before students start to use the application. This is shown in Fig. 2. Note that, tables have their concrete elements to be collected in each task.

Fig. 2. Physical space configuration for "*Aprendo Jugando*".

"*Aprendo Jugando*" was developed for Android version 4.0 and uses QR codes. On the one hand, these codes are used (for a group of students) to receive the question of a task (to collect or deposit). On the other hand, these codes are used (by this group) to indicate what concrete element is picked up in response to a collect task. That is, a group of students should read a QR code to receive a question and after that, they should read QR codes of concrete elements (see Fig. 3) to collect them. Collecting elements in this way produces that each of them is put in a virtual basket of the application. On the other side, a group should pick each concrete element (corresponding with the QR code read) up, and they put them in a physical basket. So, this means that virtual basket should reflect what a group has in their physical basket.

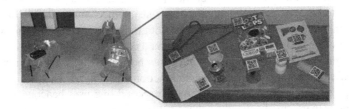

Fig. 3. Concrete elements of a collect task for "*Aprendo Jugando*".

Suppose, a group decide that a particular concrete element that was collected is not correct in order to respond to the question of their current task. If the group decides to return the collected element, then they should select this element from a list displayed on their mobile device, so, this indicates that they want to remove it from the virtual basket of collected elements. Then, they should touch the delete option. In this way, this element is removed from the virtual basket. In addition, the group has to find this concrete element inside their physical basket, and return it to their current task's table.

It should be noted that to perform a collection task, as mentioned above, a group should read the QR code of the element if they decide to collect it. However, to deposit an element into a container, a group should select an element from a list displayed on their mobile device, and also, they should pick this concrete element up from their physical basket. Then, they deposit it into a container which they think is appropriate. That is, deposit task does not involve to read the element's QR code. So, this works in a similar way to return an element because a group notes that this does not respond to their current task (as it is explained above).

According to the description above, it is noted that concrete elements were on the tables are moved (or transported) to some of the containers. Thus, every time a group finishes to use "*Aprendo Jugando*", physical space should be reconfigured as shown in Fig. 2.

In [19], authors describe how they have putted into practices of "*Aprendo Jugando*" in two primary schools. In this paper, these putting into practices will be analysed from the QR codes use perspective. It should be noted that each putting into practice was carried out with groups of three or four students. Each group have been formed freely among themselves and they had a single mobile device. The latter mentioned allows taking advantages of "face to face" collaboration to solve tasks [20]. This also allows establishing social interactions and thus favouring knowledge circulation for collaborative building of it [21].

During first putting into practice it was detected that first time that a group had to read a QR code, this was a complex action. This situation is due to the fact that use QR codes require a level of indirection to obtain a learning content. Reading a QR code involves a conscious act of students once QR codes reader application (which is embedded in the "*Aprendo Jugando*") is opened. Then, students should focus the mobile device camera, so, that it "reads" a QR code. This could be appreciated in Fig. 4, where a student reads a QR code of a task and then he/she receives information of the question associated with it (on the screen of mobile device). In this received screen, a group has a collecting elements option, when they select this option, a QR code reader is opened which allows to read QR codes of concrete elements that the group want to collect in response to their current task.

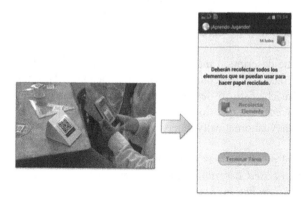

Fig. 4. Student reading a QR code of a collection task.

After second or third times that a groups interacted with this way of reading QR codes, they incorporate it without problems, because they understand how this work. In spite of, there are two different semantics associated to when QR code reader is used, one to receive the question and another to collect concrete elements, this did not impact to students when they have been using the application. The difficulty was only detected to understand how QR codes interaction was, in general, the first time.

In the first putting into practice was detected the lack of naturalness of reading QR codes for groups which as mention before involving indirect interaction with the QR code reader. For this reason, we have decided to add a scaffolding activity for the second putting into practice in a school. For this, a reduced micro application was developed only to show how to read QR codes. This micro application is called *"Exploro como Jugar"* which have been used in a students group talk in the second school before each group uses the *"Aprendo Jugando"*. This small variation (from first to second putting into practice) made it easier for students to read QR codes for the first time in *"Aprendo Jugando"* without any problem. So, students experience to read QR codes have been improved.

In this way, it can be seen that in the case of using an indirect sensing mechanism and that this requires an unknown form of interaction for students, it would be advisable to first explain it. This would mean that during the putting into practice of the application (in this case, *"Aprendo Jugando"*) the form of interaction does not become a limiting factor, thus avoiding frustrations and demotivation on the part of the students. This explanation would not be viable when what one wants to prove is either the naturalness of the interaction of the sensing mechanism for the students, where in this particular case, a previous training could affect the results.

3.2   Exploring the Behaviour of the Beacons in a Functional Prototype

After carrying out the putting into practices of *"Aprendo Jugando"* application [19], it was possible to register QR codes interaction experience. This interaction requires that a user "read" a code with their mobile devices which *"can be a tedious process to learn and apply"* [22] or *"unintuitive"* [10]. In [10, 22], authors propose to use beacons instead of QR codes. In [7] is described the use of beacons as natural evolution of QR codes.

Considering the description mentioned above, we had decided to develop a functional prototype which uses beacons only to receive each task. This have allowed to test a direct sensing mechanism to detect students' location avoiding students having to read a QR code to receive a question. In this way, when students approach to each table shown in Fig. 2, they automatically receive the corresponding question on their mobile device.

This functional prototype was systematically tested by students who were participants in *"Location-based Learning Activities"* project (in the context of *"Projects of Development and Innovation Applications with Students 2017"* of the Faculty of Informatics of UNLP, Argentina).

These tests focused on analyze how to use this direct sensing mechanism and how beacons behaved when they were located on tables which are located inside small distances from each other.

In a small and limited indoor space as a classroom, beacons presented many anomalies. Detecting that depending on:

- Beacon's orientation, its signal is affected. For example, if a beacon is oriented horizontally (as shown Fig. 5B), its signal decreases considerably respect to beacon's signal emitted when it is oriented vertically (see Fig. 5A). This is because its signal is emitted from beacon's front. For this reason, beacons can often find placed on walls of places where they are used.

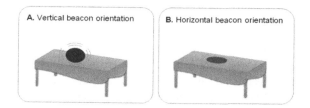

Fig. 5. Beacon's orientation on a table: vertical or horizontal.

- Mobile device's orientation, received beacon's signal could be not accuracy to the real distance to it. So, in this situation could do interpret user's location further away of real beacon's location. This is because mobile device's Bluetooth is located on one side of it. So, if a beacon is located on the same side, its signal is received without problems. However, if a beacon is located on the other side, its signal decreases considerably, this makes interpret user's location further away of real beacons's location. For Location-based Learning Applications (used inside a small indoor space), this situation generates that many times an application interpret that students are in a table but in reality students are closer to another. In Fig. 6, it shown a mobile device locates at the same distance (one meter) from two beacons. However, when a Samsung Galaxy S4 device is used to test, the right beacon is closest. This is because its Bluetooth sensor is on this side. This can vary by different mobile devices vendors and models. So, this behaviour affects how an application works, so, students could receive a question which is not appropriate to their nearest table because it was detected by another beacon due to mobile device's orientation. This kind of signal problem is addressed, for example, in [23] where authors advise to locate beacons to ten meters distance from each other. Thus, in

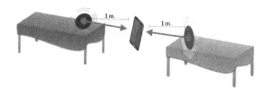

Fig. 6. Example of beacon located to right and left side of a mobile device.

this way they avoid signal conflict and it is easier to determine unambiguous locations. This condition, in case of a small indoor space, is not possible to accomplish.

- Processing capacity of mobile device, processing speed of beacons' signal could delay more to be analysed. This means depend on mobile device's vendor and model. So, user should be closer to a beacon to receive a corresponding learning task, since many times device is still processing a received signal while user is still walking. Our tests were conducted with a Samsung Galaxy S3 and a Samsung Galaxy S4. Detecting for first one device that beacons' signal is received later. So, if user kept moving he/she could receive a task when he/she was no longer near to the corresponding table.

Systematic tests carried out with this functional prototype has allowed to detect how it work in a small indoor space in which there are tables located at small distances from each other. For this mentioned case, this kind of direct sensing mechanism would not be the most recommended. Because, erroneous beacon's signal processing could trigger student receive a question which is not correspond with the real student's location. For example, student could be ask to collect certain concrete elements, but he/she is located another table (associated to another task), so, concrete elements over this table are not respond the question that he/she have received. Moreover, this kind of application's behavior could be imperceptible for students, since they may think that proposed question is suitable with the table closest to them. Take into account these results; we have decided not to advance beyond the functional prototype (which uses beacons). So, this prototype has not been put into practice with students in schools, as if we did with "*Aprendo Jugando*" which uses QR codes.

4   Discussion

In this section, some explored features related to location sensing mechanisms are discussed. Hoping that this discuss helps not only to design and create Location-based Learning Applications, but also to improve authoring tools using to generate this kind of applications.

When QR codes are using, it is indispensable to consider that code reader applications may have different sensitivity. This implies that by having a reading application open, any QR code could be read by it. This is designed in this way in order to speed up the user's task. However, when this mechanism is used inside applications, such as "*Aprendo Jugando*" where there are many concrete elements on a table, each of them with a QR code; so, one of them could be read without explicit intention. That is, it could be read a QR codes of a concrete element but may be this is not that student want. Because, they want not to collect this element. During putting into practices of "*Aprendo Jugando*", this situation mentioned before only happened to one of the groups. But, for this group this situation did not generate any inconveniences in the use of the application. It should be noted that QR code reader applications should be previously installed in a mobile device to be used in a mobile application, as it is the case of "*Aprendo Jugando*".

In the case of use beacons, it is advisable to locate them at a considerable distance from each other. Note that beacons' signal is interfered with by building characteristics (for example walls). So, for each physical space a technical test should be carried out in order to decide optimal distances according to these characteristics. If a catalog of beacons is provided, as [16], these should be placed strategically with the aim of avoid signal interfere from each other. This facilitates a proper functioning of applications based on them. In the case of beacons are inevitably require to be located close to each other, it could be possible to define an ad hoc heuristic to analyze which is the closest beacon in every moment. For this, it could use some variables such as device's orientation to evaluate if a user is on the left or on the right of the beacon. Sensing mechanisms based on signals usually function with sensed data's accuracy and a margin of error. These data allows to take better decisions (by applications) in order to decide what information or services be offer to the user. In addition, beacons emit values to indicate distance from mobile device to it; for example, one, two or three meters. So, in this case, it could decide to provide only learning content when a distance to a beacon is less than one meter. However, this last mentioned strategy to offer content not always work correctly since it depends on processing capacity of the mobile device. So, it could occur that a student is located less than one meter from a table but this situation is not detected by a mobile application which is still processing sensed data. Therefore, for each domain is required to analyze what could be the best ad hoc heuristic to process beacon's signals, and thus to determine which one is closest to a user all the time. However, it is very complex to achieve a generalized solution applicable to any physical space and any mobile device. Note that, for beacons to be detected by mobile devices, they should support BLE (*Bluetooth Low Energy*) technology.

Using QR codes to determine students' location affect application's visual interface. Because, a selectable option should be provided to open the corresponding reader (as shown in Fig. 4 to collect concrete elements). In the case of beacons, the use of them is transparent for students, since when they are near a beacon, they receive learning content (for example, a question) associated with this beacon. However, in direct sensing mechanisms, such as beacons, it should be consider the delay to receive associated information to them. Users are constantly walking, so, sometime they may receive outdated information to their current location, such as it is mentioned in [7].

It can be appreciated how each location sensing mechanism involves a different form of interaction and they require specific considerations according to how they behave. It is essential to perform in-situ functional tests to detect first if a location sensing mechanism is suitable for a physical space where a Location-based Learning Application is planned to use. Depending on this, it will be possible to perform then tests with students.

It is interesting to note that, in the last recent years, authoring tools [3, 16–18] to facilitate creation of applications which use sensing mechanisms has increased. Generating applications with these tools is very useful for teachers, but they also need to understand how sensing mechanisms work in order to choose the most appropriate for each situation. This may require teachers training in order to know how each location sensing mechanism behaves.

5 Conclusions and Future Works

An exploration of two location sensing mechanisms, such as QR codes and beacons, have been presented for Location-based Learning Applications inside small indoor spaces such as a classroom. It has been described how each mechanism behaves and some characteristics related to them have been discussed. For physical spaces where relevant locations are close to each other, beacons are not a recommended option to use as a location sensing mechanism. The exploration presented in this paper allows analyzing viability of each sensing mechanism when some specific requirements required to be covered, in this case to be used inside a small indoor space.

Taking into an account the four phases proposed [4] to the Location-based Learning Applications (conceptual design, development cycle, put into practice the development and evaluation of the put into practice), these four phases have been performed by the application presented in Sect. 3.1 ("*Aprendo Jugando*"), which uses QR codes as location sensing mechanism. However, for the functional prototype presented in Sect. 3.2, which uses beacons as location sensing mechanism, have been carried out the two first phases. So, the third phase (put into practice the development) could not be performed with students in school because beacons are not suitable as location sensing mechanism for a small indoor space. According to this, it can be observed that the phases proposed in [4] could be carrying out only if it is viable to pass to the next phase. For example, if conceptual design is not feasible to develop (due to complexity or high cost involved in it), so, in this case, the rest of the phases defined in [4] could not be addressed either.

We are working on develop an API which allows to generalize sensing mechanisms behavior, in order to be easier to develop this kind of application. So, this allows that they can evolve over time without requiring too many changes. For this, we take into account what is proposed in [13] which describes a conceptual framework based on the separation of concerns and one of these concerns involve sensing mechanisms. In this way, applications could be "listening" for user's location sensing in general, so, it do not matter what mechanism is used to sense user's location.

In the future, we will be planned to organize meeting with multidisciplinary teams to register emerging features which could contribute to detect other requirements when this kind of applications are created. So, this will be use to provide tools that allow to speed up the creation of this applications. For example, expanding the features of the tool presented in [18]. These meetings are also expected to help understand how to carry out co-design of this kind of applications when a multidisciplinary team is involved.

Acknowledgments. The authors thank Ramiro Ongaro, Juan Emilio Salaber and Andrés Gabriel Binaghi for their participation in systematic tests of the functional prototype in "*Location-based Learning Activities*" project (in the context of "*Projects of Development and Innovation Applications with Students 2017*" of the Faculty of Informatics of UNLP, Argentina), Res. HCD N° 4/17, File No. 3300-006343/17-000).

References

1. Rivero-Rodriguez, A., Pileggi, P., Nykänen, O.A.: Mobile context-aware systems: technologies, resources and applications. Int. J. Interact. Mob. Technol. **10**(2), 25–32 (2016). http://online-journals.org/index.php/i-jim/article/view/5367
2. Hargood, C., Hunt, V., Weal, M.J., Millard, D.E.: Patterns of sculptural hypertext in location based narratives. In: 27th ACM Conference on Hypertext and Social Media (HT 2016), pp. 61–70. ACM, New York (2016). https://doi.org/10.1145/2914586.2914595
3. Vera, F., Sánchez, J.A.: A model for in-situ augmented reality content creation based on storytelling and gamification. In: 6th Mexican Conference on Human-Computer Interaction, pp. 39–42, ACM, New York (2016). https://doi.org/10.1145/2967175.2967385
4. Lliteras, A.B., Challiol, C., Gordillo, S.E.: Location-based mobile learning applications: a conceptual framework for co-design. In: 12th Latin American Conference on Learning Technologies (LACLO), pp. 358–365. IEEE Press, La Plata (2017). https://doi.org/10.1109/laclo.2017.8120946
5. Emmanouilidis, C., Koutsiamanis, R.A., Tasidou, A.: Mobile guides: taxonomy of architectures, context awareness, technologies and applications. J. Netw. Comput. Appl. **36**(1), 103–125 (2013). https://doi.org/10.1016/j.jnca.2012.04.007
6. Kato, H., Chai, D., Tan, K.T.: Barcodes for Mobile Devices. Cambridge University Press, New York (2010). https://doi.org/10.1017/CBO9780511712241
7. Hartmann, K., Quirnn, A.: How useful are BLE beacons for mobile guides? In: 5th International Conference on Wireless Networks and Embedded Systems, pp. 1–10. IEEE Press, Rajpura (2016). https://doi.org/10.1109/wecon.2016.7993487
8. Zydney, J.M., Warner, Z.: Mobile apps for science learning: review of research. Comput. Educ. **94**, 1–17 (2016). https://doi.org/10.1016/j.compedu.2015.11.001
9. Alakärppä, I., Jaakkola, E., Väyrynen, J., Häkkilä, J.: Using nature elements in mobile AR for education with children. In: 19th International Conference on Human-Computer Interaction with Mobile Devices and Services, pp. 41–54. ACM, New York (2017). https://doi.org/10.1145/3098279.3098547
10. Tsai, T.-H., Shen, C.-Y., Lin, Z.-S., Liu, H.-R., Chiou, W.-K.: Exploring location-based augmented reality experience in museums. In: Antona, M., Stephanidis, C. (eds.) UAHCI 2017. LNCS, vol. 10278, pp. 199–209. Springer, Cham (2017). https://doi.org/10.1007/978-3-319-58703-5_15
11. Melero, J., Hernández-Leo, D.: Design and implementation of location-based learning games: four case studies with 'QuesTInSitu: the Game'. IEEE Trans. Emerg. Top. Comput. **5**(1), 84–94 (2017). https://doi.org/10.1109/TETC.2016.2615861
12. Google Maps. https://maps.google.com. Accessed 23 May 2018
13. Challiol, C., Lliteras, A.B., Gordillo, S.E.: Diseño de aplicaciones móviles basadas en posicionamiento: un framework conceptual. In: XXIII Congreso Argentino de Ciencias de la Computación (CACIC 2007), pp. 682–691. RedUNCI, La Plata (2017). http://sedici.unlp.edu.ar/handle/10915/63780
14. Cober, R., Tan, E., Slotta, J., So, H.J., Könings, K.D.: Teachers as participatory designers: two case studies with technology-enhanced learning environments. Instr. Sci. **43**(2), 203–228 (2015). https://doi.org/10.1007/s11251-014-9339-0
15. XML. https://www.w3.org/standards/techs/xml#w3c_all. Accessed 23 May 2018
16. Hauge, J.B.: Exploring context-aware activities to enhance the learning experience. In: Dias, J., Santos, P.A., Veltkamp, R.C. (eds.) GALA 2017. LNCS, vol. 10653, pp. 238–247. Springer, Cham (2017). https://doi.org/10.1007/978-3-319-71940-5_22

17. Pishtari, G., et al.: SmartZoos: modular open educational resources for location-based games. In: Lavoué, É., Drachsler, H., Verbert, K., Broisin, J., Pérez-Sanagustín, M. (eds.) EC-TEL 2017. LNCS, vol. 10474, pp. 513–516. Springer, Cham (2017). https://doi.org/10.1007/978-3-319-66610-5_52

18. Zimbello, A.M., Alconada Verzini, F.M., Challiol, C., Lliteras, A.B., Gordillo, S.E.: Authoring tool for location-based learning experiences. In: 4th IEEE/ACM International Conference on Mobile Software Engineering and Systems, pp. 211–212. IEEE Press, Buenos Aires (2017). https://doi.org/10.1109/mobilesoft.2017.32

19. Lliteras, A.B.: Un enfoque de modelado de actividades educativas posicionadas que contemplan elementos concretos. Master thesis, Faculty of Informatics, National University of La Plata, Argentina (2015). http://hdl.handle.net/10915/50030

20. Christensne, B.C., Giakalis, A.P., Jørgensen, N.M., Poulsen, M.K., Rehm, M.: The effect of device number and role assignment on social group dynamics in location-based learning. In: 15th International Conference on Mobile and Ubiquitous Multimedia, pp. 297–305. ACM, New York (2016). https://doi.org/10.1145/3012709.3012711

21. Suthers, D.D., Vatrapu, R., Medina, R., Joseph, S., Dwyer, N.: Beyond threaded discussion: representational guidance in asynchronous collaborative learning environments. Comput. Educ. 50(4), 1103–1127 (2008). https://doi.org/10.1016/j.compedu.2006.10.007

22. Ng, P.C., She, J., Park, S.: Notify-and-interact: a beacon-smartphone interaction for user engagement in galleries. In: IEEE International Conference on Multimedia and Expo, pp. 1069–1074. IEEE Press, Hong Kong (2017). https://doi.org/10.1109/icme.2017.8019467

23. Lin, X.Y., Ho, T.W., Fang, C.C., Yen, Z.S., Yang, B.J., Lai, F.: A mobile indoor positioning system based on iBeacon technology. In: 37th Annual International Conference of Engineering in Medicine and Biology Society, pp. 4970–4973. IEEE Press, Milan (2015). https://doi.org/10.1109/embc.2015.7319507

Proposal of an Open Hardware-Software System for the Recognition of Emotions from Physiological Variables

Mauricio Sánchez Barragán$^{(\boxtimes)}$ ⓘ,
Luis Alejandro Solarte Moncayo$^{(\boxtimes)}$ ⓘ,
and Gabriel Elias Chanchí Golondrino$^{(\boxtimes)}$ ⓘ

University Institution Colegio Mayor del Cauca, Popayán, Cauca, Colombia
mausanbar93@gmail.com,
alejandrosolarte0223@gmail.com,
gchanchi@unimayor.edu.co

Abstract. In this article, we present the design and construction of an open hardware-software system responsible for the characterization of the user context, through physiological signals such as: heart rate variability (HRV), galvanic skin response (GSR) and electromyographic signals (EMG), which allows to establish significant levels of mental stress (SI), arousal and valence, metrics important that make possible the inference of emotional states in the person. In addition, we describe the development of computational method for the inference of emotions and the mathematical calculations that involve this process. Finally, the hardware software system validation is presented through a video on demand service based on emotions, which includes a recommendation system that suggests a set of contents based on the user's emotional behavior during the interaction with the service. This system aims to serve as a reference for the construction of other services based on the study of the user's emotional behavior in different application contexts.

Keywords: Arousal · Emotions · Physiological signals and valence

1 Introduction

According to [1], the global population will have about 20.8 billion devices connected to the Internet in 2020, while for [2] thanks to the rapid advance of current and future technologies, this number could be even bigger with about 50 billion. That is why the need to interconnect and design new intelligent systems with the ability to monitor and control different inter-connected devices, in order to take advantage of profiting and processing the data obtained, thereby inferring the preferences of a user. Regarding the previous problematic, a concept that has taken force in recent years emerges, which has been called the Internet of Things [2, 3]. This trend seeks to improve the internet model, through the connection on the web between different electronic devices, called "things or objects". Thus for example, a set of devices that allow obtaining physiological information of the corporal space of a person have appeared at a commercial

V. Agredo-Delgado and P. H. Ruiz (Eds.): HCI-COLLAB 2018, CCIS 847, pp. 199–213, 2019.
https://doi.org/10.1007/978-3-030-05270-6_15

level, which are receiving the name of wearable devices. Through the data delivered by these devices, it is possible to track the activities of a person, taking advantage of this information in fields such as health, entertainment and interaction. Despite many of these devices are commercial and not open, they allow data capture but not the easy integration and customization.

In this way, and despite the benefits of the Internet of Things, it exists a set of problems that make the expansive use of this technology difficult, such as: the difficulty in personalizing intelligent services, the massive management of data and the use of the captured data, in order to obtain more precise and related information to users [4–6]. In relation to these challenges, millions of solutions emerge daily created by the leading technological companies, which are limited by the little information and freedom of the user to use and integrate with other open technologies [7]. This article aims to contribute to this problem through an open hardware-software system for the recognition of user emotions by means of wearables [5].

According to the previous challenges, there is a demand for solutions that help in the personalization of intelligent services and the characterization of the profile of users, this with the purpose of achieving a more suitable control of their environment and in turn to present recommendation strategies adapted whit the profile of a person. An alternative to the above, it is the use of context variables [8], which are understood as information that can be used to determine the state of an entity, being this: a person, place or object relevant to interactions between the user and the application [9].

The context of a person is broad, that is why it is necessary to establish the variables that allow an adequate reading of the data of users. The physiological signals can provide important and precise information, since they allow evaluating the behavior of an individual, and inferring emotions from the observations that his organism presents before a certain stimulus. Examples of these signals are: the rate of respiration, blood circulation, the galvanic response of the skin, among others [10].

In this paper we present a proposal of an open hardware-software system for the capture of user context variables such as heart rate variability (HRV or HRV, Heart Rate Variability), the galvanic response of the skin (RGP or GSR, Galvanic Skin Response), and electromyographic signals (EMG, Electromyographic). These variables were used for establishing the levels of mental stress and emotional positivity associated with the moods that can help with the characterization of behavior patterns and inference in the preferences of users. Thus, the contribution of this work is the design and implementation of an open hardware-software system for the capture of physiological signals, which through the use of wearable devices, allows the monitoring of emotional changes in a person. In this way, the possible services in different areas that can be implemented from the open hardware-software system are: recommender systems, tracking systems, assistance systems, learning systems, among others.

The rest of the article is organized as follows: in Sect. 2, a set of research works related to this research are presented; Sect. 3 includes some relevant concepts that allow a better understanding about this research; in Sect. 4, we show the methodology used in the implementation of the open hardware-software system and the method of inference of emotions; in Sect. 5, we present the development of the proposed system based on the use of open technologies; likewise, in this section the application of the proposed methodology is carried out. Finally, Sect. 7 presents the conclusions and future work obtained from the present research.

2   Related Works

The main focus of this article is the study of the analysis systems of physiological signals. Regarding to this theme, in [11] it is explained how the physiological signals relate to the mood of the user, when it performs a certain activity. The proposal raises the development of a portable system to measure parameters of the autonomous system of a person and display it in any of the output devices, using an algorithm for the recognition of stress. Also, some experimental measurements, from physiological signals such as: RGP, VFC, EMG, temperature, among others. In [12] there are the techniques for the evaluation of mental stress from VFC in the domain of time and frequency, showing the importance of this measurement for the assessment of mental stress and its relationship with the mood. In [13] there is a description of a method for the detection of mental stress using sensors and methods for the measurement of the activation of the two autonomic branches: the sympathetic and parasympathetic. In this article, two experimental studies are done, one associated with mental tasks and the other with relaxation exercises, where it's possible to observe how the heart rate is a physiological variable that is related to the mood. Likewise, in [14] it is proposed the use of open hardware platforms such as Arduino for the capture of physiological signals, which makes possible the use of open source sensors for the measurement of heart rate. Similarly, in [15] a set of techniques and advanced applications of pattern recognition are presented, showing how biomedical signals can help in the characterization and analysis of human behavior. On the other hand, in [16] there is the theory and the basic instructions for the understanding of the psychological concepts of human behavior. Likewise, this work shows the importance of emotions and adaptation methods for health care. In [17] a set of researches on human behavior are described, which expose the last contributions and gaps on this subject. Additionally, this work proposes the use of biomedical sensors as an aid in the understanding of behavior patterns. Thus, from the literature found, it is considered as a research gap, the use of physiological signals as a possible method of entry into the understanding of patterns of human behavior, taking into account the advantages of the Internet of Things.

3   Conceptual Framework

In this section we present the concepts considered in this research, among which are: physiological variables, arousal and valence.

3.1   Physiological Variables

The goal of human physiology is to provide an explanation about the characteristics and specific mechanisms of the human body. Staying alive is the result of complex control systems, which regulate activities such as breathing, circulation, senses, metabolism, and temperature among others [18]. These activities are controlled directly by the autonomic nervous system (SNA), which constitute the physiological signs that can be measured and monitored through different types of sensors.

3.2   Arousal

This emotional characteristic is defined as a general physiological and psychological activation of the organism, which appears continuously in the form of variable intensities of moods, observing from deep sleep to frenzy, panic or intense anger. In the central nervous system, the arousal/excitation usually refers to the state of excitation of neurons or increased blood flow in humans [19].

3.3   Valence

This emotional characteristic can be defined like the perception of the positivity degree of emotions in the organism, the dimension of the experience refers to the hedonic note (that is to say, the pleasure and the displeasure) that the human being perceives under different emotional conditions [19].

4   Methodology

For the design of the open hardware-software system, six phases are proposed, namely: definition of a model of emotions, study of physiological variables, selection of development tools, proposal of hardware-software module, design of the method for the inference of emotions, see Fig. 1.

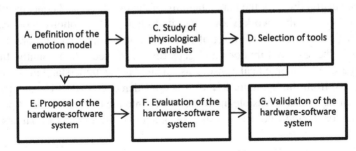

Fig. 1. Methodology for the design of the hardware-software system and method of inference, source: own

In phase A, a model of emotions was proposed based on the affective properties of *arousal* and *valence*, with the aim of classifying in the most appropriate and easy way, five of the fundamental emotions present in people, like: happiness, excitement, anger, sadness and relaxation. In phase B, there is an explanation and analysis of the physiological variables that allowed the calculation of the affective properties *arousal* and *valence*, necessary for the determination of emotional states. In phase C, there is a description of open hardware-software tools used for the capture and processing of physiological variables. In phase D, it is proposed the design of the hardware-software system that allows the capture of physiological variables and inference of emotions. This phase includes the mathematical method used for the inference of emotions.

In phase E, the evaluation of the constructed system is presented, through load and stress tests. Finally, in phase F the validation of the hardware-software system is presented through its use in video on demand service.

5 Proposal of the Hardware-Software System

In this section we present the development of each of the phases proposed in the methodology, beginning with the phase of characterization of emotions and culminating with the phase of validation of the hardware-software module.

5.1 Phase A. Definition of an Emotions Model

Emotion is a complex set of interactions between subjective and objective factors, mediated by neural-hormonal systems, which can give rise to affective experiences, such as feelings of excitement or arousal and pleasure/displeasure, leading to a behavior which is often but not always, expressive, goal-directed, and adaptive [20]. Emotions can be reduced to a specific and affective core of pleasure or displeasure. Other studies suggest models in two dimensions, such as the arousal-valence model, where the arousal can be high or low and the valence can be positive or negative, being able to characterize any emotion by its coordinates in a two-dimensional space (see Fig. 2). As an example, happiness usually has positive valence and moderately high arousal, whereas sadness has a moderately low arousal and negative valence [21].

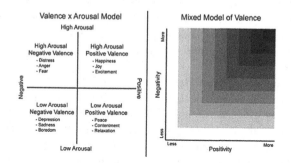

Fig. 2. Emotion models based on arousal and valence, taken from [21]

Once the concept of emotion and the possible models that help with its characterization, it was decided to adapt a model that would simplify even more the way of determining an emotion according to arousal and valence. For this, it was considered to work with arousal-valence model, since it is a good reference framework that facilitates its adaptation and application to new designs, due to its simplicity of two coordinates for the identification of emotion, and its use in environments of multimedia contents. The new model proposed in this section, is an adaptation of arousal-valence considered in other works and researches as presented in [21–24], where the five fundamental emotions are considered: happiness, excitement, anger, sadness and relaxation. Finally, each of the previous emotions has amplitude of 72° on the cartesian plane (see Fig. 3).

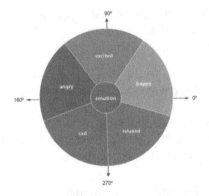

Fig. 3. Model of arousal-valence adapted to 5 emotions, source: own

5.2   Phase B. Study of Physiological Variables

After analyzing the model of emotions based on arousal and valence, it is necessary to establish the possible physiological variables that can help in obtaining these emotional parameters in a user. According to the literary review and research in the related works, it could be established that the measurement of heart rate variability allows to determine levels of mental stress that can be associated to moods according to the level of excitement arousal, besides that the galvanic response of the skin is used to calculate the intensity value of the previous parameter. It was also possible to analyze that electromyographic signals help to determine the level of positivity in emotions, or what was referred to the valence parameter. Thus, in this work these physiological variables were incorporated: heart rate, galvanic response of the skin and the electromyographic measurement, as variables to infer the user emotion.

5.2.1   Methods for Analysis of Heart Rate Variability

Once the physiological measurements that allow the inference of emotions have been chosen, the methods or metrics should be defined for the analysis of the measurements and the calculation of the emotional parameters. For this, it was decided to work with measurements in the time domain, which facilitate calculations and data processing. There are numerous statistical and mathematical methods that are useful to analyze the measurements of heart rate variability in users. The following are the methods that were considered most relevant for the present research (see Table 1). According to the literature, it has been found a relationship between the statistical measurements RMSDD and pNN50, with the level of a person's mental stress. One way to know when the user begins to increase their level of mental stress, is to observe when the metrics have a low value of RMSSD and pNN50, while, if the user begins to relax these metrics are characterized by high values.

Table 1. Measurements for analysis of heart rate variability, source: own

Measurement	Equation	Description
RMSSD	$= \sqrt{media\left[\left[RR_{i+1} - RR_i\right]^2\right]}$	It is the RMS value of the RR intervals captured [25]
pNN50	$= \dfrac{\left[\left\lvert RR_{i+1} - RR_i \right\rvert\right] * 100}{N-1}$	Percentage of consecutive RR intervals that differ by more than 50 ms from each other [25]

5.2.2 Mental Stress Index

According to [26] stress can be interpreted as a threat to the psychological integrity of an individual that gives rise to physiological responses and/or behavior. For the analysis of mental stress it is possible to use the statistical measurements of RMSDD, pNN50 and Eq. (1) of the stress index (SI) proposed by Bayevsky [25]. Bayevsky's equation is based on geometric methods using the cardio-histogram distribution curve drawn from the study of pulse variations or heart rate [25].

$$SI = \frac{AMo}{2Mo * (M * DMn)} \tag{1}$$

Where Mo is the mode or the presumable level in which the cardiovascular system is working. It refers to the RR value that the user presents more regularly in the analyzed set of measurements. Amo is the amplitude of mode, in physiological terms; it is the nominal index of activity of the chain of sympathetic regulation. It refers to the percentage of the intervals that correspond to the value of the mode in the sample taken. M * DMn is the range of variance, it is the difference between the maximum and minimum values of the cardio-intervals, it is better known as variance. In Table 2, it is possible to see the ranges of stress index that the user can present, which are associated with three moods, such as: stressed, relaxed and normal. From the Table 2, it can be concluded that the stress index allows an association of the three emotional states. In addition, the ranges of the level of *arousal* can be established according to the relationship that exists with the level of excitement.

Table 2. SI ranges associated with each state, source: own

SI range	Associated state	Arousal level
>150	Stressed	>0,5
≥ 40 y ≤ 150	Normal	$\geq 0,14$ y $\leq 0,5$
<40	Relaxed	<0,14

5.2.3   Methods for Calculating the Positivity Level of an Emotion

According to the literature and studies carried out, it has been shown that it is possible to infer the degree of positivity of an emotion according to muscle activity in specific parts of the human body, one of them is the face [27], where most of the nervous senses of the human being are found; and which can infer or reveal the mood of a user. It is therefore the need to obtain measurements of the level of muscle activity that will serve to determine the positivity level in emotions. The electromyographic signals can help in this task, since they measure the degree of muscle activity and nerve cells in the human being, it is also necessary to estimate the capture of the electrical signal of only 2 of the facial muscles, which according to the literature are activated when a positive emotion emerges on the user or, on the contrary, a negative *valence*. The facial muscles on which the capture of the signal is focused are the *corrugator supercilli* and the *zygomaticus mayor*, the first one is usually activated when the user performs expressions caused by negative emotions such as frowning when he is angry. While the second one is associated with positive emotions such as happiness, since its activation occurs when the person presents the muscular reflex of smiling [28]. Thus, the values of the *valence* parameter can be established, when analyzing which of the two muscles on the face has greater muscle activity and does a mathematical relationship to determine the values of *valence*.

For this, it is necessary to estimate a mathematical method to determine the muscle that presents greater muscular activity, one solution is to perform a linear regression with the captured data and observe the one with greater slope and variation in its data, since it can evaluate the behavior as a straight line as time goes by. In (2) it is possible to see the equation that models the behavior of data as a straight line.

$$Y = a + bX \tag{2}$$

Where Y represents each of the electromyographic values; X includes each of the incremental values in time; a is the cut point with the Y axis and b is the slope of the straight. Once Bayevsky's methods and linear regression are presented, which allow the calculation of the level of mental stress that can be associated with a value of *arousal*, and the linear regression method that permits the calculation of the level of positivity of an emotion or what refers to a *valence* value in a user, we proceed to mention the development tools that will allow the capture of physiological signals.

5.3   Phase C. Selection of Development Tools

The development tools (sensors, arduino platform, programming languages, among others) used in this research are from open hardware and software, because these allow the use of several sensors and also are useful for the implementation of web services. As mentioned above, one of the contributions of this work is an open hardware-software system for the capture of physiological variables, according to the literature and research carried out; it was decided to work with the VFC, GSR and EMG signals, which enable the obtaining the level of mental stress. Currently, there are a large number of devices that allow the capture of physiological variables, which have been used in the most part by athletes and scientific groups in recent years. In the case of the proposed hardware-software system, it was determined to work with the open hardware sensors presented in the Table 3.

Table 3. Sensors used in the taking of physiological signals, source: own

Sensor device	Description
	Hear rate sensor: The pulse sensor for Arduino is a sensor that allows the measurement of the heart rate signal (HR) and its variability (VFC).
	Galvanic skin response sensor: The grove sensor (GSR) for Arduino is a sensor that measures the electrical conductance of the skin, which varies the level of humidity.
	Electromyographic Sensor: The MyoWare sensor (EMG) allows the measuring of the electrical activity of muscles and nerve cells.

The Arduino Yún platform was used to interconnect the sensors with the user, because it allows the capture and processing online, since this platform provides the ability to connect several sensors to internet using the Wi-Fi module.

5.4   Phase D. Proposal of the Hardware-Software System

The design of the open hardware-software system consists of three functional blocks: signal capture module, signal analysis module and inference module (see Fig. 4).

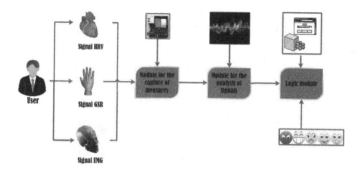

Fig. 4. Proposed hardware-software system, source: own

At the beginning, the module of signals capture obtains each one of the data of variables: VFC, GSR and EMG through the sensors connected to the Arduino Yún, and sends them to the module of analysis which is in charge of obtaining the levels of mental stress and the level of emotional positivity and associate them with a state of mind. Subsequently, the inference module is responsible for recording the values of mental stress, *arousal*, *valence* and mood in a database and providing them to the user in real time through a web application. Figure 5 shows the final hardware-software system, which considers the deployment module that refers to the web interface that will be implemented to validate the system and it is possible to observe the feedback of user's physiological variables.

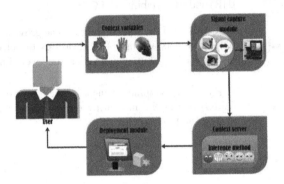

Fig. 5. Final system hardware-software feedback, source: own

5.4.1   Design of the Method for the Inference of Emotions

In Fig. 6 it is possible to find a flow chart that models the algorithm for the inference of emotions, which was developed in the Python programming language, due to its great potential in data processing.

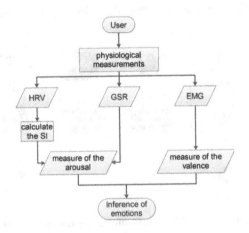

Fig. 6. Flow chart of the inference method, source: own

Initially the physiological measurements of the user are captured through the sensors mentioned in phase C, then two processes are carried out with the measurements obtained from each sensor, one of these is to calculate the mental stress index with the data of the VFC, later the value of the arousal is established according to the calculation of the level of mental stress and excitation, obtained by means of the GSR signal; parallel to this, the level of emotional positivity that allows to establish the valence is calculated, according to the stimulation of the facial muscles (corrugator supercilli and the zygomaticus mayor). Once determined the values of arousal and valence, the user emotion is inferred, according to the model of emotions proposed in phase A.

5.5   Phase E. Hardware-Software System Evaluation

In order to evaluate the response capacity and processing of the proposed system, sequential and concurrent load tests were performed, using the free tool apache benchmark. In Fig. 7 it is possible to observe the load tests carried out with 200 sequential connections, with a periodicity of 10 connections in each request, obtaining a response time ranging between 1,381 and 1,407 s, adequate time considering the number of connections and taking into account the personal use of the system.

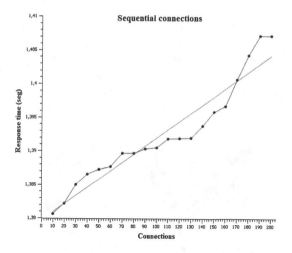

Fig. 7. Sequential connections, source: own

In turn, Fig. 8 shows the load tests performed concurrently until the system stops responding adequately. In this way, the maximum response capacity of the system was 60 simultaneous connections in a period of almost 100 s, obtaining response times ranging from 5 to 100 s.

It can be concluded that the hardware-software system proposed for the recognition of emotions can be an adequate system of personal use for the continuous monitoring of physiological variables and the inference of emotions. This taking into account that on average for an individual request the hardware-software system takes about 0.15 s, so it is considered adequate for use in services that use the inference of emotions.

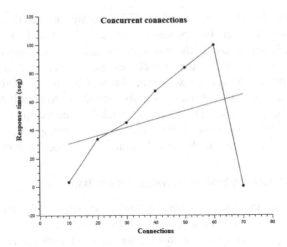

Fig. 8. Concurrent connections, source: own

5.6   Phase F. Hardware-Software System Validation

From the hardware-software system proposed, it is implemented as validation way, a video in demand service (VoD) of emotional multimedia contents, which include a recommender system (see Fig. 10). The purpose of the recommendation system is to speed up access to multimedia content, taking into account the continuous monitoring of physiological user variables such as: heart rate variability (HRV, Heart Rate Variability), the galvanic response of the skin (GSR, Galvanic Skin Response), and electromyographic signals (EMG, Electromyographic) (see Fig. 9).

Fig. 9. Physiological user variables, source: own

The physiological variables were used to establish levels of mental stress and emotional positivity, which can be related to the moods of a user, allowing to characterize its profile more adequately. The multimedia contents suggested by the recommender system were previously classified based on the musical properties of arousal and valence. In this way, it is possible to relate the multimedia contents to the emotional perception of a user, from the tracking of the physiological variables (see Fig. 10).

Fig. 10. Video on demand service, source: own

The Fig. 10 shows the prototype of the VoD service implemented, in which in "1" it is possible to see the video component that displays the content the user is currently playing. In "2" the real-time monitoring of the physiological variables of the user (VFC, GSR and EMG) and emotion inferred from the analysis of these variables is presented. Finally, in "3", it is the list of recommendations generated in real time from the emotion inferred by the physiological variables.

Additionally, the VoD service allows specific monitoring of the different physiological variables used for the inference of emotions. Thus, each of the physiological user variables considered has a graph associated in real time (see Fig. 11).

Fig. 11. Physiological variables monitoring module, source: own

6 Conclusions and Future Work

The open hardware-software system provides a solution to the problem of personalization of intelligent services that interact with the real world in an intelligent and natural way, for which it considers among its components the use of open wearables for the recognition of the user's emotions through the capture of physiological signals in real time.

The hardware-software system and the inference method developed present the advantages of being flexible and making use of open technologies for its operation, which contributes to its use in future projects and services related to ICT and health.

Variables of the user context, such as physiological permit the evaluation of behavior of an individual or infer emotions from the functioning of their organism, providing information that makes possible to determine patterns of behavior of the person.

The VFC, GSR and EMG variables are fundamental to the built system, since these allow the calculation of the stress index, establish the initial arousal level of the user, and calculate the level of emotional positivity through the valence, to finally determine the emotion of the user through the designed model of 5 emotions (Phase B).

As a future work, it is intended to include in the hardware-software system other types of physiological variables, such as the voice, the movement of the extremities, among others. The previous, in order to feed back the emotion inference module of the proposed system.

References

1. Gartner, Inc.: Gartner Says 6.4 Billion Connected "Things" Will Be in Use in 2016, Up 30 Percent From 2015 (Gartner) (10 de Noviembre de 2015). http://www.gartner.com/newsroom/id/3165317. Recuperado el 10 de Junio de 2016
2. Cisco IBSG. The Internet of Things How the Next Evolution of the Internet Is Changing Everything. Cisco (2011)
3. Buyya, R., Dastjerdi, A.V.: Internet of Things: Principles and Paradigms. Elsevier, Amsterdam (2016)
4. Cha, H., Lee, W., Jeon, J.: Standardization strategy for the internet of wearable things. In: 2015 International Conference on Information and Communication Technology Convergence (ICTC), Jeju (2015)
5. Kannan, R., Rasool, R.U., Jin, H., Balasundaram, S.: Managing and Processing Big Data in Cloud Computing. IGI Global, Hershey (2016)
6. Rose, K., Eldridge, S., Chapin, L.: The Internet of Things (IoT): An Overview. The. Internet Society, Reston (2015)
7. Pilioura, T., Tsalgatidou, A.: E-services: current technology and open issues. In: Casati, F., Shan, M.-C., Georgakopoulos, D. (eds.) TES 2001. LNCS, vol. 2193, pp. 1–15. Springer, Heidelberg (2001). https://doi.org/10.1007/3-540-44809-8_1
8. Adomavicius, G., Tuzhilin, A.: Context-aware recommender systems. In: Proceedings of the 2008 ACM Conference on Recommender Systems, New York, USA (2008). https://doi.org/10.1145/1454008.1454068

9. Moreno, M.N., et al.: Web mining based framework for solving usual problems in recommender systems. A case study for movies' recommendation. Neurocomputing (2015). https://doi.org/10.1016/j.neucom.2014.10.097

10. González, G., López, B., De la Rosa, J.L.: Managing Emotions in Smart User Models for Recommender Systems. Institut d'Informàtica i Aplicacions, Universitat de Girona, Girona, Spain (2004)

11. Sharma, T., Kapoor, B.: Intelligent data analysis algorithms on biofeedback signals for estimating emotions. In: International Conference on Reliability, Optimization and Information Technology, Baddi, India (2014)

12. Patil, K., Singh, M., Singh, G., Anjali, S.N.: Mental stress evaluation using heart rate variability analysis: a review. Int. J. Public Ment. Health Neurosci. 2 (2015). ISSN: 2394-4668

13. Choi, J., Gutierrez-Osuna, R.: Using heart rate monitors to detect mental stress. In: Wearable and Implantable Body Sensor Networks, Berkeley, CA (2009)

14. Mohana, S.R., Aradhya, H.R.: Remote monitoring of heart rate and music to tune the heart rate. In: Communication Technologies (GCCT), Thuckalay (2015)

15. Salah, A.A., Gevers, T.: Computer Analysis of Human Behavior. Springer, London (2011). https://doi.org/10.1007/978-0-85729-994-9

16. Honeycutt, A., Milliken, M.E.: Understanding Human Behavior: A Guide for Health Care Providers. Delmar Cengage Learning, Clifton Park (2012)

17. Salah, A.A., Kröse, B.J., Cook, D.J.: Human behavior understanding. In: 6th International Workshop, HBU 2015, Osaka, Japan, 8 September 2015, Proceedings, Osaka (2015)

18. Hall, J.E.: Tratado de fisiología médica. Elsevier, Barcelona (2011)

19. Heilman, K.M.: The neurobiology of emotional experience. J. Neuropsychiatr. 439–448 (1997)

20. Kleinginna, P., Kleinginna, A.: A categorized list of emotion definitions, with suggestions for a consensual definition. In: Motivation and Emotion, pp. 345–379. Plenum Publishing Corporation, Georgia (1981)

21. Jones, M., Fay, R., Popper, A.N.: Music Perception. Springer, Ohio (2010). https://doi.org/10.1007/978-1-4419-6114-3

22. Meyers, O.: A Mood-Based Music Classification and Exploration System. Massachusetts Institute of Technology, Massachusetts (2004)

23. Posner, J., Russell, J.: The circumplex model of affect: an integrative approach to affective neuroscience, cognitive development, and psychopathology. Dev. Psychopathol. 17(3), 715–734 (2005)

24. Yang, Y., Chen, H.: Music Emotion Recognition. CRC Press, Taiwan (2011)

25. Bayevsky, R.M., Ivanov, G.G., Chireykin, L.V., et al.: HRV analysis under the usage of different electrocardiography systems (methodical recommendations). Committee of New Medical Techniques of Ministry of Health of Russia, Moscow (2002)

26. Kappeler-Setz, C.: Multimodal Emotion and Stress Recognition. ETH ZURICH, Zurich (2012)

27. Dimberg, U.: Facial electromyography and emotional reactions. In: Psychophysiology, pp. 481–494. The Society for Psychophysiological Research, Inc., Upsala (1990)

28. Van Boxtel, A.: Facial EMG as a tool for inferring affective states. In: Spink, A., Grieco, F., Krips, O., Loijens, L., Noldus, L. (eds.) Proceedings of Measuring Behavior, Tilburing, pp. 104–108 (2010)

Usability Evaluation of Learning Objects with Augmented Reality for Smartphones: A Reinterpretation of Nielsen Heuristics

Beatriz de Almeida Pacheco[1]([⊠]) (iD), Marcelo Guimarães[2],
Ana Grasielle Correa[3] (iD), and Valeria Farinazzo Martins[3] (iD)

[1] Universidade Paulista, São Paulo, SP, Brazil
beatriz.pacheco@docente.unip.br
[2] Mestrado do Centro Universitário Campo Limpo Paulista,
Universidade Federal de São Paulo-(Unifesp/UAB), São Paulo, SP, Brazil
marcelodepaiva@gmail.com
[3] Programa de Pós-Graduação em Distúrbios do Desenvolvimento,
Universidade Presbiteriana Mackenzie, São Paulo, Brazil
anagrasi@gmail.com, valeria.farinazzo@mackenzie.br

Abstract. Augmented Reality Systems merge virtual content and the real world with real-time interaction and have features such as lighting conditions, sensor usage, and user position. These systems are very different from conventional applications that use mouse and keyboard; therefore, require a usability assessment to verify that they achieve their goals and their users goals, taking into account these specificities. When learning objects are constructed, it is necessary to guarantee their quality, measured by certain criteria in the pedagogical, content and technical components in addition to interaction components. The present work aims to discuss and present the usability assessment of Learning Objects developed in Augmented Reality, through an update of the usability heuristics proposed by Nielsen at the end of the 20th century, taking into account their specificities, such as the ease of manipulation of markers and degree of fidelity of the representation of the virtual objects added in the scenes.

Keywords: Usability · Learning objects · Augmented reality
Heuristic evaluation

1 Introduction

Since humans began to build tools there was an interaction between users and machines. Initially, people were tuned to fit the machines, in other words, they went through complex and time-consuming training. However, during World War II, new equipment emerged rapidly, making the traditional interaction solution difficult or even impracticable [1]. Thus, the need for analysis and orderly synthesis of the possibilities of human-computer interaction was perceived, so that the projected tools could approach the user's understanding and consequently reduce the time of adaptation to the use.

V. Agredo-Delgado and P. H. Ruiz (Eds.): HCI-COLLAB 2018, CCIS 847, pp. 214–228, 2019.
https://doi.org/10.1007/978-3-030-05270-6_16

Lazar [2] defines Human-Computer Interaction as a discipline that deals with the design, evaluation and implementation of interactive systems for people to use, and also as the phenomena that occurs around them, from the use of such solutions.

In describing the interaction between man and computer, the classic situation is a person using an interactive, graphical program on a workstation. Nowadays, however, there is a serious paradigm change to such model. With the popularization of ubiquitous computing, the emergence of new computational devices and new forms of interaction, it is noticed that there is a variation in the meaning of interaction and machine, leading to a rich space of possible research themes [3].

Augmented Reality (AR), in this sense, is a technology that "presents a virtual world that enriches instead of replacing the real world" [4]. This can be achieved through a device that overlays virtual 3D objects in real scenes, and viewed with devices such as monitors and smartphones. The basic working principle of AR is to capture real world images through cameras, recognize landmarks as markers, add and align virtual objects to them, so that if the marker moves in the real world, virtual objects, superimposed on it, move together [5].

AR has been used in several ways, among them as a tool to support teaching-learning process, since it allows the student to approach real problems, experiencing them in a highly interactive way. Another solution that has been widely used to support the teaching-learning process is the incorporation of AR into Learning Objects (LO). According to the IEEE Learning Technology Standards Committee [6], LOs are defined as digital or analogical entities of any nature, which have the characteristics of the possibility of use and reuse during the learning process supported by technologies. In this way, using AR as the learning mediator can make such applications of presumable value.

Although the Horizon Report [7] has pointed AR as one of the technologies that will influence education in the coming years, it is needed to discuss how much such AR applications in the educational context have followed minimum criteria that can guarantee its quality in relation to usability. In these terms, these applications cannot be analyzed only with Nielsen [8] or standards (such as ISO 9241-1) criteria, without taking into account the specificities of the technology. It can be seen that there is a methodological gap and criteria to evaluate such applications, since, for example, approximately 35% of the works studied by Martins, Kirner and Kirner [9] use generic criteria to evaluate AR and thus not achieving more specific results in their evaluations.

The present work aims to discuss and present the usability assessment of LOs developed in AR, taking into account their specificities, such as the ease of manipulation of markers and degree of fidelity of the representation of the virtual objects added in the scenes.

This article is organized as follows. Section 2 presents the theoretical framework that theoretically bases the research. Section 3 presents the related works. Section 4 discusses the methodology used to obtain the usability assessment criteria for LOs developed with AR. Section 5 presents the results and discussions of applied methodology. Finally, Sect. 6 concludes the paper.

2 Theoretical Framework

2.1 Usability Evaluation

Usability is a quality that products should have from the perspective of their users [10]. However, many present the lack of it, whether for historical, cultural, organizational, financial, etc. reasons, that are beyond the scope of this work. Fortunately, there are customary and reliable methods to assess where design has contributed to good or bad usability and also to judge the changes that must be made to design a product that is easy to use and useful enough to survive or even thrive in the marketplace.

In general, what makes a product succeed is to use it. Rubin [11] presents the following definition for the term usability: "When a product or service is truly usable, the user can do what he wants to do and the way he expects to be able to do it without obstacles, hesitations or questions." To be usable, a product or service must be useful, efficient, effective, satisfactory, easy to learn, and accessible.

Usability goals and objectives are typically defined in measurable terms of one or more of these attributes. However, it should be noted that making a usable product is not limited to simply generating numbers on usage and satisfaction. Although numbers can tell whether a product works well or not, there is a qualitative element difficult to capture. This has to do with interpreting the data to know how to solve a problem. Judging the various possible causes for a design problem and knowing which ones are especially likely often means looking beyond the individual data to design an effective treatment. By incorporating evaluation methods such as usability testing or heuristic evaluation throughout an interactive design process, it becomes possible to create products and services that are useful and usable and possibly even enjoyable.

In order to perform the usability evaluation, several methods are proposed. Such methods vary according to the stage of development in which they are applied, the way of collecting data and its characteristics, the analysis performed based on the data collected, among others. Among these methods, it is possible to cite the heuristic evaluation [8], which is a Usability Inspection method and was used in this study.

The Heuristic Evaluation is performed by specialists and aims to examine, according to established criteria, if the interface meets these criteria (heuristics). Once the problems are found, it is also necessary to rate them on a score ranging from 1 to 5, where 1 means that the problem is less important until 5 which means a catastrophic error.

According to Nielsen [8], it takes three to five specialists to perform the Heuristic Evaluation. In this type of assessment, first, the inspection should be performed individually. Thus, the evaluator must go through the interface several times in order to find the problems, that is, parts of the interface that are not in line with the proposed heuristics. So, it should sort the problem (between 1 and 5, being a superficial problem and one that does not affect the user experience and 5 - catastrophic, as it affects the user experience). Usually an inspection session lasts up to two hours, but depending on the size or complexity of the interface, we recommend dividing it into multiple sessions addressing specific scenarios. At the end of the evaluation, all evaluators present their lists of problems, which are consolidated into a single list, once discussed.

Nielsen [8] proposed 10 heuristics in the early 1990s, in which graphical interfaces emerged:

- Visibility of system state: the system must be able to inform what is happening in real time to the user, that is, to keep the user informed about where it is in the system and what is happening.
- Correspondence between the system and the real world: the system must use sounds, graphics and writing tone that the user uses to communicate.
- Freedom of user-friendly control: the system should provide the user with the freedom to perform actions other than rules that go against the business or interfere with other functionality.
- Consistency and standards: the system must contain consistency and visual standard (text, color, element design, sound, etc.).
- Error prevention: the system must provide means to prevent the user from performing unwanted actions.
- Recognition instead of memorizing: the system should not require the user to remember how to perform certain actions, for example, the path to find certain functionality.
- Flexibility and Efficiency of Use: it is necessary to provide different means of performing the same functionality to meet different types of users, from the layman to the experienced.
- Aesthetics and minimalist design: the system should provide only essential information to avoid overloading the user.
- Help users recognize, diagnose, and recover errors: error messages must be clear and close to the content or action that caused the error.
- Help and documentation: although the user does not like to use help and documentation, it should be available, if necessary.

These heuristics deal with fairly general criteria, sometimes requiring their reinterpretation or extension to meet the specificities of new forms of interaction of interactive systems. For example, Kawamoto and Martins [12] adapted these criteria for the evaluation of voice-based interfaces and Sutcliffe and Gault [13] to evaluate Virtual Reality systems.

Checklists can be used within the usability inspection process to focus on important aspects of the interface that should be analyzed in greater depth. This is a way to facilitate and guide the inspection work. This may make the evaluation relatively cheaper and can be adapted to the various valuation situations; for this, it is sufficient that appropriate ergonomic rules are selected. These rules (checklists) are constructed from the evaluator's experience, for years, in the development of several projects in the area or still understood as rules of "common sense" - Nielsen [14].

2.2   Augmented Reality

According to Azuma [5], the AR applications have as main characteristics: (1) combine the real world to the virtual; (2) support real-time interaction; and (3) add three-dimensional objects (3D) in the scenes. They differ from Virtual Reality applications because users maintain real-world awareness during use, while in Virtual Reality applications users are inserted into fully computer-synthesized worlds. For operation, AR applications collect and analyze the environment via the camera and perform actions in a coordinated and proactive manner, such as triggering animations according to the user's position. Whenever there is a change in the actual scene, the application handles user interactions, maps objects, and generates new images to be presented to users.

AR applications often exploit users' vision and hearing through the aggregation of 3D images and sounds as content. However, AR can also include, as content, stimuli to any of the other fundamental senses of humans, in this case touch, smell and taste. The development of AR applications demands a set of subsystems with several resources, such as:

- Interface: aims to present the real scene with the virtual objects (3D models, sounds, textures, videos) that are added. It should be designed in such a way as to provide user-friendly interaction and its use as naturally as possible, so users feel encouraged and feel free to use it;
- Tracking: responsible for handling the positioning of the user and the objects in the scene. Usually the applications of AR use markers, but it is not obligatory for all of them, because ones without markers use the feature of recognition of characteristics of objects for the insertion of the virtual elements in the real scene;
- Mapping of the scene: aims to mix the real world with the virtual objects according to the position of the elements detected in the scene;
- Interaction: it aims to receive user interactions, such as moving the camera, processing and making corresponding changes in the application. The handling of the interactions must be in real time, this way, for example, it allows 3D objects to be inserted in the scene at the moment the marker is presented to the camera.

Most educational applications with AR content are designed to be used only by the teacher who usually developed it. This is because it aims to meet an immediate demand, without considering the possibility of reuse by others. Thus, the use of the application is limited to only one context, because, due to the lack of resources for redistribution, the teacher does not make it available to others. So, the adoption of standards, such as those related to LO's, is an alternative to changing such a situation.

2.3   Learning Objects

It is possible to define LOs as digital or analogical entities, of any nature, that have as characteristics the possibility of use, reuse during the learning process supported by technologies [6]. Such a term, coined by Hodgins [15], is still often employed without clear criteria in both educational and developmental environments. Throughout more than 20 years of research in the field, however, some desirable characteristics of LOs have been defined:

- Accessibility: LO must be tagged with metadata so that it can be stored and referenced in a database;
- Reuse: once created, a LO should work in different instructional contexts;
- Interoperability: LO must be independent of the means of delivery and knowledge management systems.

In the area of Education other characteristics stand out, among them a basic premise: the pedagogical structuring of the use and measurement of results. In this sense, LOs should be responsible for connecting content (the conceptual framework to be learned), context (the environment, the rules and the interactive processes involved), and the student.

Thus, to develop a LO it is necessary to start from a pedagogical plan; organizing content, practice and testing; define the user profile; develop rules and requirements; finally, to choose the resources to be used in said object.

Therefore, here is perceived the need to choose the resources, and consequently, of the applied technologies, from a deep understanding of the content, student and context.

3 Related Work

Some papers that address usability assessment for AR systems have been found in literature. Martins, Kirner and Kirner [9] present a study based on a systematic review on the basis of more than 900 articles dealing with AR. The authors found 51 criteria for usability evaluation of AR systems, divided into nine categories (System Interaction, Application Interface, Representation, Sensory and Behavioral Aspects, Motivation and Effort, Spatial Association, Configurations and Internal Aspects, General Functionalities and others Attributes). However, in this work, mobile work was not considered.

Zainuddin, Zaman and Ahmad [16] described the heuristic evaluation of a didactic material for the deaf in learning science using Augmented Reality, called PekAR-Mikroorganism. The questionnaire of the heuristic evaluation of usability was divided into four constructions: (i) interface design, (ii) educational design, (iii) interactive design of AR and (iv) video sign language design. The paper does not present the questions constructed to evaluate these four aspects, but presents a rather limited version of the experts' suggestions: Interface design (Include a shortcut button. The type and size must be consistent. Include the source of the microorganisms video (e.g. youtube link). Increase the time for reading text in microorganisms video. Do not use big pictures in the background because these pictures distract the users); educational design (Use correct spelling and correct punctuation); AR Environment (Include the repeat button, Delete unimportant information, Freeze 3D object for 5 s); Sign language video (Using the correct sign language that is commonly used by the deaf community. Sign language video must be consistent (on the left) and button on the right).

In Brazil, Guimarães and Martins [17] present two usability evaluation techniques adapted to AR applications - usability testing and heuristic evaluation. The heuristic evaluation brings the criteria proposed by Nielsen [8] and adapted to the context of applications of AR and other criteria (precision, ease of use, configuration of environment, satisfaction). The paper brings a case study showing how to perform such techniques.

Carvalho [21] presented a model for the development, packaging and distribution of AR applications. The author also presented a tool capable of packaging AR contents in the LO format in the SCORM (Sharable Content Object Reference Model) standard and exporting them to compatible tools. The authors tested the solution in two case studies, comparing it with traditional teaching and with multimedia objects. However, the model needs to be applied in more contexts to demonstrate its validity.

With the ample incentive to the construction and availability of LO, it becomes necessary to develop methodologies of production and evaluation of these materials. In literature it is possible to find guidelines for the usability assessment of LO in [22, 23]. The methods used have been the traditional ones used in the area of Human-Computer Interaction (HCI), such as Heuristic Assessment [23, 24], instructional design [25], besides initiatives to create specific guidelines for the construction and evaluation of this type of digital educational material [23, 26, 27] and reusability [28].

In global terms, there are papers that explore these concepts, but none of them like this one. Rodriguez et al. [29] explore usability assessment of Learning Objects for mobile objects with two-dimensional interfaces. Selviany et al. [30] work with Augmented Reality for mobile, but focus their work on the creation of a model, not on the evaluation of objects in development or already developed. Sumadio and Rambli [31] focus their work on evaluating objects in augmented reality, but do not study those developed for mobile devices. Magalhães et al. [32] use Augmented Reality applied to the teaching/learning environment, not necessarily on mobile devices and with an evaluation process. And Finaly, Ivanc et al. [33] work on usability evaluation of a LMS mobile web interface, but they don't consider Augmented Reality in this process.

Some of these initiatives highlight the phases of the LO development and evaluation process, such as storyboard definition, creation of the object navigation map and evaluation that tests the operation and usability of LO in focus. When performing a usability assessment, it is recommended to measure the degree of adequacy to the target audience, content quality, level of accomplishment of objectives, ease of use, presentation form (layout, navigation) and didactic and pedagogical issues associated with object of learning.

According to Mussoi et al. [34], when evaluating the usability of a LO, it is important to consider the following factors: technical usability and pedagogical usability. Technical usability focuses on assessing the following factors: accessibility, memorization and learning, usage control, help, graphic layout, consistency, efficiency, memory overhead and errors. While pedagogical usability focuses on: learner control, cooperative learning, applicability, added value, motivation, prior knowledge assessment, flexibility, and feedback.

However, many papers point to a number of difficulties in using and reusing these LOs, making them simply inoperable or inaccessible digital content. Braga [28], for example, identified a series of factors that can negatively impact the quality of a LO and, consequently, its reuse: pedagogical didactic difficulties; contextualization difficulties; recovery difficulties; installation difficulties; portability difficulties; usability difficulties; difficulties in accessibility; low precision; low reliability.

Considering all these aspects inherent in the quality, usability and reuse of a LO, it is essential to establish guidelines in the development and evaluation of these objects to be effective for education.

4   Methodology

The usability criteria for LOs in AR were listed based on the authors' experience in developing and evaluating AR systems and LOs. These criteria were selected from what Nielsen [8] proposed, reinterpreted and also in new criteria [9, 17] applied to the context of AR, AR for mobile devices and also LOs.

In order to develop specific usability metrics for LOs in AR, a material was developed in which it was possible to add questionings from the selected criteria. A three-hour mini-course was then prepared for a LO-focused target audience in order to teach them how to perform usability assessments of AR Systems. For each criterion presented, it was discussed how this criterion for AR could be applied to LOs.

Among the criteria presented, it is possible to highlight:

- The 10 heuristics of Nielsen [8] were used, but re-read in the context of AR, from AR for mobile devices and for LOs. For example, for the "Aesthetics and Minimalist Design" heuristics, questions have been raised, such as: (a) Is the quantity of virtual objects in the scene satisfactory or excessive? (b) Are contents arranged on the screen in a simple and objective manner in relation to the context? (c) Design and layout of buttons and interactive objects of the application are consistent with their action?
- Indication of other criteria for:
    - AR: Accuracy, Easy configuration of equipment and system;
    - Smartphones: Easy to use, Legibility and layout, Compatibility between different platforms, Few steps to reach the goal;
    - LO: Educational Quality.

Finally, a LO with AR was presented that contained several usability problems in order so the target audience could identify it using the presented criteria. The LO in question is called MyARGalaxy and is available in the Google Play Store.

5   Results and Discussion

In an audience formed by educators and developers, in a Latin American community linked to the development of LO with AR, eight people had access to the material and participated in the discussions fostered during the course from the concepts of usability (tests and heuristic inspection). Participants were asked to highlight issues related to the use of AR in mobile devices to increase the teaching-learning process for the purpose of mapping aspects that were characteristic of such applications. Some figures have been inserted to facilitate understanding; they refer to one of the learning objects discussed in Sect. 4. Among the questions, organized here from the heuristics proposed by Nielsen [8], stand out:

Systems Status Visibility:

- Proportion of superimposed three-dimensional objects and commands;
- Neutrality of colors in front of the real world;
- How and where do I point the camera on my phone?

- User guidance on what to do.

Figure 1 presents a usability problem linked to the lack of color neutrality.

Fig. 1. Lack of color neutrality. Source: myargalaxy.com

- Systems Compatibility with the Real World:
  - Persistence of positioning of superimposed elements to the real world regardless of the speed of camera movement.
- Consistency and standards:
  - Positioning of control elements.

Figure 2 presents a good example of consistency and patterns, since the back icon always appears in the same place as the screen.

Fig. 2. Good example of consistency and patterns. Source: myargalaxy.com

- Freedom and User Control
  - The user must have control of the activity he is performing, but often the controls are hidden due to the size of the interface.

Figure 3 shows a screen where the user receives information on how to manipulate the application, however, the user can not trigger the control elements, for example, there is no "exit" button from the video display.

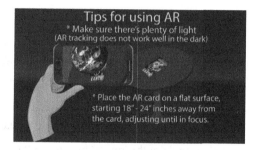

Fig. 3. Bad example of user control and freedom. Source: myargalaxy.com

- Error Prevention:
  - Error messages should be simple and concise. It becomes a challenge to provide complementary guidance in an interface with few visual control elements.
- Flexibility and efficiency of use:
  - Allow the user to interact with the system in different ways, either by touching a virtual object, pressing the smartphone keypad or voice input (and recognizing the command).
- Aesthetics and Minimalist Design:
  - Restrict the use of visual elements (control) and colors so that they do not detract from the interaction.

Figure 4 shows a screen of a heavily polluted AR application visually with a very strong contrasting color variation. The images and the links are mixed in the background of the image and it is not possible to identify when an element is a link, hindering the interaction. There is, for example, a link called "Get myARgalaxy Cards" that is not highlighted in the interface.

Fig. 4. Bad example of aesthetics and minimalist design. Source: myargalaxy.com

- Recognize rather than remember:
  - How to create an iconographic system that does not interfere with the main interaction. For example, the user should look at an icon and quickly understand what action/information is related to it. For example, help button with an interrogation icon, arrows indicating the direction of navigation, etc., as shown in Fig. 2.
- Help users recognize, diagnose, and recover wrong actions:
  - Should simple commands return to the previous stage appear?

Figure 5 presents a good example of this metric by making the return button visible on the home page.

- Help and documentation:
  - Step-by-step help tutorial;
  - How and where to start;
  - How to find the bookmarks.

Fig. 5. Good heuristic example "Helping users recognize, diagnose and recover wrong actions". Source: myargalaxy.com

Figure 6 presents a good example of the inclusion of a tutorial explaining how to use the application and where to find the markers.

- Help and documentation:
  - Step-by-step help tutorial;
  - How and where to start;
  - How to find markers.

Fig. 6. Good heuristic example "Help and Documentation". Source: myargalaxy.com

Figure 6 presents a good example of integrating a tutorial explaining how to use an application and where to find the markers.

In addition to the suggested complements for the evaluation of LOs in AR, new specific heuristics were proposed. Among them, one can present:

- Precision:
  - Does the system, with or without a marker, present the objects in the proper position?
  - Are virtual objects mixed with the real world properly (texture, scale)?
  - Is the tracker system stable?
- Easy configuration of equipment and system:
  - Does the system guide the user of the steps to use it? Enable camera, print bookmark, etc.
- Easy to use:
  - Is it easy to interact with the system even if you have to hold the device (smartphones)?
  - Is it easy to interact with the system even with a reduced screen size (smartphones)?
  - Is there muscle fatigue?
- Legibility and layout:
  - Can the user easily identify what is to click and what is not?
  - Can you identify when you need to enter information into the system?
  - Can the user identify when to wait for the system to perform a task?

Figure 7a and b show the application screen and it is not clear what is clickable and what is image.

- Compatibility between different platforms:
  - Is the system available on different platforms?
  - Do you offer the same functionality on different platforms?
  - Do you offer the same forms of interaction on different platforms?
- Few steps to reach the goal:
  - Can the user access all system resources quickly?
  - Can the user perform all functions with a single interaction type?
- Educational quality:
  - Do the virtual objects inserted in the scene together with the possible actions contribute to the teaching-learning process?

Fig. 7. (a) Bad legibility and (b) layout example. Source: myargalaxy.com

From the above, one can see that Nielsen's heuristics are somewhat generic and, even after two decades, are still valid. However, it can be seen that the intrinsic characteristics of the AR systems must be considered and adapted to these heuristics. These characteristics refer mainly to questions of insertion of virtual objects in composition with real objects, how to perform interaction in an intuitive and easy way and iconographic system.

Regarding the evaluation to be for AR in mobile devices, factors should also be considered, such as: reduced screen size and the three-dimensional information that must be presented; the fact that one hand is holding the device or there is muscle fatigue.

6 Conclusions

Educational content packaged in LO format can contribute to the entire teaching-learning process, from facilitating development, through the reuse of previously prepared material, to the opening of possibilities of using materials in formats that require time and knowledge of specific tools for elaboration, as is the case of AR. Therefore, it is reasonable to promote the development of educational content of AR in LO format.

However, if you really want to know if LOs with AR content generates gains for those involved, especially for learners, it is necessary to evaluate them. To do so, it is necessary to collect, analyze and quantify or qualify the results according to a predetermined quality standard.

Although usability is one of the criteria for the success or failure of the applications, little is known about users' opinions and their satisfactions and frustrations in the use of educational content with RA. This work presented usability criteria for LO in AR from a re-reading of the heuristics proposed by Nielsen [8] and also from new specific criteria for AR and LO, such as whether the quantity of virtual objects is satisfactory or excessive in the scene or even if the Design and layout of the buttons and interactive objects of the application are consistent with their action.

The importance of this work is due precisely to the still restricted number of works on how to evaluate LOs in the context of AR, in usability issues. It is realized that many LOs are constructed without taking into account the real need for the use of AR technology and also without taking into account the needs of the target audience.

It can be noticed in this work that the heuristics of Nielsen [8] are quite generic but must be re-read to fit the specifics of educational AR applications and their target audience. Thus, other heuristics were necessary to contemplate other aspects of this type of applications.

As future work, a methodology can be created to perform usability tests, so that end users can be included to evaluate LOs that uses AR.

References

1. Dix, A., Finlay, J., Abowd, G.D., Beale, R.: Human-Computer Interaction, 3rd edn. Pearson Education Limited, Haddington (2004)
2. Lazar, J., Feng, J.H., Hochheiser, H.: Research Methods in Human-Computer Interaction. Morgan Kaufmann, Cambridge (2017)

3. Hewett, T., et al.: ACM SIGCHI curricula for human-computer interaction. Technical report. ACM Press, New York (1992)
4. Bryson, S., et al.: Knowledge-based augmented reality. Commun. ACM **26**(7), 56–62 (1993)
5. Azuma, R., Baillot, Y., Behringer, R., Feiner, S., Julier, S., MacIntyre, B.: Recent advances in augmented reality. IEEE Comput. Graph. Appl. **21**(6), 34–47 (2001). https://doi.org/10.1109/38.963459
6. IEEE - Institute of Electrical and Electronics Engineers. Learning Object Metadata (2005). http://grouper.ieee.org/groups/ltsc/wg12/. Acesso 02 fev. 2018
7. NMC, NMC Horizon Project Short List: 2013 Higher Education Edition, Austin, Texas, The New Media Consortium (2012). https://www.nmc.org/publication/nmc-horizon-report-2013-higher-education-edition/. Acesso 15 dez. 2017
8. Nielsen, J.: Heuristic evaluation. In: Nielsen, J. (ed.) Usability Inspection Methods. Wiley, New York (1994)
9. Martins, V.F., Kirner, T.G., Kirner, C.: Subjective usability evaluation criteria of augmented reality applications. In: Shumaker, R., Lackey, S. (eds.) VAMR 2015. LNCS, vol. 9179, pp. 39–48. Springer, Cham (2015). https://doi.org/10.1007/978-3-319-21067-4_5
10. Shackel, B.: Usability-context, framework, definition, design and evaluation. In: Human Factors for Informatics Usability, pp. 21–37 (1991). https://doi.org/10.1016/j.intcom.2009.04.007
11. Rubin, J., Chisnell, D.: Handbook of Usability Testing: How to Plan, Design, and Conduct Effective Tests. Wiley, New York (2008)
12. Kawamoto, L.S., Martins, V.F.: Requirements and guidelines for the evaluation of voice user interfaces. In: Lazinica, A. (ed.) User Interfaces. InTechweb (2009)
13. Sutcliffe, A., Gault, B.: Heuristic evaluation of virtual reality applications. Interact. Comput. **16**(4), 831–849 (2004). https://doi.org/10.1016/j.intcom.2004.05.001
14. Nielsen, J.: Usability inspection methods. In: Conference Companion on Human Factors in Computing Systems. ACM (1994)
15. Hodgins, W.: The future of learning objects. In: Proceedings of the 2002 eTEE Conference, Davos, Switzerland (2002). doi:10.1.1.162.2852
16. Zainuddin, N.M.M., Zaman, H.B., Ahmad, A.: Heuristic evaluation on augmented reality courseware for the deaf. In: 2011 International Conference on User Science and Engineering (i-USEr). IEEE (2011)
17. Guimarães, M.P., Martins, V.F.: A checklist to evaluate augmented reality applications. In: 2014 XVI Symposium on Virtual and Augmented Reality (SVR). IEEE (2014)
18. Unity 3D. https://unity3d.com/pt. Acessado em 07 fev. 2018
19. Ogre3D. https://www.ogre3d.org/. Acessado em 07 fev. 2018
20. Northrup, P.T.: Learning Objects for Instruction: Design and Evaluation: Design and Evaluation, 300p. Information Science Publishing (2007)
21. Carvalho, B.A.: Modelo de Desenvolvimento de Aplicações de Realidade Aumentada para Empacotamento e Distribuição no formato de Objetos de Aprendizagem. Dissertação (Mestrado em Ciência da Computação) - Faculdade Campo Limpo Paulista, Brasil (2017)
22. Rocha, A.R., de Campos, G.H.B.: Avaliação da qualidade de Software Educacional. Em Aberto **12**(57), 23–45 (1993)
23. Silveira, M.S., Carneiro, M.L.F.: Diretrizes para a Avaliação da Usabilidade de Objetos de Aprendizagem. In: Brazilian Symposium on Computers in Education (Simpósio Brasileiro de Informática na Educação-SBIE) (2012)
24. Gomes, F.J.L., Lima, J.V., Nevado, R.A.: Definindo orientações de usabilidade para o desenvolvimento de objetos de aprendizagem para TV Digital. RENOTE-Revista Novas Tecnologias na Educação **5**(2), 1–9 (2006)

25. Ramos, F., Santos, P.K.: A contribuição do Design Instrucional e das Dimensões da Educação para o desenvolvimento de Objetos de Aprendizagem. In: Anais do Workshop de Informática na Escola, pp. 1–8 (2006)
26. Cazella, S.C., Behar, P., Schneider, D., Silva, K.K., Freitas, R.: Desenvolvendo um Sistema de Recomendação de Objetos de Aprendizagem baseado em Competências para a Educação: relato de experiências. In: Brazilian Symposium on Computers in Education (Simpósio Brasileiro de Informática na Educação-SBIE), pp. 1–10 (2012)
27. Reategui, E., Finco, M.D.: Proposta de diretrizes para avaliação de objetos de aprendizagem considerando aspectos pedagógicos e técnicos. RENOTE- Revista Novas Tecnologias na Educação **8**(3), 1–10 (2010)
28. Braga, J.C., Dotta, S., Pimentel, E., Stransky, B.: Desafios para o Desenvolvimento de Objetos de Aprendizagem Reutilizáveis e de Qualidade. In: Anais do Workshop de Desafios da Computação Aplicada à Educação, pp. 90–99 (2012)
29. Rodriguez, A.P., Dominguez, E.L., Velazquez, Y.H.: Usability assessment of mobile learning objects by high school students. IEEE Latin Am. Trans. **14**(2), 1044 (2016)
30. Selviany, A., Kaburuan, E.R., Junaedi, D.: User interface model for Indonesian animal apps to kid using augmented reality. In: International Conference on Orange Technologies (ICOT) (2017)
31. Sumadio, D.D., Rambli, D.R.A.: Preliminary evaluation on user acceptance of the augmented reality use for education. In: Second International Conference on Computer Engineering and Applications, vol. 2 (2010)
32. Jayasinghe, J.A.S.S., Hewagamage, K.P.: An innovative mobile learning framework for the field of Agriculture extension Sri Lanka. In: Sixteenth International Conference on Advances in ICT for Emerging Regions (ICTer) (2016)
33. Magalhães, P., Castro, A., Carvalho, C.V.: Augmented reality applied to the teaching/learning environment. In: 6th Iberian Conference on Information Systems and Technologies (2011)
34. Ivanc, D., Vasiu, R., Onita, M.: Usability evaluation of a LMS mobile web interface. In: Skersys, T., Butleris, R., Butkiene, R. (eds.) ICIST 2012. CCIS, vol. 319, pp. 348–361. Springer, Heidelberg (2012). https://doi.org/10.1007/978-3-642-33308-8_29
35. Mussoi, E.M., Flores, M.L.P., Behar, P.A.: Avaliação de objetos de aprendizagem. In: Congresso Iberoamericano de Informática Educativa, Santiago, Chile, Anais, (2010). Author, F.: Article title. Journal 2(5), 99–110 (2016)

World of Knowledge: An Application for Learning Assistance in the Reading Process for Children in the Literacy Period

Pedro H. M. Arthur[1]([✉]) [iD], Allain Hortis[2] [iD], Henrique O. Cury[1] [iD],
Vinicius F. Gomes[4] [iD], Marcelo de Paiva Guimarães[3] [iD],
and Valéria Farinazzo Martins[4] [iD]

[1] California Trinity University, Los Angeles, USA
`pedrohma95@gmail.com`, `henrique.cury09@gmail.com`
[2] Mestrado Profissional em Computação Aplicada e Programa de Pós-Graduação
em Distúrbios do Desenvolvimento, Mackenzie Presbyterian University,
São Paulo, Brazil
`allainhortins@gmail.com`
[3] Federal University of São Paulo-(Unifesp/UAB),
Mestrado do Centro Universitário Campo Limpo Paulista, São Paulo, Brazil
`marcelodepaiva@gmail.com`
[4] Mackenzie Presbyterian University, Rua Pietro Longhi, 200,
São Paulo 05863240, Brazil
`vine.fgomes@gmail.com`, `valeria.farinazzo@mackenzie.br`

Abstract. To learn to read the child must understand a process that involves sensory, emotional, intellectual, physiological, neurological as well as cultural, economic, and political aspects. Reading is the correspondence between the sounds and the graphic signals, through the deciphering of the code and the understanding of the concept or idea. Reading difficulties can occur in a variety of ways during the learning process, and acquisition of this is an extremely important factor in favoring future knowledge. The purpose of this paper is to present an application based on two different approaches - conventional (mouse/keyboard) and non-conventional (gesture) interaction (using Kinect device) that allows to assist children in the reading process. The application is a game focused on three storybooks for kids. Details about the development approach (requirements analysis, project, implementation and tests) used are presented. We also present a usability test for conventional and nonconventional devices with 15 children in the literacy period.

Keywords: Kinect · Teaching-Learning process · Usability
Gestural interfaces · Serious game

1 Introduction

Reading is the correspondence between the sounds and the graphic signals, through the deciphering of the code and the understanding of the concept or idea [1]. The process of learn to read is complex and multi-dimensional. It involves sensory, emotional,

V. Agredo-Delgado and P. H. Ruiz (Eds.): HCI-COLLAB 2018, CCIS 847, pp. 229–243, 2019.
https://doi.org/10.1007/978-3-030-05270-6_17

intellectual, physiological, neurological as well as cultural, economic, and political aspects. Moreover, learn to read is a developmental process which each child learns at their own unique pace. Then, create a solution that allows children to understand the relation between letters and sound is a challenge [2].

Reading difficulties are common and they are best addressed when caught at a young age. Overcome these difficulties is an extremely important factor in favoring future knowledge. According to Homer [3] & Mol and Bus [4], reading keeps on of the most relevant activity for supporting literacy development and fostering language skills.

On the other hand, digital solutions are affecting the way that children live. They are altering children relationships with the learning process of reading, including during the literacy period. Hence, the use of digital technologies is an opportunity to improve the learning process integrating successful reading practices into effective experiences with new technologies, using more natural ways to interact with, such as voice and gestural interfaces [5].

Real-time gesture recognition [6, 7] can be used as a control for games to assist the reading process for children in the literacy period, improving the learning activities through interactive scenarios. The success of gesture recognition in serious games for children is demonstrated in diverse examples [3, 8–10]. Interfaces based on gesture interaction can provide new possibilities form embedding dynamic in-game activities that maintain children interested in their tasks (e.g., reading activity). However, the interaction solution must not distract the children during their learning activity, then it is necessary to guarantee a good design between the interface, users and activities [3].

This paper aims to present the World of Knowledge ("Mundo do Saber"), an application for learning assistance in the reading process for children in the literacy period. It is based on storybook for kids. It was already added the storybooks "Little Red Riding Hood" [11] and "Three Little Pigs" [12]. During the read activity, the child can activate a function called "Read to me" to the application reads the words, highlighting them one by one. Then, the child can associate the sound and the word, simulating the adult's actions monitoring the child's reading. Each storybook is divided in chapters which each one has questions about reading comprehension and spelling. In application, motivational game mechanisms were also implemented (e.g. scoring, awards, and penalties). This application supports conventional (keyboard and mouse) and non-conventional (gesture) interaction devices. The approach used to create the World of Knowledge allows to add others storybook narratives. We also present a usability test with 15 children in the literacy period. These students were divided into group I (public school students from a poor community and belonging to a Non-governmental organization (NGO)) and group II (private school students with a level socioeconomic average-high.)

This paper is organized in the following sections: Sect. 2 presents concepts related to the teaching process of reading; Sect. 3 discusses some related work regarding the use of gesture interaction within educational applications; Sect. 4 shows the development processes used to create the World of Knowledge; Sect. 5 discusses the usability test; and, finally, Sect. 6 presents the conclusions and future perspectives.

2 The Teaching Process of Reading

The process of reading involves the following phases [13]:

- Decoding: during this phase the child perform the recognition of the written symbols and their connection with their meaning. It can be said that this phase of visual identification, not loading the symbols or words of semantic load;
- Understanding: after decoding, this phase occurs when the child captures the information from text that is presented, that is, from where he/she takes his/her theme and main ideas. For understand the text, it is necessary a previous knowledge on the subject;
- Interpretation: during this phase the critical capacity of the child is used. The child makes judgments about what he/she reads;
- Retention: it is responsible for storing the most important information in long time memory. The retention step occurs on two levels. It can come directly from the use of simple understanding of the text which allows the child retain theme and the most important topics. Already, at a second level, the retention occurs after the interpretation.

These phases are covered by the World of Knowledge application. The phases Decoding and Understanding are treated with the functionality "Read to me" which the text read appears highlighted on the screen. The phases Interpretation and Retention occurs when the children answer the questionnaires. Details are presented in next sections.

3 Related Work

Diverse works presented the use of gesture interaction in educational context, focusing on learning difficulties about how gesture interaction can assist the teaching-learning process.

Alves et al. [10] developed an application based on gesture interaction to assist the literacy process. Their program shows letters and images of geometric forms. The children must move the letter over the corresponding image. This work covers the phase Decoding of the process of reading. This application was evaluated by 5 professors. They did not present user evaluation.

Martins et al. [9] presented an educational game to assist children to spell words during the literacy process. Gesture interaction was adopted as motivational factor. During the game, the child visualizes the image of an object and hear the pronunciation, then the student choose the correct writing (two options are presented) using gesture movements. They evaluated the applications with children. Although, this application also covers just the Decoding phase of the process of reading.

Homer et al. [3] conducted an experiment comparing the language and reading of children. One group had a story read to them by an adult and another the story was read by a virtual character. The interaction was done using a gesture interface. They emphasized that gesture interaction is a motivating factor for children. The application presented covered the phases Decoding, Understanding and Interpretation of the process of reading.

4 Development

The application World of Knowledge is composed of storybooks for kids which allows a child to entertain himself using conventional and non-conventional interaction devices during the literacy period. New storybooks can be added dynamically without modify the application. Each storybook is divided into chapters, and each chapter has its owns questionnaire.

The application also has a speech synthesizer module, in which the book can be read to the child, when the button "Read to me" is clicked. Then, the text appears on the screen and it is highlighted the word being read at the moment, simulating the manual method in which an adult read to a child by pointing a finger at the word being read, giving to them written-to-spoken word correspondence. This also supports directional.

The application provides forward and backward controls of the storybook pages, allowing to move to any page that the child wants to remember details. It also has some game features (e.g., point accumulation, progress bars, tips, and rewards), allowing the children to compete with each other for the highest score. A reading score list is presented at the end of each storybook.

The interaction can be accomplished by interface devices, as Kinect, mouse, and keyboard. The support of unconventional devices (Kinect) aims to apply an intuitive to user interaction with the application. Through the gesture detection is possible navigate between pages, select the options and execute all interactions gestures, precisely using child hands as a cursor. Depending on hand gesture, the child can move the cursor and perform left click, right click, drag, select and scroll up and down. It is a mouse simulation system which performs all the functions performed by a mouse corresponding to child hand movements and gestures. The World of Knowledge requires just left click to interact.

4.1 Development Process

The application World of Knowledge was developed using the Iterative model [14]. This model suited to the World of Knowledge development because we aimed to add new storybooks during the application life. Then, it was not possible to begin the process development with a complete requirements specification. The application World of Knowledge has a core which new storybooks can be added. This solution allowed to add new storybooks during the design and implementation of each new iteration, enhancing the versions iteratively until the implementation be deployed.

Requirements Analysis

For the definition of functional and non-functional requirements, there were several meetings with a child literacy teacher with large experience with learning drawbacks in childhood. She participated of all phases of the project development cycle. The following requirements were identified:

- The application should allow the children chosen a storybook;
- Each storybook must contain a questionnaire after the end of each chapter.

- The function "Read to me" which each word is pronounced and highlighted must be always available;
- The applications must allow the child to exit or change the storybook at any time during reading;
- The children must be free to move to any page (backward and forward);
- The application must have a score system (questionnaire) for storing the information of the best ranked child;
- The child can or not to answer the questionnaire.

In addition to the functional requirements, it was defined the following non-functional requirements:

- Each storybook is divided in any chapter which should not be long, so as not to distract and demotivate children;
- The questionnaire should be appropriate to Literacy audience. They can not have a high difficulty regarding spelling and understanding;
- Questionnaires must only involve questions that refer to the current chapter;
- The reader's score must be presented in all questionnaires;
- Just storybooks for kids must be added into the World of Knowledge application;
- Gestures performed by the child to explore and select actions must not cause muscle fatigue.

4.2   Project

The World of Knowledge application was implemented using the programming language C# in order to apply the platform .NET Framework 4 [15]. Also, the development Kit Kinect SDK 1.8 [16] was applied, besides the Kinect for Xbox 360 device [17]. Kinect Magic Cursor software [18] was used to be the intermediary between the user and Kinect. The application environment was created using the game engine Unity 3D [19]. The development was done on computers running Windows 7 and Windows 10 operating systems. The computer used in the development was a Positive Master, Intel Core i3-2330 M processor, 4 GB RAM, Intel 3000 Graphics Driver and 455 GB HD space.

The function "Read to me" was done using Microsoft Speech Platform [20]. It was necessary also to use the Cortana (personal assistant of Windows) [21] to support Portuguese (Brazilian) reading - the application was tested by Brazilian children.

Figure 1 gives an overview of the World of Knowledge architecture. The top layer represents the application interface that it is based on conventional (mouse/keyboard) and non-conventional interaction (gesture). This learning environment supports storybook for kids. Nowadays, it is available the "Three Little Pigs" and "Little Red Riding Hood". For add a new storybook it is necessary to configure a file text with a story and a questionnaire. Each storybook chapter is also configured in this file text. World of Knowledge is implemented using a game engine, a gesture recognition solution and a speech resource.

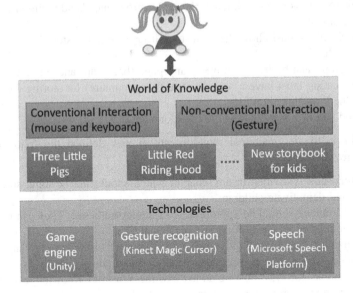

Fig. 1. World of knowledge software architecture.

4.3   Implementation

Figure 2 depicts a screenshot of the World of Knowledge interface which the child can choose a storybook. He/she just must click over a storybook image. The image is associated with each storybook is described in the text file.

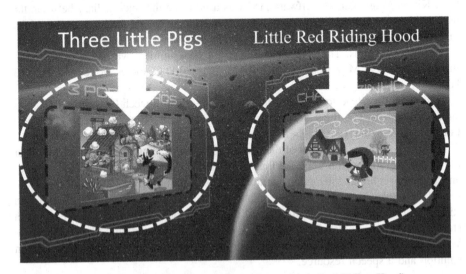

Fig. 2. Storybook choice (Three Little Pigs or Little Red Riding Hood)

Figure 3 depicts the first "Little Red Riding Hood" chapter. The child can navigate through the pages (backward or forward) and activate the "Read to me" function. The child score is presented on top.

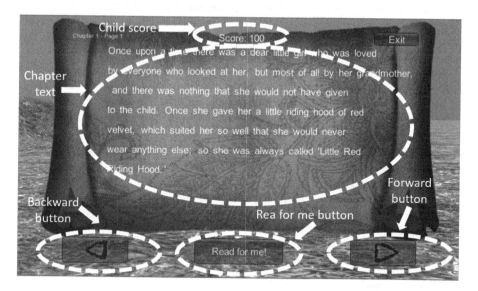

Fig. 3. A chapter

At the end of each chapter a question appears based on the contents of the chapter (Fig. 4). A chapter can have more than one question - this resource is configured in the text file. The child can or not answer the question. Each question has three alternatives.

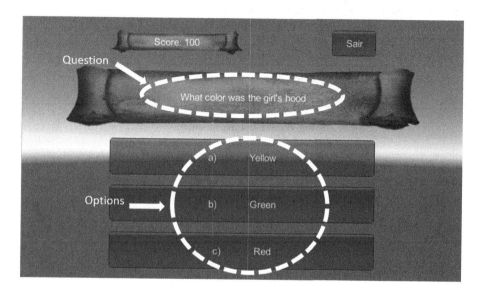

Fig. 4. Question of a chapter

5 Methodology of Tests with Final Users

A usability test with 15 Brazilian children (of both genders) in the literacy period which some have difficulties in the reading process. They had the parents' approval. The tests were carried out in uncontrolled environments, without access to devices or sensors that aid in the analysis process or other elements available in a usability laboratory. The tests were applied between October 16 and November 23, 2016.

A pilot test was performed with two adults, in which the need for a screen with a relatively large dimension for optimum use of the application was identified, since it has the reading objective. Even with a large font size, it was necessary to use screens larger than 30 inches or projector for the tests, where the projected screen resolution should be greater than 1360×768 pixels.

The children were divided into two groups: group I (public school students from a poor community and belonging to an NGO - 7 children) and group II (private school students with an average to high socioeconomic status - 8 children). Before performing on-site tests, the children were submitted to pre-test questionnaires to identify personal information related to the use of the technologies used. Figure 5 depicts the pre-test questionnaire.

1.What is your name? _____
2.How old are you?
3.What is your gender? ( ) male ( ) female
4.Have you ever played a computer game? ( ) yes ( ) no
5.How many times have you played a computer game during last week?   ( ) once ( ) twice ( )three times or more
6.Have you ever played a game with gesture interaction ? ( ) yes ( ) no
7.How many times have you played a game with gesture interaction?   ( ) once ( ) twice ( )three times or more

Fig. 5. Pre-test questionnaire

The children from group I had never used gesture interaction (Kinect) and felt highly motivated to use the application. The children from group II had already used gesture interaction with commercial games. All children were invited to use the application until they had finished the activity (finalize the reading of the storybook and answer the questions).

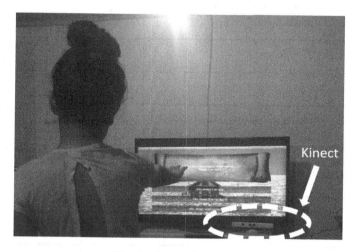

Fig. 6. Gesture interaction

The test using gesture interaction required a computer, a Kinect and a TV. These components were not available at the NGO school, then the group I performed the usability test using mouse and keyboard. The private school had the hardware required, then the group II did the usability test using gesture interaction. Figure 6 shows the gesture environment setup in which it was kept distance greater than 1.8 meters between the Kinect and the child.

Post-test questionnaires were applied to analyze user satisfaction of both groups. It was applied immediately after the child's interaction with the application, to obtain the results regarding the child's satisfaction. Because they were children, we adopted the Likert [22] scale of 3 points. Figure 7 shows the questions used for this test.

Question	Disagree	Indifferent	Agree
Were you able to use gestures without difficulty? (just group 2)			
Did you like the scenarios and menus of the game?			
Did you like the custom pointer?			
Did you like the size of the letters?			
Were you able to read the story completely?			
Were you able to answer the questionnaires without difficulty?			
Were you able to use the "Read to me" function without difficulty?			
Do you like the speed of the computer talking when using the "Read to me" function?			
Do you consider the experience motivating?			
Would you use the World of Knownlodege again to read other stories?			
What did you like most in the application?			
What did you don't like most in the application?			
What would you add in the application?			

Fig. 7. Post-test questionnaire

6 Findings and Discussion

Figures 8 (group I) and 9 (group II) depict the results obtained in the post-test questionnaires. Figures 10 (group I) and 11 (group II) show the average reading times of a storybook, from beginning to end, separated by age. Figure 12 presents general results (group I and II).

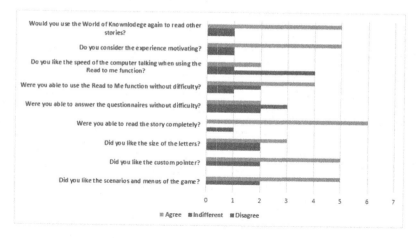

Fig. 8. Mouse/Keyboard interaction results (group I)

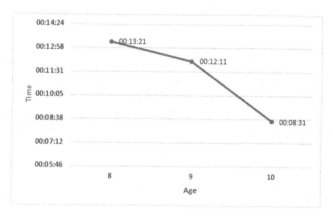

Fig. 9. Time spent completing the task, divided by age (group I)

Only one child from group I could not read the story completely, even though the function "Read to me" had been added as an aid. It was noticed that most were able to use the function, but they did not like the speed of the computer's speech. In relation to interaction using gestures (group II), five children reported that they considered the function good, while two felt indifferent and one did not like it. This issue is non-applicable to group I. On the appearance of the scenarios and menus, ten liked, four felt indifferent and one did not like it. A custom pointer was created, eight children liked it, five felt indifferent, and two others did not like it. As to the size of the letters, seven children liked it, three felt indifferent and another five did not like the size, implying the difficulty and delay in completing the reading of the stories.

Regarding the times of use for reading a story, data was presented within expectations based on the difficulties children would have to read depending on their level of learning.

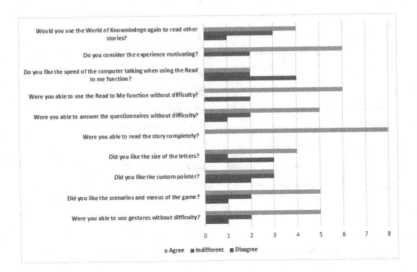

Fig. 10. Gesture interaction results (group II)

The feedback reported by the children related to the difficulty of the questionnaires, shown at the end of each chapter, was positive, with seven children reporting that they were good, five felt indifferent and three did not like it. When asked if the experience was motivating, eleven children liked it and said yes, three others felt indifferent and one did not like it. He also wondered if they would use the game to read another story, nine children agreed, four were indecisive, and two did not agree. The results show that the devices supported was easily assimilated.

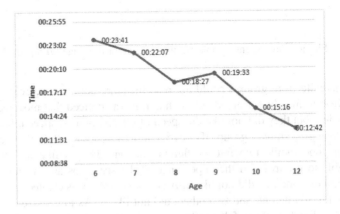

Fig. 11. Time spent completing the task, divided by age (group II)

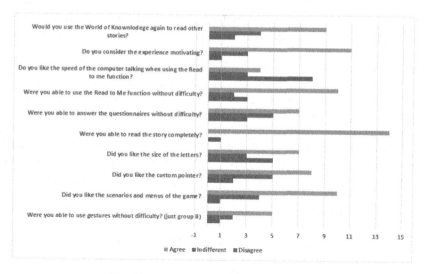

Fig. 12. General results of groups I and II

7 Conclusions

This work presented the World of Knowledge, an interactive learning environment that can motivate and help children in the reading process. The interaction can be done using conventional and non-conventional devices. Nowadays, it was added the story-books for kids "Three Little Pigs" and "Little Red Riding Hood". New storybooks for kids can be added dynamically without modify the application. It is necessary just configure a text file.

The World of Knowledge uses as a motivational factor the support of natural interfaces (gestural interface) as well as game characteristics (such as accumulating points, using points and obtaining tips) in order to aid the process of acquisition and reinforcement of reading. From the results of the usability tests, it was concluded that the children who used the application, would use it again and did not find great difficulty in interacting with the interface of gestures.

Throughout the tests, it was noticed that most of the children the private school (group II) already had contact with some type of game based on gesture interaction and that, in short, they had facility to use the World of Knowledge application and to understand the gestures necessary to use the game in the right way, enjoying all its features.

The most positive points for the children who used the application were the size of the letters, reading the story, the ease of answering the questionnaires and the "Read to me" functionality. Also, as part of the feedback, the children found the motivational application for the learning process and reinforcement of reading, a large part (80%) were able to answer the questionnaires related to the stories without difficulty and 60% of them would use the World of Knowledge.

It was also noticed that there were difficulties (implementation and quality) related to the "Read tor me" functionality, the synthesized voice for reading by the computer. A native Windows library was used that limited the application's speech capabilities, especially regarding tone of voice, pronunciation, and reading pace, and required manual configuration on each of the computers used for testing, as well as limiting operational system chosen. As a result, negative points were obtained through feedback from children, where 53.3% of users disliked the pace at which the story was read, providing a level of contentment below expectations to help children.

In a comparison, it can be concluded that the children who study in public school showed more enthusiasm during the tests (even without the use gesture interaction), since the interaction with games and computer applications is a less frequent experience in their daily life and, by gold side, children who study in private college, where experience and contact is more frequent, had higher expectations than the games presented.

In short, it was concluded that the application met the expectations regarding the requirements raised and the experience of the users, who were able to use 100% of the application and its available functionalities.

For future work, the improvement in "Read to me" functionality. This resource is dependent of the speech synthesizing, showing limitations because it uses native speech libraries from the Microsoft Windows operating system. Other storybooks for kids should be added also.

References

1. Coelho, M.T.: Problemas de aprendizagem. Editora Ática S.A, São Paulo (2009)
2. DePriest, D., Barilovits, K.: LIVE: Xbox Kinect©s virtual realities to learning games. In: 16th ANNUAL TCC Worldwide Online Conference, Hawaii, pp. 48–52 (2011)
3. Homer, B.D., et al.: Moved to learn: the effects of interactivity in a Kinect-based literacy game for beginning readers. Comput. Educ. **74**, 37–49 (2014). https://doi.org/10.1016/j.compedu.2014.01.007
4. Mol, S.E., Bus, A.G.: Bus.: to read or not to read: a meta-analysis of print exposure from infancy to early adulthood. Psychol. Bull. **137**, 267–296 (2011). https://doi.org/10.1037/a0021890
5. Wigdor, D., Wixon, D.: Brave NUI World: Designing Natural User Interfaces for Touch and Gesture, 1st edn. Morgan Kaufmann Publishers Inc., San Francisco (2011)
6. Kurakin, A., Zhang, Z., Liu, Z.: A real time system for dynamic hand gesture recognition with a depth sensor. In: 2012 Proceedings of the 20th European Signal Processing Conference (EUSIPCO), Bucharest, pp. 1975–1979 (2012). https://doi.org/10.1109/itsc.2015.381
7. Baoliang, W., Zeyu, C., Jing, C.: Gesture recognition by using Kinect skeleton tracking system. In: 2013 5th International Conference on Intelligent Human-Machine Systems and Cybernetics (IHMSC), vol. 1, pp. 418–422 (2013). https://doi.org/10.1109/ihmsc.2013.106
8. Boutsika, E.: Kinect in education: a proposal for children with autism. Procedia Comput. Sci., 123–129 (2014). https://doi.org/10.1016/j.procs.2014.02.015

9. Martins, V.F., Sampaio, Paulo N.M., Niedermeyer, A., de Paiva Guimarães, M.: Usability evaluation of a gestural interface application for children. In: Marcus, A. (ed.) DUXU 2016. LNCS, vol. 9747, pp. 587–596. Springer, Cham (2016). https://doi.org/10.1007/978-3-319-40355-7_56

10. Alves, R.S., Araújo, J.O.A., Madeiro, F.: AlfabetoKinect: Um aplicativo para auxiliar na alfabetização de crianças com o uso do Kinect. In: Anais do Simpósio Brasileiro de Informática na Educação, vol. 23, No. 1 (2012). http://dx.doi.org/10.5753/cbie.sbie.2012.%25p

11. Little Red Riding Hood. https://americanliterature.com/childrens-stories/little-red-riding-hood. Accessed 4 June 2018

12. The Three Little Pigs. https://americanliterature.com/childrens-stories/the-three-little-pigs. Accessed 4 June 2018

13. Cabral, L.S.: Processos psicolinguísticos de leitura e a criança. Letras de hoje **21**(1), 7–20 (1986). http://revistaseletronicas.pucrs.br/ojs/index.php/fale/article/view/17425. Accessed 4 Aug 2018

14. Larman, C., Basili, V.R.: Iterative and incremental developments. A brief history. Computer **36**(6), 47–56 (2003). https://doi.org/10.1109/mc.2003.1204375

15. Microsoft .NET Framework 4. https://www.microsoft.com/pt-br/download/details.aspx?id=17851. Accessed 4 Aug 2018

16. Kinect for Windows SDK v1.8. https://www.microsoft.com/en-us/download/details.aspx?id=40278. Accessed 6 June 2018

17. Kinect for Windows Sensor Components and Specifications. https://msdn.microsoft.com/library/jj131033.aspx. Accessed 6 June 2018

18. Renton, D.: Kinect Magic Cursor and Xremote. https://drenton72.wordpress.com/2012/08/16/kinect-magic-cursor-and-xremote. Accessed 6 June 2018

19. Unity 3D. https://unity3d.com. Accessed 4 June 2018

20. Surface Pro. https://www.microsoft.com/en-us/cortana. Accessed 4 June 2018

21. Cortana. https://www.microsoft.com/en-us/cortana. Accessed 4 June 2018

22. Likert, R.: A technique for the measurement of attitudes. Arch. Psychol. **140**, 1–55 (1932)

XP / Architecture (XA): A Collaborative Learning Process for Agile Methodologies When Teams Grow

Luis Freddy Muñoz-Sanabria[1(✉)] ⓘ, Julio Ariel Hurtado Alegría[2] ⓘ, and Francisco Javier Álvarez Rodriguez[3] ⓘ

[1] Fundación Universitaria de Popayán, Cauca, Colombia
lfreddyms@fup.edu.co
[2] University of Cauca, Popayán, Cauca, Colombia
ahurtado@unicauca.edu.co
[3] University of Aguascalientes, Aguascalientes, Mexico
fjalvar@correo.uaa.mx

Abstract. Agile methodologies have proven their effectiveness in small teams; among them, Extreme Programming (XP) as the most used by the software industry and the scientific community. However, there are reports that report problems in applying agile parameters when the development team grows, and the project becomes more complex. The software architecture emerges as a mechanism to solve complexity and collaboration problems for complex projects and large development teams. This research proposes a method based on criteria of collaboration and Extreme Programming (XP) called Xp / Architecture (XA), to apply agile methods when the equipment grows, taking advantage of the capacity of the architecture methods proposed by the system engineering institute (SEI). Different XP teams work collaboratively in coordination with a team that incorporates agile architectural practices. The XA method was applied to three software projects, obtaining as a result, that the proposed model allowed to adhere Extreme Programming to larger teams and maintained the productivity proposed by the agile methodologies.

Keywords: Software architecture · Collaboration · Agile methods
Software process · Extreme programing

1 Introduction

Much of the software development companies are composed of VSEs (Very Small Enterprises) [1] where generally most of the agile practices available in different reports they do not apply directly to these companies.

The competitiveness of software companies must demonstrate that they have productive development teams deliver quality products [2]; therefore, agile methodologies became a response to the industry through rapid development and quality in environments of great uncertainty. Agile methodologies directly address quality problems that come from understanding the requirements [3, 4] through short development cycles, oriented to value and with the active participation of the client. Extreme Programming - XP [4]

© Springer Nature Switzerland AG 2019
V. Agredo-Delgado and P. H. Ruiz (Eds.): HCI-COLLAB 2018, CCIS 847, pp. 244–257, 2019.
https://doi.org/10.1007/978-3-030-05270-6_18

as reported scientific papers, is one of the most successful agile methodologies for small development teams, however, presents problems of coordination when the team size grows [5], i.e., it is not possible scalability [6], since the agile practices are diluted in the development of the project. Scale a method refers to ex-tending its application in a larger or complex context for which it was initially pro-posed. Normally the scale is related to the complexity of the problem and the size of the team, so any solution strategy should consider technical elements and management in order to facilitate the methodical decomposition of the project into simpler, manageable and constructible units. Here, architecture is one of the key concepts to solve the problem in a draft medium or high complexity tries to use agile methodologies [7]. The absence of an orientation towards architecture in agile methodologies, does not allow early design decisions that will have a profound impact on the entire project will take. A competitive software industry should be able to increase its pro-duction capacity in the long term, i.e. must be able to re-use components, structures and design decisions, as well as obtain products that can then be properly maintained [8]. To achieve this, it is necessary to establish collaborative prac-tices among team members, so that, while growing, properly coordinated the project. This article pre-sent XP / Architecture (XA): A collaborative learning process agile method-ologies when teams grow, a process model XP-based software and architecture-centric, oriented medium complexity projects and teams over 16 people seeking to enhance the productive capacity of organizations. XA introduces a holistic and collaborative model, which facilitates the coordination of a set of development teams, small and satellites working independently with XP around a group of agile architecture. The proposed model has been validated using a case study involving embedded application in three software development projects.

The remainder of this paper is organized as follows: Sect. 2 presents the main scalability of agile methods work, Sect. 3 introduces the XA process, which involves specifying values, equipment, practices and processes. Section 4 presents the application of the model in three academic studies, an embedded case study and analysis of results. Finally, Sect. 5 presents the conclusions, limitations and future work.

2   Related Works

In this session, the most relevant works on the different proposals that have tried to scale agile methodologies to larger teams are described.

Thus Kornstädt and Sauer [9] based on real experiences show that a common architectural view allows to solve communication problems in agile development project. Although a process that combines agile methods with methods of architecture is proposed, the idea that architecture is an important method to scale agile device is supported. Hadar and Silberman [7] present the C3A method, which is based on the use of reference diagrams and the implementation of the architecture in XP, a set of component contracts and a methodology that aligns the schedule and the granularity of the tasks. However, this method does not explicitly define the practices regarding the development of requirements and architecture design, also reported cases of application. Jensen et al. [10] use a similar mechanism to user stories to represent the requirements and architectural decisions in XP in order to raise one based on the stories of developers architecture. These stories express the specific demands of refactoring and are a tool for planning. In addition, these stories allow developers to reflect on the system design, to have a shared understanding of architecture. However, the stories of developers are not used to define an architecture according to the quality requirements are not explicitly integrated architecture practices or empirical results are presented. Donald J. Reifer et al. [11] collected the criteria of several experts who say it is not possible to scale agile methods but mixed metaphors (agile and rigorous) are used. These authors propose an architectural team and subdivide the rest of the team into smaller teams of developers, clarifying that depending on the size of the software, communication and the other principles of the agile postulate can be made so complex that in the customer relationship and XP teams the objectives of the system may be lost.

Regarding the studies that productivity and quality of developments with XP is measured, very little is reported in the literature. [12] reported a case study in which a productivity of 0,003 individual user stories hour (32 user stories at 3.5 months by a team of 14.7 people) was reached. Another study of case study is reported by [13], where the productivity of an XP team is 17 NLOC-P- (NLO-PH - Number of lines of code per person per hour).

3 Methodology

3.1 Extension XP practices Architecture

Xp / Architecture (XA) is an agile methodology based on collaborative environments, sustained by the values and principles of extreme programming (XP), which adds some architectural practices, whose primary purpose of making usable XP projects of medium complexity (problem / solution) and with larger traditional teams. In the Fig. 1. shows how the great project team is decomposed by a set of smaller teams XP around a team XA architecture. Thus, the dynamics of the XA model are a combination of the dynamics present in these groups and their interrelationships. Therefore, the description of this holistic model is based on the practices and values of XP and these transcend the intra-group dynamics of the architecture group and the inter-group dynamics of the entire team.

Therefore, to XA they are very important the 4 values proposed by the agile [4] manifesto, and XA also proposes a new value that will be part of the pillars that will guide agile development projects of medium complexity:

- *Team organization XP:* Because of the magnitude of the project, this new value is aimed at awareness of holistic organization of teams XP, where each team follows the values and principles of XP [7] and at least one team will have more emphasis on software architecture, the which will follow the practices defined in XA extended. The teams that follow the principles of XP are called XP teams and the team that also follows the architectural practices is called the XA team.

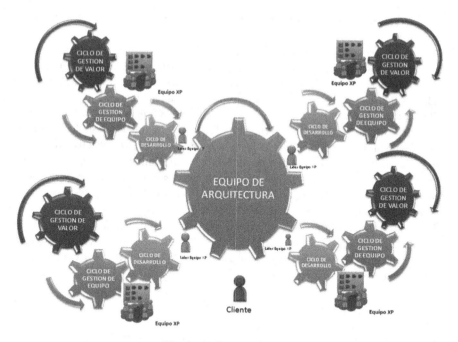

Fig. 1. Holistic model XA

- *The communication:* Based on a high interaction between XP teams work, team members XA and these with the customer, communication requires establishing channels for knowledge flows from emerging form. The customer must be an active member of the XA team as a permanent source of system requirements. This team is made up of one member from each XP computer, which in turn make their respective clients in XP computer. Customer project will be called Customer and Customer XA every XP team member turn the XA team will be called Client XP. XP clients are agents that establish the inter-group relationship and are therefore key elements of communication in XA.

- *Simplicity:* Applied to all aspects of XA, from the initial phase with very simple and basic practices-based architectures, including code refactoring. XA, the important thing is to do what the customer needs and the easiest way, but without losing the possibility of continuous integration and value.

- *Feedback*: It happens in two stages; the first by the XA team to the customer, in order to provide advance on system development and meet its assessment, and from the XP client to the XP computer in contributions to the development of the project. The second moment occurs between each member of XP teams and team members architectural XA, in order to provide progress on the development of sub-system and know their appreciation, and from the XP client to the XP computer in contributions to the development of the sub-project.

- *Courage*: To meet the continuous changes that occur in the course of the activity, which involves all members of both the XA team like the XP computers.

- In addition to the twelve (12) practices that characterize XP [14], other character-ized XA:
- *Agile management architecture*: Each team XA and XP have a project leader who is managed in an agile way. For integrating management practices XA project leader meets regularly (daily management meeting) with the leaders of each XP project to address the problems and approaches to project management.
- *Unification of code on computers XA*: As with the XP teams exists for the archi-tecture team collective code ownership [15], but in order to do less complex development and meet the agile criteria in each team there is collective ownership of code sub-system that is in charge (collective ownership of code remains practice on each team). XA architecture supports practices for distribution subsystems, requirements and subsequent validation and integration. XA can be seen as an agile team that outsources component development teams XP.
- *Mechanism to distribute requirements:* Having established an increase in the architecture, the XA team, you will share the XP computers subsystem requirements taking advantage of the interaction of a member XA and XP client computer and thus maintaining the philosophy of XP.

3.2   The Life Cycle XA

- *Exploration:* XA members of the team with the client (XA) meet to set initial system requirements. In this phase the system is delimited (Fig. 2).

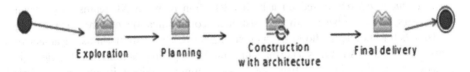

Fig. 2. Phases method XA

- *Planning:* XA team members set the objectives of the phase and build early ver-sions of the system architecture.
- *Architecture construction*: Based on the previous phase, the system requirements are prioritized, and a skeleton of architecture raised by the architectural team for these requirements is developed, the system is modularized and requirements for XP teams participating in the project are distributed. The definition of architecture is developed parallel to the development of the XP computers. It is continuously integrating the system. As in XP this construction is done iteratively and incre-mentally ensuring continuous customer feedback.
- *Final delivery:* The XA team delivers customer of the final product, although has made incremental validations; You should fully evaluate the product.

An iteration of XA shown in Fig. 3. In this iteration of XA is embedded iteration XP, which is executed by the computer XP. The main activities have been parallelized in order to give freedom to the teams perform these tasks according to the emerging dynamics.

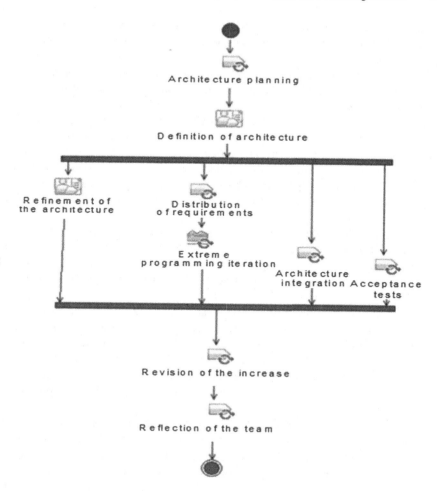

Fig. 3. A iteration method in XA

3.3   XA Architecture Practices

XA maintains the simplicity of XP, the metaphor of the system and refactoring. Also they applied as methods adapted architecture: Attribute-Driven Design ADD and [16] QualityattributeWorkshops (QAW) [17]. These practices have been combined and packed with practical base XP in previous work [8, 18] and this has been taken as a reference point to get through this research fragments process concerning architectural topics as shown then:

- *Game Planning:* User stories resulting from the dynamics of XP are complemented by quality attribute information provided by the QAW which takes into account the quality scenarios, stories denominated XA architecture. Prioritizing the stories of architecture and refinement of these provide additional information for the customer and developers choose the user stories in each iteration. In the exploration phase

and planning they are identified and selected stories for key architectural architecture very useful in choosing user stories during practice game planning XP
computers.

- *Customer site:* Customer concept is extended to accommodate the participation of
  other participants (e.g. Computer maintenance, management) in order to verify the
  system requirements and technical solutions beyond an owner of the business
  requirements. This is done in some of the daily meetings of the XA team. Each XP
  team maintains this practice, where his client is the architecture team.
- *Metaphor system:* The Add method provides an approach for defining recursive
  refinement of architecture in terms of decomposition of the system into smaller
  modules. XA uses this approach to break the system simple and allegorical shape
  the world of the problem and provide a comprehensive map to distribute product
  requirements.
- *Simple design:* The Add method provides an architecture at a high level sufficient to
  ensure a competent design abstraction, and user stories and architecture, so that the
  risks associated with the project are mitigated. You have a high-level design will
  facilitate the integration and independence of XP teams in their designs, so they can
  keep intact this practice inside.
- *Refactoring:* Architecturally it facilitates rapid development of solutions while in
  parallel ADD provides architectural tactics and strategies for longer-term solution,
  firing architectural refactoring requirements. This facilitates the technical requirements may arise incrementally backed by the ability of trading practices and
  refactoring requirements in XP computers. The refactorings in XA, are architectural
  type in order to locate the greatest impact potential changes as early as possible in
  the project.
- *Collective ownership of code:* XP keeps each team through its subsystem development. The XA team further define architectural elements code and synchronize
  tasks performed by teams XP, for it is necessary to have an application repository
  and version management to ensure work on these restrictions.
- *Development directed by tests:* It is extended by the development of early integration testing. Early integration tests are defined to test the behavior abstract
  architecture before it is implemented, providing an idea of the mechanisms should
  be defined as a form of implementation requirements. The tests are performed by
  implementing the abstract behavior concretely with example code (required by the
  test case) before this behavior is developed by the XA team and released the XP
  computers.

3.4   Main activities concerning XA architecture

Like XP [19], XA proposed activities which are part of their life cycle and highlight the
practices described above in the following activities carried out concurrently (see
Fig. 4):

- *Analyze architectural requirements:* this activity based on quality criteria QAW in
  which identifies and analyzes the stories of architecture in order to address issues as
  early as possible prioritization and decomposition of the system. To identify stories

Analizar requisitos arquitectónicos   Diseñar arquitectura   Implementar arquitectura

Fig. 4. Main activities related to architecture in the iteration of architecture

of the architect, the XA team identifies and defines user stories and architecture, based schemes and non-formal, visible through the radiator computer information XA devices. During the game planning, architecture stories are prioritized and expressed by a measurable objective. User stories and quality requirements in the histories of architecture, which specify a direct situation as performance, security and availability, as well as indirect situations like changeability and scalability.

- *Architecting:* The architectural design of initial proposals called Architectures candidates. In these, the XA team raises initial sketches of architectures based on business knowledge, technology and their previous experiences. Architectures candidates are evaluated using scenarios architectural histories in order to determine their viability and feasibility. According to the evaluation, selection of candidate architectures, where the architecture team took as a candidate architecture those most conducive to the development of the project is done. Candidates based on these architectures, the system architecture is detailed exhibiting a set of design decisions that will be placed on the radiator of information,

- *Implement the architecture:* It is to implement the interfaces, abstract behavior and document API in order to turn them into the main artifacts of architecture description. The implementation follows the development strategy led by tests: once developed the concept of architecture, each XP computer, encodes testing their designs and designs themselves, so that early on can show the client functional modules. The addition to defining the level of programming services firm, interfaces must associate information regarding the quality of them, their restrictions and decisions that led to that specification. Architecture implementation also requires implementing and documenting code-level testing, abstract behavior and skeletal concrete behavior The API documentation is necessary for the team XA present to XP computers, strategies and specifications arising from architectural decisions. Level documentation of the same code is based on the criteria agile XP and will be made incrementally as architectural and non-architectural code grows.

4   Case Studies

XA was applied in embedded case study within two academic projects and one industry, keeping the guidelines of empirical research studies case where a phenomenon within its real context [9] is studied.

4.1   Design Case Study

The objective of this case study was to evaluate the ability of XA to scale to large groups as part of a large development project regarding a short development time. To design this research, the proposed Runenson and Host [20] was followed, for it broke the main research question being solved: How to scale an agile process in projects of medium complexity and equipment of medium development?. Along with the review of the scientific literature related, defined as a hypothesis: XA remain in the case study the order of the indices of productivity and satisfaction reported for XP, but projects of medium complexity and with equipment more than 10 ± 2 people. To support this research indicator were defined (See Table 1).

Table 1. Indicators, Metrics, Information Sources, Instruments

Indicator	Measurements	Information sources	Instruments
Satisfaction	Acceptance na-Level of Participation NP-	Customer and Equipment	Poll
Quality	Conformance Level NC- Satisfaction level NS-	Customer and Product	Survey and Registration of defects
Productivity	Productivity P-	Management artifacts	Burndown chart

To collect information on this case study were used and designed the following instruments:

- *Surveys:* applied to client computers XP and XA equipment in order to investigate the degree of customer involvement, their commitment to the project and XA team and satisfaction with the method and product. Knowing the degree of acceptance of the proposed agreement between the team members and the degree of responsiveness and dynamism model against the project and other stakeholders' model.
- *Artifacts:* as the product checklist to assess coverage requirements, the template defect to assess the quality and architecture assessment to evaluate the quality of the proposed architecture.

4.2   Project 1: Project Manager Research Systems Engineering Program FUP

Case Scenario: XA was applied to a group of 18 students in the fifth year of the program Systems Engineering University Foundation of Popayan, under laboratory software engineering, where the development of a distributed application development is proposing a prototype registration and tracking system research projects. The development was carried out with J2EE technology, Web Services and JUnit. The client was a teacher of the institution designated by the curriculum committee.

Development of the case: For the implementation of XA, students received an initial 12-h training divided into three parts. The first part addressed the topic of agile methodologies (XP), in order to unify terms of reference. In the second part the theme of architecture was addressed, particularly as regards its concepts, views, styles and ADD and QAW methods. In the third part, they were presented XA, revealing the group parameters and tools to be carried out for the project course. To support training and development of the project they were given two technical reports developed specifically to introduce XP and XA. The project was developed in classes with 4-h sessions covering a total of 48 h of development.

Students are self-organized into 3 teams XP 6 members; each team chose to XA its client / architect representative. The XA team was organized by the three representatives of the XP computers. In the dynamics of the project, while XA met with the client of the project, radiators XP teams organized their information (billboards) in a visible place for everyone. In all sessions (12) 4 h each a 15-min meeting between the client and the team XA was developed at the beginning to get customer feedback. The client had a very high commitment, was available within the institution and actively participated in the development of requirements. In addition, XA and XP teams continued planning practices iteration and daily work according to the provisions of XP and XA.

During the project development information as planned was collected. The dynamics corresponds to the proposed model, as was noted during the development of the case a commitment by each of the team members to follow proposed by the XA model practices, achieving an adherence of 82%, which can be considered acceptable in order to assess the results of the case study.

4.3   Project 2: Research System FUP

Project context: For the latter case, XA was applied to a group of 18 students who were characterized because 60% of them had completed subjects and performed with the institution a diploma in software development and the remaining 40% graduates of programs Systems Engineering different universities in the city interested in the subject and the work proposal for the project. This group is also proposing the development of a large-scale application. The project to develop as with the first group consisted of a distributed for registration and monitoring of research projects implementation. What made development with PHP technologies and jquery-UI library for MySQL database and Apache web server as. Again in this case, the client was designated by the curriculum committee, representative of Systems Engineering program at the Center for Studies and Research and who knew the dynamics of the project and requirements for application development teacher.

Project development: For the implementation of XA, students received an initial 12-h training divided into three parts. The first part addressed the topic of agile methodologies (XP), in order to unify terms of reference. In the second part the theme of architecture was addressed, particularly as regards its concepts, views, styles and ADD and QAW methods. In the third part, they were presented XA, revealing the group parameters and tools to be carried out for the project course. To support training and development of the project they were given two technical reports developed specifically to introduce XP and XA. The project was developed in classes with 4-h sessions covering a total of 48 h of development.

Students are self-organized into 3 teams XP 6 members; each team chose to XA its client /architect representative. The XA team was organized by the three representatives of the XP computers. In the dynamics of the project, while XA met with the client of the project, radiators XP teams organized their information (billboards) in a visible place for everyone. In all sessions (12) 4 h each a 15-min meeting between the client and the team XA was developed at the beginning to get customer feedback. The client had a very high commitment, was available within the institution and actively participated in the development of requirements. In addition, XA and XP teams continued planning practices iteration and daily work according to the provisions of XP and XA. During the project development information as planned was collected. The dynamics corresponds to the proposed model, as was noted during the development of the case a commitment by each of the team members to follow proposed by the XA model practices, achieving an adherence of 82%, which can be considered acceptable in order to assess the results of the case study.

4.4   Project 3: CRM Doubleclick

This project corresponds to an application for a foreign customer to academia and software all requirements and commercial complex. The company for which the application was developed called doubleclick, dedicated to establishing telematic services, and those who did not have an information system in the area of customer service. The problem was that the company support the performing telephone and call flow increasingly becomes greater. This is an area that, as the customer ordered, requires agility in the process of providing information, offer new products and services through a web platform. A team of 22 participants was delegated to develop a CRM to strengthen customer processes.

Project development: The 22 participants did not know the XA methodology for the project, were given training in XP / architecture 16 h. Two working days in 8 days and 4 h one day to the next. They were also trained on agile methodologies focusing on Extreme Programming (XP), in order to unify terms of reference. Finally, it was also trained in the areas of architecture, since it needed the group particularly know the basics, views, styles and methods of architecture proposed by the SEI (Software Engineering Institute), emphasizing ADD (Attribute- driven Design) and QAW (Quality Attribute Workshop).

Case Scenario: Developers are self-organized into 3 teams 6 members XP and XA team of 4 members. Each team chose his client / architect to XA representative. The XA team was organized by the three representatives of XP teams and 4 more members who were only in the XA team. In the dynamics of the project, while XA met with the client of the project, radiators XP teams organized their information (billboards) in a visible place for everyone. In all sessions (12) 4 h each a 15-min meeting between the client and the team XA was developed at the beginning to get customer feedback. The client had a very high commitment, was available within the institution and actively participated in the development of requirements. In addition, XA and XP teams continued planning practices iteration and daily work according to the provisions of XP and XA. During the project development information as planned was collected. The dynamics corresponds to the proposed model, as was noted during the development of the case a commitment by each of the team members to follow proposed by the XA model practices, achieving an adherence of 82 \%, which can be considered acceptable to assess the results of the case study.

5   Results

XP productivity teams were among 0.010y 0.017 HU-PH (User Stories by Person Time) While the XA teams were 0.007 HA-PH (Stories Architecture per person) Timerespectively, which is significantly better than that reported by [12] where productivity was 0.003 HU-PH (32 user stories at 3.5 months by a team of 14.7 persons). On the other hand, according to [13], the productivity of an XP team is 17 NLOC-PH (number of lines of code per person per hour) was significantly better than a project developed in the traditional way (10.3 NLOC-person-hour). In this case study, they developed 12600 NLOC reaching a productivity of 14.58 NLOC, lower than that reported by [13] using XP but maintaining order productivity and better than that reported using the traditional approach. These results preliminarily validate the hypothesis that the productivity of equipment XA maintain order XP productivity of teams reported in the literature (See Table 2).

Table 2. Results

INDICATOR	PROJECT 1	PROJECT 2	PROJECT 3
Acceptance level of XA	100%	100%	100%
Customer Participation Level	95%	97%	90%
Product compliance level	70%	87%	90%
Satisfaction of requirements	95%	97%	95%
XP productivity equipment	HU-0010 PH	HU-0017 PH	HU-0017 PH
XA productivity equipment	0.007 HA-PH	0018 HA-PH	0013 HA-PH
Adherence method XA	82%	93%	95%

6   Conclusions, Limitations and Future Work

This article has presented XA, a collaborative learning process for agile methodologies extending XP practices and scale to larger teams and more complex projects. Preliminarily scale method when applied in two academic cases and collaboration enabled learning agile practices when compared with other studies. Then it was necessary to verify the model in an industrial context, where the variables presented in these exercises are quite demanding to be controlled. Among the main findings of this qualitative case study we have:

- The model could specify that communication between the XA equipment and XP computers is one of the parts most at risk due to equipment size therefore it should prioritize this aspect proposing strategies and / or methods that allow it to be smooth clear and consistent. XA team members must know and clearly manage the project objectives and requirements of customer business.

- The collaborative process needs about driving forces that are continually vigilant of agile methodology, so that representatives of the XA team should not only be the element of connection between the computer architecture and XP computers, but must be motivators team and client.
- The collaboration worked, at the end of each iteration, there was a new knowledge (value added) learned by each team member. XA team members understand their role in ensuring the integrity of the holistic model, generated stories architect and mechanisms for establishing the requirements of all XP computers.
- XP /Architecture was able to demonstrate that you can work collaboratively with agile methodologies, although teams grow. In the case studies, team size remained productivity.

The case study presented here has established that to corroborate the results of this research will be necessary to consider other variables of context as established by [12] to make a more objective comparison, for example, the expertise of the participants. All these considerations are now being taken to improve the design of future case studies and experimental case.

Although the collaborative process proved effective in the case studies raised, research has some limitations due to the type of comparisons and measurements found in the literature; since the literature in most cases are not reported or reported without characterizing the context of case studies. It seeks for a next phase of this work make a controlled to establish a closer and more reliable comparison experiment. It is also expected to apply XA other cases industry, where a richer feedback would be obtained.

References

1. Fedesoft. News ICT: (2011). http://www.fedesoft.org
2. Canos, J.H., Penadés, C.: Agile methodologies in software development. In: VIII Conference on Software Engineering and Databases (JISBD) (2003). 123456789/476
3. Costello, R.J., Liu, D.B.: Metrics for requirements engineering. J. Syst. Softw. (1995). https://doi.org/10.1016/0164-1212(94)00127-9
4. Beck, K., Andres, C.: Extreme Programming Explained: Embrace Change, 2nd edn. Addison-Wesley Professional, US (2004). ISBN: 0-201-61641-6
5. Pendharkar, P.C., Roger, J.A.: The relationship between software development software development team size and cost. Commun. ACM **52**(1), 141–144 (2009). https://doi.org/10.1145/1435417.1435449
6. Nord, R.L., Tomayko, J.E.: Architecture-centric software development agile metodsand. IEEE Softw. **23**(2), 47–53 (2006). https://doi.org/10.1109/MS.2006.54
7. Hadar, E., Silberman, G.M.: Architecture agile methodology: long term short term strategy interleaved with practics. In: 23rd ACM in Companion to the SIGPLAN Conference on Object-Oriented Languages and Applications Programming Systems be. Companion OOPSLA 2008, pp. 641–652. ACM, New York (2008). https://doi.org/10.1145/1449814.1449816
8. Abrahamsson, O.S., Ronkainen, .J.: Agile software development methods: review and analysis. VTT Electr. (2002). https://doi.org/10.1007/978-3-642-12575-1_3

9. Kornstadt, A., Sauer, J.: Tackling offshore challenges with agile communication architecture-centric development. Working in Proceedings of the Sixth IEEE/IFIP Conference on Software Architecture, ser. WICSA 2007. IEEE Computer Society, Washington, DC (2007). https://doi.org/10.1109/WICSA.2007.39

10. Jensen, R.N., Møller, T., Sönder, P., Tjørnehøj, G.: Architecture and design in eXtreme programming; introducing "Developer Stories". In: Abrahamsson, P., Marchesi, M., Succi, G. (eds.) XP 2006. LNCS, vol. 4044, pp. 133–142. Springer, Heidelberg (2006). https://doi.org/10.1007/11774129_14

11. Reifer, D.J., Maurer, F., Erdogmus, M.H.: Scaling agile methods. IEEE Softw. 20(4), 12–14 (2003). https://doi.org/10.1109/MS.2003.1207448

12. Layman, L., Williams, L., Cunningham, L.: Exploring Extreme Programming in context: an industrial case study. In: Proceedings of in the Agile Development Conference, to be. ADC 2004, pp. 32–41. IEEE Computer Society, Washington, DC (2004). https://doi.org/10.1109/ADEVC.2004.15

13. Maurer, F., Martel, S.: On the productivity of agile software practices: an industrial case study. In: International Workshop on Software Engineering Economics-Driven Researh (EDSER). 10.1.1.19.1925 & type = cc

14. Wells, D.: Extreme Programming to Gentle Introduction (2012). http://www.extreme-programming.org (2002)

15. Beck, K., Beedle, M., Bennekum, A.V., Cockburn, A., Cunningham, W.: Manifesto for agile software development (2009). http://www.agilemanifesto.org

16. Wojcik, R., et al.: Attribute-Driven Design (ADD), Version 2.0. Software Engineering Institute, no. CMU / SEI-2006-TR-023 (2006). 10.1.1.97.5395

17. Barbacci, M.R., Ellison, R.J., Lattanze, A.J., Stafford, J.A., Weinstock, C.B., Wood, W.G., Quality Attribute Workshops QAW -third Edition, Carnegie Mellon, Technical report CMU / SEI-2003-TR-016 (2003). 10.1.1.208.5450

18. Muñoz, F., Hurtado, J.: XP / Architecture. Technical report, IDIS-TR-002 (2011)

19. Dyb, T., Dingsøyr, T.: Empirical studies of agile software development: a systematic review. Inf. Softw. Technol. 50(9–10), 833–859 (2008). https://doi.org/10.1016/j.infsof.2008.01.006

20. Runeson, P., Host, M.: Guidelines for conducting and reporting case study research in software engineering. Empirical Softw. Eng. 14(2), 131–164 (2009). https://doi.org/10.1007/s10664-008-9102-8

21. Muñoz, F., Hurtado, J.: XA: an extension for supporting XP architecture practices. In: 2012 7th Colombian Digital Object Identifier Computing Congress (CCC), 10.1109/Colombian CC.2012.6398012 (2012). https://doi.org/10.1109/2012.6398012

Author Index

Printed in the United States
By Bookmasters